HOW WOULD YOU MOVE MOUNT FUJI?

Also by William Poundstone

BIG SECRETS

THE RECURSIVE UNIVERSE

BIGGER SECRETS

LABYRINTHS OF REASON

THE ULTIMATE

PRISONER'S DILEMMA

BIGGEST SECRETS

CARL SAGAN: A LIFE IN THE COSMOS

HOW WOULD YOU MOVE MOUNT FUJI?

Microsoft's Cult of the Puzzle

HOW THE WORLD'S SMARTEST COMPANIES SELECT THE MOST CREATIVE THINKERS

William Poundstone

Little, Brown and Company
Boston New York London

First Edition

The third quotation on p. vii is used by permission of The Metropolitan Museum of Art: Huang Binhong (1865–1955); *Insects and Flowers;* Chinese, dated 1948; Album of ten leaves; ink and color on gold-flecked paper; 12½ × 14 in. (31.8 × 35.6 cm); The Metropolitan Museum of Art, Gift of Robert Hatfield Ellsworth, in memory of La Ferne Hatfield Ellsworth, 1986 (1986.267. 204a-j).

Library of Congress Cataloging-in-Publication Data

Poundstone, William.
    How would you move Mount Fuji? : Microsoft's cult of the puzzle : how the world's smartest companies select the most creative thinkers / by William Poundstone.
        p. cm.
    Includes bibliographical references and index.
    ISBN 0-316-91916-0
        1. Employment interviewing. 2. Microsoft Corporation. I. Title.

HF5549.5.I6 P68 2003
    658.3'112 — dc21   2002040619

10 9 8 7 6 5 4 3 2 1

Q-FF

Designed by Meryl Sussman Levavi/Digitext
Printed in the United States of America

To my father

"Like any other value, puzzle-solving ability proves equivocal in application. . . . But the behavior of a community which makes it preeminent will be very different from that of one which does not."

— Thomas Kuhn
The Structure of Scientific Revolutions

"As, in a Chinese puzzle, many pieces are hard to place, so there are some unfortunate fellows who can never slip into their proper angles, and thus the whole puzzle becomes a puzzle indeed, which is the precise condition of the greatest puzzle in the world — this man-of-war world itself."

— Herman Melville
White-Jacket

"To understand that cleverness can lead to stupidity is to be close to the ways of Heaven."

— Huang Binhong
Insects and Flowers

Contents

1. The Impossible Question   3

2. The Termans and Silicon Valley   23

3. Bill Gates and the Culture of Puzzles   50

4. The Microsoft Interview Puzzles   78

5. Embracing Cluelessness   91

6. Wall Street and the Stress Interview   111

7. The Hardest Interview Puzzles   118

8. How to Outsmart the Puzzle Interview   121

9. How Innovative Companies
   Ought to Interview   130

Answers   147

Acknowledgments   247

Notes   249

Bibliography and Web Links   257

Index   263

HOW WOULD YOU MOVE MOUNT FUJI?

One

The Impossible Question

In August 1957 William Shockley was recruiting staff for his Palo Alto, California, start-up, Shockley Semiconductor Laboratory. Shockley had been part of the Bell Labs team that invented the transistor. He had quit his job and come west to start his own company, telling people his goal was to make a million dollars. Everyone thought he was crazy. Shockley knew he wasn't. Unlike a lot of the people at Bell Labs, he knew the transistor was going to be *big*.

Shockley had an idea about how to make transistors cheaply. He was going to fabricate them out of *silicon*. He had come to this valley, south of San Francisco, to start production. He felt like he was on the cusp of history, in the right place at the right time. All that he needed was the right people. Shockley was leaving nothing to chance.

Today's interview was Jim Gibbons. He was a young guy, early twenties. He already had a Stanford Ph.D. He had studied at Cambridge too — on a Fulbright scholarship he'd won.

Gibbons was sitting in front of him right now, in Shockley's Quonset hut office. Shockley picked up his stopwatch.

There's a tennis tournament with one hundred twenty-seven players, Shockley began, in measured tones. *You've got one hundred twenty-six people paired off in sixty-three matches, plus one unpaired player as a bye. In the next round, there are sixty-four players and thirty-two matches. How many matches, total, does it take to determine a winner?*

Shockley started the stopwatch.

The hand had not gone far when Gibbons replied: One hundred twenty-six.

How did you do that? Shockley wanted to know. *Have you heard this before?*

Gibbons explained simply that it takes one match to eliminate one player. One hundred twenty-six players have to be eliminated to leave one winner. Therefore, there have to be 126 matches.

Shockley almost threw a tantrum. That was how *he* would have solved the problem, he told Gibbons. Gibbons had the distinct impression that Shockley did not care for other people using "his" method.

Shockley posed the next puzzle and clicked the stopwatch again. This one was harder for Gibbons. He thought a long time without answering. He noticed that, with each passing second, the room's atmosphere grew less tense. Shockley, seething at the previous answer, now relaxed like a man sinking into a hot bath. Finally, Shockley clicked off the stopwatch and said that Gibbons had already taken *twice* the lab average time to answer the question. He reported this with charitable satisfaction. Gibbons was hired.

Find the Heavy Billiard Ball . . .

Fast-forward forty years in time — only a few miles in space from long-since-defunct Shockley Semiconductor —

to a much-changed Silicon Valley. Transistors etched onto silicon chips were as big as Shockley imagined. Software was even bigger. Stanford was having a career fair, and one of the most popular companies in attendance was the Microsoft Corporation. With the 1990s dot-com boom and bull market in full swing, Microsoft was famous as a place where employees of no particular distinction could make $1 million before their thirtieth birthday. Grad student Gene McKenna signed up for an interview with Microsoft's recruiter.

Suppose you had eight billiard balls, the recruiter began. *One of them is slightly heavier, but the only way to tell is by putting it on a scale against the others. What's the fewest number of times you'd have to use the scale to find the heavier ball?*

McKenna began reasoning aloud. Everything he said was sensible, but somehow nothing seemed to impress the recruiter. With hinting and prodding, McKenna came up with a billiard-ball-weighing scheme that was marginally acceptable to the Microsoft guy. The answer was two.

"Now, imagine Microsoft wanted to get into the appliance business," the recruiter then said. "Suppose we wanted to run a microwave oven from the computer. What software would you write to do this?"

"Why would you want to do that?" asked McKenna. "I don't want to go to my refrigerator, get out some food, put it in the microwave, and *then* run to my computer to start it!"

"Well, the microwave could still have buttons on it too."

"So why do I want to run it from my computer?"

"Well maybe you could make it *programmable?* For example, you could call your computer from work and have it start cooking your turkey."

"But wouldn't my turkey," asked McKenna, "or any other food, go bad sitting in the microwave while I'm at work? I could put a frozen turkey in, but then it would drip water everywhere."

"What *other* options could the microwave have?" the recruiter asked. Pause. "For example, you could use the computer to download and exchange recipes."

"You can do that now. Why does Microsoft want to bother with connecting the computer to the microwave?"

"Well let's not worry about that. Just *assume* that Microsoft has decided this. It's your job to think up uses for it."

McKenna thought in silence.

"Now maybe the recipes could be very complex," the recruiter said. "Like, 'Cook food at seven hundred watts for two minutes, then at three hundred watts for two more minutes, but don't let the temperature get above three hundred degrees.'"

"Well there is probably a *small* niche of people who would really love that, but most people can't program their VCR."

The Microsoft recruiter extended his hand. "Well, it was *nice* to meet you, Gene. *Good luck with your job search.*"

"Yeah," said McKenna. "Thanks."

The Impossible Question

Logic puzzles, riddles, hypothetical questions, and trick questions have a long tradition in computer-industry interviews. This is an expression of the start-up mentality in which every employee is expected to be a highly logical and motivated innovator, working seventy-hour weeks if need be to ship a product. It reflects the belief that the high-technology industries are different from the old economy: less stable, less certain, faster changing. The high-technology employee must be able to question assumptions and see things from novel perspectives. Puzzles and riddles (so the argument goes) test that ability.

In recent years, the chasm between high technology and old economy has narrowed. The uncertainties of a wired, ever-shifting global marketplace are imposing a start-up mentality throughout the corporate and professional world. That world is now adopting the peculiar style of interviewing that was formerly associated with lean, hungry technology companies. Puzzle-laden job interviews have infiltrated the Fortune 500 and the rust belt; law firms, banks, consulting firms, and the insurance industry; airlines, media, advertising, and even the armed forces. Brainteaser interview questions are reported from Italy, Russia, and India. Like it or not, puzzles and riddles are a hot new trend in hiring.

Fast-forward to the present — anywhere, almost any line of business. It's your next job interview. Be prepared to answer questions like these:

How many piano tuners are there in the world? If the Star Trek *transporter was for real, how would that affect the transportation industry? Why does a mirror reverse right and left instead of up and down? If you could remove any of the fifty U.S. states, which would it be? Why are beer cans tapered on the ends? How long would it take to move Mount Fuji?*

In the human resources trade, some of these riddles are privately known as impossible questions. Interviewers ask these questions in the earnest belief that they help gauge the intelligence, resourcefulness, or "outside-the-box thinking" needed to survive in today's hypercompetitive business world. Job applicants answer these questions in the also-earnest belief that this is what it takes to get hired at the top companies these days. A lot of earnest believing is going on. To an anthropologist studying the hiring rituals of the early twenty-first century, the strangest thing about these impossible questions would probably be this: *No one knows the answer.* I have spoken with interviewers who use these questions, and they have enthusiastically assured me not only that they *don't* know the "correct answer" but that *it makes no difference* that they don't know the answer. I even spent an amusing couple of hours on the Internet trying to pull up "official" figures on the number of piano tuners in the world. Conclusion: There are no official figures. Piano-tuner organizations with impressive websites do not know how many piano tuners there are in the world.

Every business day, people are hired, or not hired, based on how well they answer these questions.

The impossible question is one phase of a broader phenomenon. Hiring interviews are becoming more invasive, more exhaustive, more deceptive, and meaner. The formerly straightforward courtship ritual between employer and employee has become more one-sided, a meat rack in which job candidates' mental processes are poked, prodded, and mercilessly evaluated. More and more, candidates are expected to "prove themselves" in job interviews. They must solve puzzles, avoid getting faked out by trick questions, and perform under manufactured stress.

"Let's play a game of Russian roulette," begins one interview stunt that is going the rounds at Wall Street investment banks. "You are tied to your chair and can't get up. Here's a gun. Here's the barrel of the gun, six chambers, all empty. Now watch me as I put *two* bullets in the gun. See how I put them in two adjacent chambers? I close the barrel and spin it. I put the gun to your head and pull the trigger. Click. You're still alive. Lucky you! Now, before we discuss your résumé, I'm going to pull the trigger one more time. Which would you prefer, that I spin the barrel first, or that I just pull the trigger?"

The good news is that the gun is imaginary. It's an "air gun," and the interviewer makes the appropriate gestures of spinning the barrel and pulling the trigger. The bad news is that your career future is being decided by someone who plays with imaginary guns.

This question is a logic puzzle. It has a correct answer (see page 147), and the interviewer *knows* what it is. You had better supply the right answer if you want the job. In the context of a job interview, solving a puzzle like this is probably as much about stress management as deductive logic. The Russian roulette question exemplifies the mind-set of these interviews — that people who can solve puzzles under stress make better employees than those who can't.

The popularity of today's stress- and puzzle-intensive interviews is generally attributed to one of America's most successful and ambivalently regarded corporations, Microsoft. The software giant receives about twelve thousand résumés each month. That is amazing when you consider that the company has about fifty thousand employees, and Microsoft's turnover rate has been pegged at about a third of the industry average. Microsoft has more cause to be selective than most companies. This is reflected in its interview procedure.

Without need of human intervention, each résumé received at Microsoft is scanned for keywords and logged into a database. Promising résumés lead to a screening interview, usually by phone. Those who pass muster get a "fly back," a trip to Microsoft's Redmond, Washington, headquarters for a full-day marathon of famously difficult interviews.

"We look for original, creative thinkers," says a section of the Microsoft website that is directed to college-age applicants, "and our interview process is designed to find those people." Six recent hires are pictured (three are women, three are black). "Your interview could include a technical discussion of the projects you've worked on, an abstract design question, or general problem-solving puzzles or brainteasers. The types of questions you'll be asked vary depending on the position you're looking for, but all are meant to investigate your capabilities and potential to grow. It's important for us to find out what you can do, not just what you've done."

Another company publication advises bluntly: "Get over your fear of trick questions. You will probably be asked one or two. They are not exactly fair, but they are usually asked to see how you handle a difficult situation."

Riddles and Sphinxes

"Not exactly fair"? It's little wonder that some compare this style of interviewing to fraternity hazing, brainwashing, or the third degree. As one job applicant put it, "You never know when they are going to bring out the guy in the chicken suit."

Another apt analogy is that familiar type of video game where you confront a series of odd and hostile characters in a series of confined spaces, solving riddles to get from one space to the next. Not many make it to the highest levels; for most, after three or four encounters, the game is over.

As classicists point out, those video games update the ancient Greek legend of Oedipus and the sphinx. The sphinx devoured anyone who couldn't answer her riddle: "What is it that walks on four legs in the morning, two legs at noon, and three legs in the evening?"

Oedipus solved the riddle by answering "Man." A baby crawls on all fours, an adult walks on two legs, and the elderly use a cane as a third leg. It was, in other words, a trick question.

The sphinx tale puzzles people even today. *Why didn't they just shoot it?* is the reaction of most college students. The principal source for the story, Sophocles's *Oedipus Rex,* is a realistic and psychologically nuanced tragedy. There the man-eating she-monster is as out of place, one scholar noted, as Godzilla would be if he were to lumber into the New York of Coppola's *Godfather* trilogy. Still, *something* about this crazy story strikes a chord. We all undergo tests in life. Maybe we succeed where all others have failed — or maybe not; at least, it's a common fantasy. There is something familiar in the banality of the riddle too, and in the weirdness of its poser. They remind us that the tests of life are not always reasonable and not always fair.

Tales of people proving their mettle by solving riddles exist in cultures around the globe. The "ordeal by trick question" was possibly raised to the highest art by the monks of Japanese Zen. Zen riddles are the antithesis of the Western logic puzzle, though one might describe them as demanding an extreme sort of outside-the-box thinking. A student of Zen demonstrates worthiness by giving a sublimely illogical answer to an impossible question. Zen master Shuzan once held out his short staff and announced to a follower: "If you call this a short staff, you oppose its reality. If you do not call it a short staff, you ignore the fact. Now what do you wish to call this?" In traditional Zen teaching, the penalty for a poor answer was a hard whack on the head with a short staff.

So Microsoft's "not exactly fair" questions are not exactly new. The company has repackaged the old "ordeal by riddle" for our own time. With its use of puzzles in its hiring decisions, Microsoft plays to the more appealing side of the digital generation mythos — of maverick independence and suspicion of established hierarchies. Puzzles are egalitarian, Microsoft's people contend, in that it doesn't matter what school you attended, where you worked before, or how you dress. All that matters is your logic, imagination, and problem-solving ability.

For of course Microsoft is an egalitarian meritocracy. It is ruthless about hiring what it calls the "top ten percent of the top ten percent." Microsoft's interviews are carefully engineered to weed out the "merely" competent who don't have the Microsoft level of competitive drive and creative problem-solving ability. It is estimated that less than one in four of those flown up to Redmond for a day of interviews receive a job offer. Like most riddle-bearing sphinxes, Microsoft's human resources department leaves a high body count.

Blank Slate

Microsoft is a fraught place. It represents the best and worst of how corporate America lives today. The software company that Bill Gates and Paul Allen founded was one of the great success stories of the last quarter of the twentieth century. The Justice Department's 1998 antitrust suit against Microsoft has not entirely dimmed that reputation. Maybe the opposite: Microsoft is now *bad*, and as we all know, *bad* is sometimes *good*. People have misgivings about Microsoft, just like they do about pit bulls and the Israeli Army. People also figure that if Microsoft hires this way, well, it may push the ethical envelope, but it must *work*.

Microsoft's role in changing interview practice is that of a catalyst. This influence owes to a shift in hiring priorities across industries. With bad hires more costly than ever, employers have given the job interview an importance it was never meant to have.

There was a time when a corporate job interview was a conversation. The applicant discussed past achievements and future goals. The interviewer discussed how those goals might or might not fit in with the company's. If the applicant was "put on the spot," it was with one of the old reliable human resources chestnuts such as "describe your worst fault."

At many companies, that type of low-pressure interview is on its way out. The reasons are many. References, once the bedrock of sound hiring practice, are nearing extinction in our litigious society. The prospect of a million-dollar lawsuit filed by an employee given a "bad reference" weighs heavily on employers. This is often dated to 1984, when a Texas court ruled that an insurance salesman had been defamed when his employer, insurance firm Frank B. Hall and Company, was asked for a reference and candidly rated the salesman "a zero." The court added a few zeros of its own to the damage award ($1.9 million).

Employment attorneys observe that awards of that size are rarer than the near hysteria prevailing in human resources departments might suggest. They also allow that — theoretically — the law protects truthful references. It is tough to argue against caution, though. "We tell our clients not to get involved in references of any kind," said Vincent J. Appraises, former chair of the American Bar Association's Labor and Employment Law Section. "Just confirm or deny whether the person has been employed for a particular period of time and that's it. End of discussion."

Equally problematic for today's hirers is the generically positive reference letter. Some companies are so terrified of lawsuits that they hand them out indiscriminately to any employee who asks. It's no skin off their nose if someone else hires away an inept employee.

With references less common and less useful, hirers must seek information elsewhere. The job interview is the most direct means of assessing a candidate. But the ground rules for interviews have changed in the past decades. It is illegal in the United States for an interviewer to ask an applicant's age, weight, religion, political view, ethnicity, marital status, sexual preference, or financial status. Nor can an interviewer legally inquire whether a job seeker has children, drinks, votes, does charity work, or (save in bona fide security-sensitive jobs) has committed a major crime. This rules out many of the questions that used to be asked routinely ("How would your family feel about moving up here to Seattle?") and also a good deal of break-the-ice small talk.

Hiring has always been about establishing a comfort level. The employer wants to feel reasonably certain that the applicant will succeed as an employee. That usually means sizing up a person from a variety of perspectives. In many ways, today's job candidate is a blank slate. He or she is a new person, stripped of the past, free of social context, existing only in the present moment. That leaves many employers scared.

One popular website for M.B.A. recruiting offers a "Social Security Number Decoder for Recruiters." Based on the first three digits, it tells where a job candidate was living when the social security number was issued. "The point being . . ." you ask? Well, it's one way of telling whether someone is lying about his past — a way of spotting contradictions when employers can't pose direct questions.

The Two-Second Interview

There are other, more serious reasons to worry about the American way of hiring. In the past decade, the traditional job interview has taken hits from putatively scientific studies. An increasing literature asserts the fallibility of interviewers.

Two Harvard psychologists, Nalini Ambady and Robert Rosenthal, did a particularly devastating experiment. Ambady had originally wanted to study what makes teachers effective. She suspected that nonverbal cues — body language and such — were important. To test this, she used some videotapes that had been made of a group of Harvard teaching fellows. She planned to show silent video clips to a group of people and have them rate the teachers for effectiveness.

Ambady wanted to use one-minute clips of each teacher. Unfortunately, the tapes hadn't been shot with this end in mind. They showed the teachers interacting with students. That was a problem, because having students visible in the clips might unconsciously affect the raters' opinions of the teachers. Ambady went to her adviser and said it wasn't going to work.

Then Ambady looked at the tapes again and decided she *could* get ten-second clips of teachers in which no students were visible. She did the study with those ten-second clips. Based on just ten seconds, the raters judged the teachers on a fifteen-item list of qualities.

Okay, if you *have* to judge someone from a ten-second video clip, you *can*. You probably wouldn't expect such a judgment to be worth anything.

Ambady repeated the experiment with five-second clips of the same teachers. Another group of raters judged them. Their assessments were, allowing for statistical error, identical to the ratings of the people who saw the ten-second clips.

Ambady then had another group view two-second clips of the same teachers. Again, the ratings were essentially the same.

The shocker was this: Ambady compared the video-clip ratings to ratings made by the students of the same teachers after a semester of classes. The students knew the professors much better than anyone possibly could from a silent video clip. No matter — the students' ratings were in close agreement with those of the people who saw only the videos. Complete strangers' opinions of a teacher, based on a silent two-second video, were nearly the same as those of students who had sat through a semester of classes.

It looks like people make a snap judgment of a person within two seconds of meeting him or her — a judgment *not* based on anything the person says. Only rarely does anything that happens after the first two seconds cause the judger to revise that first impression significantly.

All right, but the raters in this study were volunteer college students. Who knows what criteria they used to rate the teachers? Who knows whether they took the exercise seriously?

A more recent experiment attempts to treat the hiring situation more directly. Another of Rosenthal's students, Frank Bernieri (now at the University of Toledo), collaborated with graduate-student Neha Gada-Jain on a study in which they trained two interviewers for six weeks in accepted employment interviewing techniques. Then the two people interviewed ninety-eight volunteers of various backgrounds. Each interview was fifteen to twenty minutes, and all the interviews were captured on tape. After the interview, the trained interviewers rated the subjects.

Another student, Tricia Prickett, then edited the interview tapes down to fifteen seconds. Each fifteen-second clip showed the applicant entering the room, shaking hands with the interviewer, and sitting down. There was nothing more substantial than that. You guessed it — when another group rated the applicants just on the handshake clip, their opinions correlated strongly with those of the two trained interviewers who had the full interview to work from.

This would be *funny* if it weren't *tragic*. These studies suggest that the standard job interview is a pretense in which both interviewer and interviewee are equally and mutually duped. The interviewer has made up her mind by the time the interviewee has settled into a chair. Maybe the decision is based on looks, body language, or the "cut of your jib." What's certain is that it's not based on anything happening inside the job candidate's head. The questions and answers that follow are a sham, a way of convincing both that some rational basis exists for a hiring decision. In reality, the decision has already been made, on grounds that could not possibly be more superficial.

Human resources experts categorize interview questions with terms such as "traditional" and "behavioral." Traditional questions include the old standards that almost any American job seeker knows by heart. *Where do you see yourself in five years? What do you do on your day off? What's the last book you've read? What are you most proud of?*

Traditional-question interviews walk a tightrope between concealment and disclosure. They often invite the candidate to say something "bad" about himself, just to see how far he'll go. These questions seem to be about honesty. Really, they're about diplomacy. What you're most proud of might be your comic-book collection. That's not necessarily what the interviewer wants to hear, and you probably know that. There are safer answers, such as "the feeling of accomplishment I get from doing something — it could be anything —

really well." The trouble with the traditional interview is that both sides are wise to the game. Practically everyone gives the safe answers. The interviewers nod, not believing a word of it.

This has led to the rise of behavioral questions. These ask the candidate to describe a past experience bearing on character and job skills. An example (used at Microsoft) is "Describe an instance in your life when you were faced with a problem and tackled it successfully." Another is "Describe a time when you had to work under deadline and there wasn't enough time to complete the job." The rationale for asking behavioral questions is that it's harder to fabricate a story than a one-liner.

Unfortunately, traditional and behavioral interview questions do almost nothing to counter the two-second snap judgment. These are soft, fuzzy, and ambivalent questions. Rarely addressed is what you're supposed to make of the answers. It's mostly gut instincts.

Ask yourself this: "Is there any conceivable answer to a traditional interview question that would cause me to want to hire someone on that answer alone? Is there any possible answer that would cause me to *not* want to hire someone?"

I guess you can imagine alarming answers that might betray the candid psychopath. But most of the time, job candidates give the cautious and second-guessed answers everyone expects. With half-empty or half-full logic, an interviewer can use any answer retroactively to justify the first impression. Rarely does an answer challenge that first impression.

This probably makes some interviewers comfortable. It may not be the best way to hire. It is far from clear that traditional and behavioral questions are a good way of spending the always-too-limited time in a job interview.

Future Tense

Microsoft's interviewing practices are a product of the pressures of the high-technology marketplace. Software is about ideas, not assembly lines, and those ideas are always changing. A software company's greatest asset is a talented workforce. "The most important thing we do is hire great people," Microsoft CEO Steve Ballmer has stated more than once.

But how do you recognize great people? It is harder than ever to equate talent with a specific set of skills. Skills can become obsolete practically overnight. So can business plans. Microsoft is conscious that it has to be looking for people capable of inventing the Microsoft of five or ten years hence.

Microsoft's hiring focuses on the future tense. More than most big companies, Microsoft accepts rather than resists the "job candidate as blank slate." Its stated goal is to hire for what people can do rather than what they've done.

Because programming remains a youthful profession, Microsoft hires many people out of college. There is no job experience to guide hiring decisions. Nor is Microsoft overly impressed by schools and degrees. "We fully know how bogus [graduate school] is," one senior manager is reported to have said. This attitude has changed somewhat — Harvard dropout Bill Gates now encourages potential employees to get their degrees — but Microsoft has never been a place to hire people because they went to the right schools.

Microsoft is also a chauvinistic place. The private suspicion in Redmond seems to be that Sun, Oracle, IBM, and all the other companies are full of big, lazy slobs who couldn't cut it at Microsoft. The only kind of "experience" that counts for much is experience at Microsoft. So even with job candidates who have experience, the emphasis is on the future tense.

Microsoft does not have a time machine that lets its human resources people zip ten years into a subjunctive future to see how well a candidate will perform on the job. Predictions about future performance are perforce based largely on how well candidates answer interview questions.

"Microsoft really does believe that it can judge a person through four or five one-hour interviews," claims former Microsoft developer Adam David Barr. Barr likens the interview process to the National Football League's annual draft. Some teams base decisions on a college football record, and others go by individual workouts where the college players are tested more rigorously. At Microsoft, the "workout" — the interview — is the main factor in hiring all but the most senior people.

Why use logic puzzles, riddles, and impossible questions? The goal of Microsoft's interviews is to assess a general problem-solving ability rather than a specific competency. At Microsoft, and now at many other companies, it is believed that there are parallels between the reasoning used to solve puzzles and the thought processes involved in solving the real problems of innovation and a changing marketplace. Both the solver of a puzzle and a technical innovator must be able to identify essential elements in a situation that is initially ill-defined. It is rarely clear what type of reasoning is required or what the precise limits of the problem are. The solver must nonetheless persist until it is possible to bring the analysis to a timely and successful conclusion.

What This Book Will Do

The book will do five things. It will first trace the long and surprising history of the puzzle interview. In so doing, it will touch on such topics as intelligence tests for employment, the origins of Silicon Valley, the personal obsessions of Bill Gates, and the culture of Wall Street.

The book will then pose the following question: Do puzzle interviews work as claimed? Hirers tout these interviews, and job candidates complain about them. I will try to supply a balanced discussion of pros and cons — something that is often missing from the office watercooler debates.

The book will present a large sample of the actual questions being used at Microsoft and elsewhere. Provided your career is not on the line, you may find these puzzles and riddles to be a lot of fun. Many readers will enjoy matching their wits against those of the bright folks in Redmond. For readers who'd like to play along, there's a list of Microsoft puzzles, riddles, and trick questions in chapter four (most of which are in widespread use at other companies as well). A separate list of some of the hardest interview puzzles being asked at other companies is in chapter seven. I will elaborate in the main narrative on some of these questions and the techniques used to answer them but will refrain from giving answers until the very end of the book. The answer section starts on page 147.

The final two chapters are addressed in turn to the job candidate and the hirer. There is a genre of logic puzzle in which logical and ruthless adversaries attempt to outsmart each other. This is a good model of the puzzle interview. Chapter eight is written from the perspective of a job candidate confronted with puzzles in an interview. It presents a short and easily remembered list of tips for improving performance. Chapter nine is written from the opposite perspective — that of an interviewer confronted with a candidate who may be wise to the "tricks." It presents a list of tips for getting a fair assessment nonetheless.

If this appears a paradox, it is only because these interviews have been touted as being difficult or impossible to "prepare" for. Most logic puzzles exploit a relatively small set of mental "tricks." Knowing these tricks, and knowing the unspoken expectations governing these interviews, can help a candidate do his or her best.

The hirer, in turn, needs to recognize the possibility of preparation and structure the interview accordingly. The merits of puzzle interviews are too often defeated by the hazing-stunt atmosphere in which they are conducted and by use of trick questions whose solutions are easily remembered. Chapter nine gives a proposal for how innovative companies ought to interview. I will show how this type of interview can be improved by refocusing on its original goal of providing information that the hirer can use.

Two

The Termans and Silicon Valley

In his early days as a brash celebrity entrepreneur, Bill Gates was often quoted as saying that IQ is all that matters. IQ was a loaded, retro, non-PC concept. Gates's endorsement of it was like contemporary vogues for cigars, martinis, and thick, bloody steaks. His hiring philosophy, he explained, was that he could teach a smart person to do anything. So Microsoft valued intelligence above all, placing less emphasis on skills or experience.

This is still the Microsoft philosophy. One of the more conventional questions sometimes asked in Microsoft interviews alludes to it: "Define 'intelligence.' Are you intelligent?"

This is not a trick question (except in that an affirmative answer to the second part loses its conviction if you flub the first part). What is intelligence, anyway?

Lewis Terman and IQ

No one has done more to define intelligence and make mental assessments a part of hiring than Stanford psychologist Lewis M. Terman (1877–1956). It was Terman who popularized the concept of IQ, created the classic IQ test, and promoted intelligence testing tirelessly. Terman's credo was that every schoolchild and every employee should be tested for intelligence. At the zenith of his influence, a large proportion of American schools and employers agreed.

By an odd historical coincidence, Terman and his son, Frederick, are also closely tied to the founding of Silicon Valley as a high-tech haven; to the discrediting of IQ tests as culturally biased and thus to their abandonment by employers; and, just possibly, to the puzzle interview as we know it today.

Lewis Terman was the extremely bright son of an Indiana farmer. An itinerant phrenologist felt the bumps on young Terman's skull when he was about ten years old. The phrenologist predicted good things for the boy.

Feeling an outsider because of his intellect, Terman grew to be fascinated by the whole idea of intelligence and how it might be measured. After drifting through careers and ending up on the West Coast, Terman took a teaching job at Stanford in 1910. Founded only nineteen years earlier, Leland Stanford's school did not enjoy nearly the reputation it has today. Within a few years, Terman established himself as the university's first star faculty member. Terman put Stanford, and for that matter the apricot-growing valley in which it nestled, on the intellectual world map.

He did this with innovative work on intelligence testing. Terman translated into English the pioneering intelligence test that had been devised by French educator Alfred Binet. As is often the case with translations, Terman put a different spin on Binet's original.

The Binet test had been intended to identify mentally handicapped children for the Parisian school system. Terman was more interested in "gifted" children (he coined that term). Terman also wanted a test that could be used for adults. He therefore had to add "harder" test items than Binet had used. He ended up substantially revising and extending Binet's test. Terman gave his university a boost by naming his test the "Stanford Revision and Extension" of Binet's Intelligence Scale (now shortened to Stanford-Binet). The first version was published in 1916. Greatly revised, it is still being used today.

Terman defined intelligence as the ability to reason abstractly. You may not feel this definition says a whole lot. It was nonetheless reverentially quoted in the twentieth-century literature of intelligence testing. Today, it would probably satisfy Microsoft's interviewers as a definition of intelligence. Terman's main point was that intelligence is not knowledge of facts but the ability to manipulate concepts.

To test that ability, Terman used most of the types of questions for which intelligence tests are known. There were analogies, synonyms and antonyms, and reading-comprehension questions. There were also a few logic puzzles.

In the first two decades of the twentieth century, logic, word, and number puzzles enjoyed a popularity that is probably impossible to understand in our media-saturated age. This was the epoch in which the crossword puzzle was invented (1913). Well before daily crossword puzzles, there were logic-puzzle columns in major newspapers and in such unlikely magazines as the Woman's Home Companion. Puzzle columnists (the two big ones were American Sam Loyd and Briton Henry Ernest Dudeney) were pop-culture celebrities. The prevailing puzzle-mania is captured in a 1917 book where Dudeney wrote:

When a man says, "I have never solved a puzzle in my life," it is difficult to know exactly what he means, for every intelligent individual is doing it every day. The unfortunate inmates of our lunatic asylums are sent there expressly because they cannot solve puzzles — because they have lost their powers of reason. If there were no puzzles to solve, there would be no questions to ask; and if there were no questions to be asked, what a world it would be!

In adding puzzles to his intelligence test, Terman was apparently making the test more accessible — and seconding the common view that puzzles were a metaphor for life.

The original Stanford-Binet was administered orally (much like a job interview!). Two of the puzzles from Terman's 1916 test went like this:

A mother sent her boy to the river and told him to bring back exactly 7 pints of water. She gave him a 3-pint vessel and a 5-pint vessel. Show me how the boy can measure out exactly 7 pints of water, using nothing but the two vessels and not guessing at the amount. You should begin by filling the 5-pint vessel first. Remember, you have a 3-pint vessel and a 5-pint vessel and you must bring back exactly 7 pints.

An Indian who had come into town for the first time in his life saw a white man riding along the street. As the white man rode by, the Indian said — "The white man is lazy; he walks sitting down." What was the white man riding on that caused the Indian to say, "He walks sitting down"?

Terman claimed that he invented the first puzzle, though it is clearly an adaptation of similar measuring problems that appeared in Dudeney's and Loyd's columns. This puzzle leaves little doubt about what constitutes a right answer. The second puzzle lends itself to a multiplicity of creative answers. It thereby illustrates one of the oldest complaints people have about intelligence tests. According to Terman, the one and only right answer to the second puzzle was bicycle. He noted that the most common "incorrect" answer was horse. That was wrong, apparently because an Indian would be familiar with a horse. For reasons less clear, Terman also rejected automobile, wheelchair, and (an amusing bit of outside-the-box thinking) a person riding on someone's back.

One of the reasons for the popularity of Terman's test was that the scores were expressed as a catchy number — the intelligence quotient, or IQ. Psychologist William Stern had earlier proposed dividing a child's "mental age" by the chronological age to get a "mental quotient" that would tell how smart the child is. Terman appropriated this idea, multiplying the ratio by 100 and calling it the intelligence quotient.

This scheme doesn't work so well with adults. What would it mean to be thirty and have a mental age of fifty — that you hate house music and are starting to forget things? Terman solved the age problem simply by adjusting his test's scoring so that 100 was average for a person of any age.

That was not the only adjustment he made. As Terman assembled more and more IQ test scores, he discovered some interesting patterns. One was that girls scored higher than boys. Another was that whites scored higher than blacks, Mexicans, and recent immigrants.

Terman decided that the first finding revealed a flaw in the test while the second finding represented a real fact about human beings. He went back and looked at what questions had the biggest gender gap. He tossed out questions that favored girls and/or added questions that favored boys until the gender difference vanished. There was nothing underhanded about this tweaking. It is part of creating any good psychological test.

The interethnic differences in IQ scores were several times larger than those between genders. Terman had no interest in adjusting the test to minimize these differences. He was a white male, and if the test said whites were smarter, then it just confirmed what most white males in 1916 America already assumed. That, at least, is one possible interpretation. Another is that Terman wanted to believe the ethnic differences were "real," because otherwise they would be a humbling demonstration that it really isn't so easy to measure intelligence. Intelligence testing is founded on the assumption that certain tasks or puzzles gauge "true" intelligence, independent of education, social station, or culture. That there were substantial intercultural differences in IQ scores could have been seen as evidence of the test's inadequacy.

Terman didn't see it that way. Nor did most of America. The Stanford-Binet ushered in a national obsession with IQ testing that continues, in attenuated form, to the present day.

IQ Tests in the Workplace

It was not long before intelligence tests were used in the workplace. Robert M. Yerkes, a Harvard psychologist specializing in animal behavior, convinced the Army to test its recruits for intelligence. In 1917 Terman, Yerkes, and a number of like-minded psychologists got together in Vineland, New Jersey, to create an IQ test suitable for Army recruits. Since the team was working largely from Binet and Terman's questions, the members whipped out their test in a mere six weeks. Some 1.75 million inductees took the test in the World War I era. The Army scores were given not in IQ points but as lettered classes, A through E (like a report card, or like the lettered grades of clones in *Brave New World!*). Based on the scores, inductees were assigned suitable responsibilities. Yerkes was not shy about claiming that these intelligence tests "helped to win the war."

The Army experiment lent almost patriotic prestige to intelligence testing. Within a few years, nearly every major American school system had adopted some kind of intelligence testing. Ellis Island immigrants were welcomed to the New World with IQ tests. Companies routinely used IQ tests to decide which people to hire and which to promote.

This was largely Terman's doing. He argued that any business of five hundred to one thousand people should have a full-time psychologist on staff to administer IQ tests and thereby assign people to jobs. (This was the weird beginning of "human resources.") As to *how* you were supposed to use IQ scores to match people and jobs, Terman had most exacting ideas. He believed there was a minimum IQ needed for every profession, and he expended considerable effort in determining that minimum.

Terman and associates went around Palo Alto plying shop girls, firemen, and hobos with IQ tests. An optimal employee, Terman concluded in 1919, would have the necessary minimum intelligence and not too much extra: "Anything above 85 IQ in the case of a barber probably represents so much dead waste." People who were *too* smart for their jobs tended to "drift easily into the ranks of the antisocial or join the army of Bolshevik discontents."

Terman's dream was to transform America into an ideal meritocracy where everyone, from feebleminded to brilliant, would be slotted into suitable jobs through IQ tests.

Terman's increasing prestige allowed Stanford to assemble a world-class psychology department. That department was especially known for psychometrics — putting numbers to human attributes through tests. As the years passed, Terman became a rich man from his intelligence tests.

There were, to be sure, some studies showing that IQ scores were not that good at predicting school or job performance. These studies hardly registered on the consciousness of the public, or of Terman.

Speaking of Bolsheviks, the Sputnik-era emphasis on science education countered any lag in American interest in testing. Baby boomers were treated to a renewed wave of schoolroom IQ assessment. Identifying future math and science geniuses early, and putting them into special programs for the gifted, was promoted as a way of competing with the Soviets.

Frederick Terman and Silicon Valley

The story now turns to Lewis Terman's son, Frederick. You will see the name "Terman" all over Stanford's buildings today. It is mostly Frederick who is being immortalized. The younger Terman, an electrical engineer, was a professor, a dean, and later the acting president of Stanford. As much as anyone, he is responsible for the stature that Stanford has today.

Frederick's main contribution to American culture was as original as his father's. Hoping to bridge the divide between the academy and the business world, he dreamed of starting an industrial park in Palo Alto next to the university. In 1938 he convinced two of his former engineering students, William Hewlett and David Packard, to set up shop in a Palo Alto garage. Their first product was audio oscillators; Walt Disney's studio bought eight to use on the soundtrack of *Fantasia*.

Terman also convinced Stanford to set aside a big plot of unused land where other students and professors could start their own businesses. It would help both the university and the local business community, Terman argued. This was a totally novel idea at the time.

In 1956 Terman bagged another high-profile entrepreneur: William Shockley. Shockley felt unappreciated at Bell Labs and let it be known that he intended to start a company to commercialize transistor technology. Terman astutely recognized the importance of Shockley's ideas. He pulled all possible strings to get Shockley to set up shop near Stanford. Terman also helped Shockley recruit an impressively talented group of engineers, most from back east.

"If Shockley had been a better manager," said biographer Joel Shurkin, "he'd be one of the richest people in the world today. He would have been the match for Bill Gates." As it was, Shockley had all of Gates's competitive instinct and none of his business sense.

Shockley was a man of passionate and idiosyncratic interests. One of them was ant farms. He raised ants as a boy and, later, as a middle-aged man. He tried to train them. Shockley's notion of a well-run technology company was itself a little like an ant farm. His key values were confinement and transparency. Shockley was a hard-driving micromanager who believed in inspecting his employees from all possible angles.

The Shockley Interview

Shockley's management started with the hiring interview. He insisted that every job candidate take an intelligence test. Some East Coast candidates were tested by a New York testing firm. In most cases, Shockley administered the tests himself at the company offices. The candidates were not recruited from a help-wanted ad in the local paper. They were a handpicked group of the most talented engineers and scientists in the world. People such as Gordon Moore (later of "Moore's Law" fame and cofounder of Intel) remember having to take these tests as Shockley timed them. Shockley decided Moore was smart enough to hire.

These interviews included logic puzzles. For the record, Shockley's preoccupation with quick answers was not all bluster. During his interview at Shockley Semiconductor, crystallographer Jay Last described a vexing problem that had plagued his graduate research at MIT. Shockley thought a moment and announced the answer. The right answer.

Last also interviewed at Bell Labs, where he was given some friendly advice: *You don't want to work for Bill Shockley.*

Being hired at Shockley Semiconductor (as Moore and Last were) was a mixed and short-lived blessing. Shockley's management techniques graded into paranoia. He regularly taped meetings so that he could review them at leisure for signs of insubordination. Shockley's wife, Emily, was a psychiatric nurse who would sometimes sit silently in a corner, taking Madame DeFarge–like notes.

One day an office assistant scratched her hand on a small, pointed piece of metal in a door. It drew a little blood. This convinced Shockley that the company had been booby-trapped by an unknown saboteur. He bullied two low-level employees into taking polygraph tests. Everyone save Shockley and his wife found this outrageous. The polygraph exams vindicated the two employees.

Shockley next decreed that *everyone* would have to take a polygraph exam. The engineers flatly refused. One of them, Sheldon Roberts, examined the offending piece of metal under a microscope. It turned out to be a thumbtack whose head had broken off.

The company's exasperated engineers staged a mass resignation in 1957. Fortunately for area real estate values, they didn't go far. The "Traitorous Eight," as Shockley called them, went on to found Fairchild Semiconductor, Intel, and other early Silicon Valley companies.

Deprived of its talent, Shockley's company withered. It never shipped a successful product. For the rest of his life, Shockley watched former employees achieve all that he had dreamed of. They advanced semiconductor technology by orders of magnitude (using silicon, and certain other ideas Shockley had championed early on). They accumulated some of the most incredible personal fortunes in the history of American capitalism while wealth forever eluded Shockley. In 1963 Shockley opted out of the business world. He took a teaching post at Stanford, where he taught a course on a pet subject, creativity and problem solving.

Shockley also brooded over IQ and race. Starting in 1964, he began claiming that differences in group IQ scores proved that African Americans and other minorities were intellectually inferior to whites. This was not a new idea. Many if not most of the major early proponents of intelligence testing in America were what we'd now call foaming-at-the-mouth white supremacists. From the outset, Lewis Terman had believed that the differing average IQ scores of ethnic groups implied real differences in intelligence. Yerkes had wanted to keep Jews from immigrating to the United States, citing low IQ scores of barely English-speaking immigrants.

But by the time of the 1937 revision of the Stanford-Binet, Lewis Terman had backed away from that sort of talk. It's not clear whether he changed his views or simply decided it politic — for himself, IQ testing, and Stanford — to keep his views private. The rise of Nazism had dampened American enthusiasm for "scientific" demonstrations of racial superiority.

Shockley was a walking time warp. He was saying what Lewis Terman and company had said in the 1920s, only he was doing it at the height of the 1960s' civil rights movement. This earned Shockley a lot of press. As a Nobel laureate, he was hard to dismiss as a "nut," and he appeared to enjoy the limelight. He was also publicity-savvy enough to keep coming up with newsworthy twists whenever the media threatened to lose interest.

At one point, Shockley modestly proposed that the government offer a reward to low-IQ people for having themselves sterilized. The payment was to be $1,000 for every IQ point below 100. (But since the *really* stupid might not be able to do the math, he also suggested "bounties" for those who recruited low-IQ people for the program, and a trust fund to dole out the money.)

Not neglecting the upside of his eugenic equation, Shockley donated sperm to an exclusive California sperm bank that claimed to be breeding geniuses by supplying Nobel-worthy sperm to suitable young women. The women did not have to have won Nobel prizes.

By the time of Shockley's 1989 death, he had succeeded in equating IQ testing with racism in the public consciousness. He alienated almost everyone who knew him, including the bearers of his own genetic legacy. Shockley's estranged children learned of his death by reading about it in the newspaper. Shockley died convinced that his statements on genetic inferiority would prove a more valuable legacy than the transistor.

The IQ Disenchantment

The Shockley affair was only the most flamboyant episode in America's gradual disenchantment with intelligence testing. From the 1930s onward, schools and employers began to realize that IQ testing was not the panacea that Terman had made it out to be.

In 1964 New York City decided to drop IQ testing in its schools. The race issue was a big part of it. Educators complained that the culture gap between the mostly white male test makers and minority test takers resulted in lower IQ scores for minority students. By stigmatizing minority children as low IQ, intelligence testing did real harm. Kids were needlessly put in special education classes; their parents were told not to expect much. Test scores became a self-fulfilling prophecy. New York's action was followed by school districts in other cities.

Companies abandoned intelligence tests in employment as well. They were spurred by a handful of lawsuits in which the tests were held to be unfairly discriminatory, and finally by a 1971 Supreme Court decision that banned IQ tests in most types of hiring.

You might think that intelligence tests are "so twentieth century." We're way beyond that now — right? Wrong.

Intelligence tests are probably as widely used as ever in education and the workplace. It's just that you can't call them that anymore. The biggest and most profitable example is the Scholastic Aptitude Test. What is aptitude for higher education if not intelligence? The SAT's roots can be traced directly back to the World War I Army tests. Princeton psychologist Carl Brigham, who was part of Yerkes's panel, designed the first SAT using the Army tests as a model. The SAT is not only the nation's most widely used intelligence test but the foundation of a major industry in coaching students for an exam that supposedly measures unchangeable aptitude.

"Is pre-employment testing legal?" This is the first question on the FAQ page of the website for Wonderlic, a major supplier of intelligence tests for employers. The short answer is yes. The Wonderlic site mentions Equal Employment Opportunity Commission guidelines stipulating that tests used in employment be fair, valid, and work related. Wonderlic says its tests are all three. A diverse group of corporate customers agrees. Even the NFL feels it important to test recruits for intelligence. A while back, the press leaked one item on the NFL's version of the Wonderlic Personnel Test. You are given the number series

$$8 \quad 4 \quad 2 \quad 1 \quad \tfrac{1}{2} \quad \tfrac{1}{4}$$

and asked "What number should come next?" San Francisco 49ers president Carmen Policy explained: "A player needs a baseline mental capacity to play this game."

IQ, the number (a more doubtful concept than intelligence testing per se), remains an unshakable part of American culture. IQ quizzes are among the most popular features on the Web and in magazines. Mensa, the high-IQ club, claims one hundred thousand members that can be found on every continent except Antarctica. Shortly after President George W. Bush took office, an e-mail hoax made the rounds, claiming to give the IQs of American presidents. The younger Bush was supposedly the dumbest. People took the hoax seriously; it fooled even seemingly high-IQ types such as *Doonesbury* cartoonist Garry Trudeau.

Thermometers and Beauty Contests

Like many other psychological ideas or instruments, intelligence testing is seen differently by the scientific community than by the public. (Another example is Shockley's equally beloved polygraph.) The scientific standing of IQ has never been especially solid and has eroded since Terman invented it.

To Terman, intelligence tests were supposed to be something like thermometers. Before the invention of the thermometer, temperature was a totally subjective concept. "Is it just me, or is it hot in here?" There was no way of separating temperature from people's subjective and often contradictory discourse about temperature.

The invention of the thermometer changed all that. It showed that there was a real physical something underlying all this talk about how hot or cold you feel. Jack may be "burning up" and Jane may be "freezing." Both can check the thermometer and agree that it reads 68°F. The thermometer also refined our understanding of what "hot" and "cold" mean. Put a thermometer in a bottle of Red-Hot Pepper Sauce, and you'll find the temperature is exactly the same as the surrounding air. That tells us that the "heat" of pepper sauce is a different, illusory kind of heat.

Terman hoped IQ tests would do the same for intelligence. They'd show that there was something solid and real beneath all our fuzzy impressions. In 1916 this was a reasonable conjecture.

It hasn't worked out that way, though. Instead of thermometers, intelligence tests have been more like beauty contests. Yes, people who score well on IQ tests are intelligent (and every Miss America is gorgeous!). By encapsulating some subjective but widely shared notions of intelligence, IQ tests succeed reasonably well in distinguishing broad degrees of intelligence — just as beauty contests do with beauty. What IQ tests have failed to do is demonstrate a simple, objective reality underneath it all. A century of intelligence testing has hardly told us anything we didn't already know about intelligence — any more than a century of beauty contests has told us anything new about beauty. Like beauty, intelligence is one of those words that is useful because it can be applied so freely and loosely.

This intrinsic vagueness undercuts the whole idea of a scientific measurement of intelligence. People who design psychological tests have to concern themselves with "validity." How do you prove that your test measures what you claim it measures? The only way to prove that IQ tests work is to show that people who score well on such tests are in fact intelligent to the degree indicated by the test. But how do you gauge intelligence, quantitatively, except by a test?

It would be great if you could attach an IQ meter to someone's brain and read off a number. The existence of such a meter would demonstrate once and for all that IQ is real. Then you could rate intelligence tests by how well people's scores correlate with IQ meter readings. You could even evaluate single questions (such as logic puzzles asked in job interviews) to see how good they are at predicting IQ. You could eliminate cultural bias by making sure that people of widely different cultures but the same IQ (measured by the meter) score the same on IQ tests.

Needless to say, the IQ meter is fantasy. The only quantitative measures of intelligence we have are test scores. Historically, most IQ tests have been "validated" by showing that their scores agree with those of Terman's Stanford-Binet test. You don't have to be a statistician to see that that's a case of the snake biting its own tail.

The credibility of intelligence tests rests on the common-sense assumption that people who answer difficult questions correctly are smarter than those who don't. What's wrong with that? The answer is that there's nothing wrong with that, provided you're willing to accept intelligence tests as a fuzzy and subjective gauge of a fuzzy and subjective concept — a beauty contest, so to speak. The trouble is, Terman, and everyone else, has taken intelligence tests more seriously than that. They've been promoted as a scientific measurement, starting with that two- or three-significant-figure IQ. The usual notion of intelligence testing folds in a lot of other assumptions that are not so commonsensical and that may be wrong.

One assumption is that the test questions measure what they are supposed to measure without introducing irrelevant bias. Terman tweaked his test to close a gender gap but not the interethnic differences. He probably felt that he didn't set out to write "racist" questions, so why should he change his test? In the absence of any objective measure of intelligence, there is no certain way of saying whether this was justified. If, on the other hand, Terman had chosen to take it as an axiom that all large ethnic groups have the same average intelligence, then he would have concluded that his test was seriously biased and needed to be adjusted or discarded. Far from being just unfortunate "public relations," the Shockley debacle highlighted an important theoretical problem with intelligence testing. With no objective reality to keep test designers "honest," intelligence becomes whatever the test designer wants it to be. Who makes up the questions *does* matter.

IQ tests also promote a conception of intelligence that may not be accurate. Terman and many other psychologists of his time believed that there was one basic kind of "general intelligence" underlying all useful thought (hence, one number can measure it). The statistical arguments used to support this have been contested, and many alternate models have been put forth. To give just one widely promoted example, in 1983 Howard Gardner proposed that there are seven distinct kinds of intelligence: linguistic, logical-mathematical, spatial, bodily kinesthetic, interpersonal, intrapersonal, and musical. Therefore, a dancer may have great bodily kinesthetic intelligence and score terribly on her math SATs.

This theory probably squares better with common experience (people who are good at one thing are not always good at other things) than Terman's view. To an age that values diversity, Gardner's model may be easier to swallow than that of a monolithic intelligence. In fact, the latest update of the Stanford-Binet nods to the contemporary marketplace by offering four specialized scores in addition to a composite IQ. But Gardner's model, much like its predecessors, is difficult to confirm or extend. In so many ways, measuring intelligence is nailing Jell-O to a wall.

The Mensa Paradox

One unexpected illustration of the fallibility of intelligence testing is due to Mensa. The club, founded in Britain in 1946, requires that applicants supply signed and notarized (!) proof that they have scored in the top 2 percent on the Stanford-Binet or other approved intelligence tests. Yet you often hear of a Mensa paradox. This is the observation that many of the club's brainy members are, well, average people in average jobs.

"There are Mensans on welfare and Mensans who are millionaires," reports the club's website. "Mensa has professors and truck drivers, scientists and firefighters, computer programmers and farmers, artists, military people, musicians, laborers, police officers, glassblowers. . . ."

Sneering at the middling success of some Mensa members has become a cliché of almost any magazine piece on the society. If these people are so smart, why aren't they rich, or famous, or Nobel-prize winners, or simply more successful at something than they are?

The suggestion that many high-IQ people are losers is as old as IQ testing. Lewis Terman attempted to challenge it by organizing a famous study of 1,528 high-IQ children. He hoped to show that such kids were not the "freaks" that some thought and would prove to be natural leaders later in life. Eighty years later, Terman's study is still going on. His successors at Stanford have followed Terman's "whiz kids" throughout life and have vowed to continue until the last one drops dead.

The high-IQ subjects ranged from a pool cleaner and a convicted forger to doctors, lawyers, and the creator of TV's *I Love Lucy* (Jess Oppenheimer). Ironically, the young William Shockley was tested for Terman's study but didn't score high enough to make the cut. Oh, well — none of those who did have won a Nobel prize.

I suppose the Mensa paradox says more about our society's overweening emphasis on intelligence than about high-IQ people themselves. From Lewis Terman to Bill Gates, people have been trying to drum into all of us the importance of intelligence. It's hard not to take some delight in seeing this credo subverted. "Mensa member mucks up," ran one recent headline in the London *Independent*. "A Mensa member who turned burglar was caught when he left a trail of muddy footprints to his own front door."

A 1968 study tried to use Terman's group to investigate why so many intelligent people aren't successes. Melita Oden, an associate of Terman's, identified the 100 "least successful" of Terman's now-aging prodigies and compared them to the 100 "most successful." Okay, "success" is even more subjective than "intelligence." Oden defined it the way that most prospective in-laws might: The successful ones were those who used their intellectual abilities in their jobs to achieve something of broadly recognized value (developing a classic sitcom, say). The least successful were those whose jobs did not make use of the intellectual talent they possessed (like cleaning pools). Oden found no significant IQ differences between the successes and failures in this already high-IQ group. The distinguishing qualities were early parental encouragement and factors such as confidence and persistence.

This finding is hardly more than common sense. It nonetheless goes some way toward explaining the Mensa paradox. It suggests that motivational factors are something distinct from intelligence. You can have one, the other, both, or neither. The PowerPoint slide of this would be two overlapping circles (or really, two *fuzzy* overlapping circles). One circle represents the intelligent people. Another circle is the confident, persistent, motivated people. "Successful" people mostly fall in the area where the two circles overlap.

Are Puzzle Interviews IQ Tests?

Puzzle interviews are a reaction to this post-IQ world we live in. When discussing their interview questions, Microsoft's people shy away from the word "intelligence," with its baggage of racism and high-IQ pool cleaners. Microsoft's interview puzzles are said to measure hipper, sexier things: *bandwidth, inventiveness, creative problem-solving ability, outside-the-box thinking.* Microsoft's interviewing style is championed as being diversity conscious and especially as being more relevant to the business world than anything so déclassé as an intelligence test.

Ignore the spin, and similarities to an intelligence test are inescapable. Microsoft's interviewers pose a puzzle about measuring water with 3- and 5-gallon containers that is extremely similar to the puzzle in the original Stanford-Binet. The Microsoft interviewing technique known as the Challenge (to be discussed in the next chapter) also occurs in the original Stanford-Binet. Aside from the specifics, the whole idea of testing a general, context-independent problem-solving ability is similar to Terman's conception of intelligence as the ability to reason abstractly.

As far as I can tell, the major verbalized difference has to do with motivation. Microsoft does not see itself as a place for high-IQ ne'er-do-wells. One of the claimed merits of its interviews is that they test motivation and persistence. Logic puzzles and other Microsoft questions pose tasks with a beginning, middle, and end. Answering these questions means encountering and surmounting obstacles. The successful solver must be persistent as well as smart. In that respect, so it's said, a logic puzzle is a better predictor of workplace success than other intelligence-test items such as analogies, synonyms, or sentence-completion tasks.

Do Puzzle Interviews Work?

It was the talented group that Shockley, using puzzles, recruited that founded Silicon Valley. Another talented group, also recruited with puzzles, built much of today's software industry. That helps explain the popularity of the puzzle interview, but by no means is everyone sold on it. Microsoft's style of interviewing is a controversial topic almost anyplace that high-technology hirers and employees compare notes.

"I enjoy puzzles, but I would really be cheesed off if getting a non–puzzle-solving job depended on them," read a message posted on the kuro5hin.org newsgroup. "It's about as stupid as making sure that FBI agents can routinely win at Super Mario Bros. just in case they need to rescue a kidnapped princess."

That puzzles are hermetic and irrelevant is probably the most common complaint expressed. "In general, I think logic puzzles are good at one thing — determining how well a person is able to solve a logic puzzle," says Chris Sells, who operates a website devoted to Microsoft interview questions.

"Performance on brainteasers says a lot about your experience working mathematical puzzles and very little about whether you will be a valuable employee," wrote John Mongan and Noah Suojanen in *Programming Interviews Exposed*, a 2000 guide for job seekers. Mongan and Suojanen judge Microsoft-style questions to be "cheap shots that don't prove much of anything."

Another frequent complaint is that the puzzle interviews constitute a "fraternity initiation." They measure not competence but how well one fits into a clubbish culture. "Everyone who works there had to answer those questions," says Sells. "And by God, they're gonna make the next guy answer those same stupid questions."

Attitudes toward Microsoft's interviews are a lot like those toward fraternity hazing: a lot more favorable among people who've been through it successfully than for the guy who got stranded in a freezing cornfield in his underwear and didn't make the cut. "The weird thing was, I loved it," said Zeke Koch, a program manager for Microsoft Office, of his "grueling" nine-hour interview. "I had a blast. I love solving puzzles and being put on the spot, where I have to think on my feet."

Of course, these interviews are more "fun" for the person who gets to ask the questions, as former Microsoft program manager Joel Spolsky concedes. Employers like puzzle interviews. They give hirers more information on which to base their decision. Besides, they're in the comfortable position of power, watching someone else squirm. Job candidates have little reason to cheer puzzle interviews. They're harder than other kinds of interviews. In practice, the chance of getting a job offer is often less than with a traditional interview — certainly in Microsoft's case, where they fly in a small army of candidates every week.

"The [Microsoft] interviewing process really emphasizes just how different they think they are," says Sells. "They tend to get the exact folks they're looking for, the ubergeeks. They are people who have spent some of their time, while growing up, obsessing over logic puzzles, stretching their brains. And that's really what Microsoft is looking for: a certain way of thinking, a certain level of technical expertise, and certain other qualities that fit into their culture."

In general, puzzle interviews raise shrugs with psychologists and cognitive scientists. They pose the same insoluble validation problem that intelligence tests do. The only way to prove the validity of Microsoft's interview techniques, says Princeton's Philip Johnson-Laird, would be for the company to hire a group of people regardless of how they did on the puzzles and hypothetical questions. Then, after years on the job, they could compare the performance of the good and not-so-good puzzle solvers. Even then, there would be the real problem of deciding, quantitatively, how "successful" each person had been on the job.

As with IQ tests, the rationale for puzzle interviews starts and ends with "It stands to reason . . ." *It stands to reason* that people who are good at logic puzzles are smart and will be good at solving problems that arise on the job. At least, a lot of people feel that way.

Scientific objections are halfway to the point. IQ tests purport to be a scientific measurement. As such, their fallibility is a debilitating flaw. Microsoft-style puzzle interviews purport merely to be effective. That is a different and less stringent claim.

All that any interviewing technique does is to sort candidates into two lists, the "hires" and the "no hires." Of these two lists, the hires is by far the more important. An interviewing technique is usually judged to be good when the hires turn out to be practically all good employees, with few or no unsuitable people.

The composition of the no hires list is almost beside the point. It might be that an interviewing technique falsely knocks a lot of good, capable people onto the no hires list. That is not necessarily a problem. At least, it's not a problem from the employer's perspective, assuming there are enough people on the hires list to fill the openings, and the technique is "fair" by equal opportunity employment law criteria. Job candidates, on the other hand, may object to a technique that falsely rejects too many people and makes such interviews a waste of their time.

The real test of an interviewing technique is how it compares with other interviewing techniques. Hiring is not a particularly scientific process anywhere. At most companies, it's seat-of-the-pants intuition. If Microsoft did not judge job seekers (in part) on their performance on puzzles and riddles, then they would have to give more weight to something else — answers to "softer" traditional and behavioral questions, small talk, the firmness of a handshake. It is hard to see how that would be a fairer or more effective way of hiring.

There is virtually no controversy about traditional interview questions such as "Why should we hire you?" Why these questions get a free ride is hard to say. The studies that have been done of traditional interviewing, such as those by Ambady, Bernieri, Gada-Jain, and Prickett, are damning.

Coders such as Mongan, Suojanen, and Sells tend to believe that the best way of assessing programming ability is to have the candidate do programming exercises in the interview. They are probably right. Why bring in a debatable correlation between puzzle-solving ability and coding ability when you can assess coding ability directly? Of course, Microsoft does require developers to write code in interviews.

But puzzles shouldn't be (and mostly aren't) presented as a weirdly indirect test of coding ability. They are intended to test a robust facility for solving problems with logic and imagination — something needed by program managers, say, or by attorneys, investment bankers, corporate managers, and hundreds of other noncoding jobs.

The relevant question to ask about puzzle interviews is whether the people who are sorted onto a hire list in this manner will make better employees than those on the hire lists produced with other interviewing techniques. Not many would dispute that puzzle interviews are better than traditional interviews at identifying good problem solvers, *assuming you can't test a specific skill set* in the interview. This is a statement that is not so much about how effective we know puzzle interviews to be but about how ineffective we know traditional interviewing techniques to be. The strongest argument for puzzle interviews is that everything else is worse.

The unease many feel toward the puzzle interview owes more to its aims than its means. Given the mental image of Shockley timing puzzle solvers with a stopwatch, you have to ask: Has it really come to that? Is it so important for compa-

nies to get the best and brightest that we allow hiring interviews to turn into puzzle-solving competitions?

These are questions that each company must answer
on its own. Running a company today is a difficult balancing
act. The global economy dictates a lean, nimble style of management. At the same time, companies are not just capitalist
machines. They have a human side, a miniature society with
expectations about how employees and potential employees
should be treated. In innovation-based industries, that human side is a company's main asset. With it comes a pressure
to challenge traditional notions of social decorum in order to
gain a competitive edge. People such as Bill Gates speak to
us today because they voice, in exaggerated form, the pressures (paranoia, even) we all feel in our mutable and inter-
connected global marketplace. For a struggling start-up — or
even for one of those $400 billion businesses that perpetually
fears missing the next technological boat — ends tend to justify means. This is the ambivalent fascination of the puzzle
interview, which is in some ways a cry of desperation.

Prehistory of the Puzzle Interview

The early history of logic puzzles on job interviews is
difficult to trace. Most of the people I spoke with in re-
searching this book were relatively young, and worked or interviewed at companies with little institutional memory. No
one, including human resources experts, was able to say
where the idea came from or where it began.

What does seem clear is that Microsoft could not have
"invented" the idea. Shockley used puzzles in interviews
around 1957. Other than that, the earliest datable use of logic
puzzles in job interviews that I came across was from 1979.
Steve Abell (now president of brising.com, a software con-

sulting firm) recalls interviewing at Hewlett-Packard that year and being asked to solve a logic puzzle. That might suggest that puzzle interviews were a Silicon Valley phenomenon.

The first question put to Abell in that Hewlett-Packard interview was "You have eight coins, and one of them is lighter than the others. Find the light coin in two weighings of a pan balance." With minor differences, this is a question Microsoft interviewers use today. In 1979 Microsoft was fifteen people in Albuquerque headed by a twenty-three-year-old kid. It's hard to believe that Hewlett-Packard paid any attention to Microsoft's hiring practices. The opposite influence is more probable. As with so many other things, Microsoft seems to have appropriated an idea that was already in the air and made it famous.

Three

Bill Gates and the Culture of Puzzles

The family of Seattle attorney William Gates II was a big believer in organized fun. Wife Mary arranged family skits and Sunday evening tournaments of bridge, Password, or trivia games. "The play was quite serious," Gates II told *Time* magazine. "Winning mattered." One of Bill III's favorite pastimes was Risk, a game whose playing board is a map of the world. The goal is to conquer countries and achieve world domination. After the young Gates discovered computers in high school, one of his first programs was designed to play Risk.

At the dinner table, attorney Gates would present and dissect topical issues for the family's edification. He posed probing questions to Bill and his sisters, and they were expected to provide well-reasoned answers. The children were awarded a quarter for every A on their report card. Should they get straight As, they earned the extra perk of being allowed to watch television on weeknights.

By all accounts, Bill Gates has never lost his taste for

games and puzzles. In true *Citizen Kane* fashion, Bill and wife Melinda while away evenings at home with jigsaw puzzles, often huge puzzles that have been handcrafted from costly rare woods. The Gateses often buy two identical puzzles, one for each of them, in order to see who completes it first.

Between courses at dinner parties, Bill will tell everyone present to turn over his or her place mat and draw a map of the United States. Whoever draws the most accurate map wins. Steve Ballmer is great at this game. He plays it on airplanes. (In 1926 Florence Goodenough, one of Terman's students, devised the "Draw-a-Man" test for children. The accuracy of the drawings was held to correlate closely with IQ scores. This was one of the most widely used psychological tests through the 1940s.)

In 1986 Bill Gates bought a four-house vacation compound on the Hood Canal, a U-shaped inlet of the Puget Sound. There, family and Microsoft employees play "Microgames," whimsical competitions where winning matters. In the "sing down" game, you're given a word, and you have to come up with songs that prominently use that word. One time the word was "sea." As longtime Gates friend Ann Winblad recalled it, Bill disappeared onto the nighttime beach during this game. A while later, a familiar voice rose out of the mists: "Puff, the magic dragon . . ."

When Microsoft people travel on business, they can expect scant time for unstructured sightseeing or hobnobbing with foreigners. Instead, the company arranges to keep them with their own kind, playing highly competitive games. At Microsoft's 1989 Global Summit in Geneva, the game was a scavenger hunt. Each team got a horse-drawn coach to carry its members around the city as they searched for odd items. Gates participated along with everyone else. His brainstorm was to ditch the company-supplied carriage and take a taxi. Team members split the cab fare; Gates's team came in third.

It will perhaps come as no surprise that Gates does not like to lose in social games any more than he does in the game of business. A game of charades once ended with Gates accusing another player of cheating (Gates was losing). A friendly Internet bridge game with Warren Buffett ended abruptly — "The miserable little cheat unplugged his computer to avoid losing!" is Buffett's story.

Math Camp

A similar attitude toward winning permeates Microsoft. Microsoft's people are "hard core," to use the term made famous by the antitrust trial. E-mails from Gates and other Microsoft executives showed approximately what competitors had claimed all along, that Microsoft is a Vince Lombardi–esque place where winning is everything. The goal is to be hard core, to wage "jihad," to "cut off the air supply" of competitors. The software business is a vast game, and money is how you keep score. As one rival software executive griped: "Basically what Microsoft is trying to do is tax every bit transition in the whole world. When a bit flips, they will charge you."

In some ways, Microsoft is a changed place since the antitrust suit. Microsoft people edit their words more — certainly their e-mail, where employees are advised to avoid obscenities and "full concepts." Some of the top talent have left in various degrees of disenchantment. Gates has stepped back from day-to-day management.

Yet the hypercompetitive ethos remains. One term Microsoft insiders have for it is "math camp." That describes the kind of place where high-IQ males (mostly) insist that everyone else is stupid and they alone know the right answer to every question. Possibly Bill Gates's most famous saying is "THAT'S THE STUPIDEST THING I'VE EVER HEARD!!!" A runner-up is "Why don't you just give up your stock options and join the peace corps?!?"

This spirit of one-upmanship is evident in the company's puzzles, games, and practical jokes. Paradoxically, these diversions are both a respite from the pressures of business and a particularly concentrated form of them. Microsoft employees returning from vacation or leave can expect to find their offices ingeniously sabotaged. Offices have been filled with Styrofoam peanuts, Dixie cups half full of water, ten thousand soft-drink cans, or the colored plastic balls used in McDonaldland play areas. One office was sodded wall-to-wall. Others have been transformed into "farms," with real livestock such as a rooster, a horse, or a potbellied pig. In one case, the floor was raised to window level; in another, the office was transformed into a bathroom. Arguably the most imaginative fate awaited program manager Jabe Blumenthal. He came back from vacation to find that his office had disappeared entirely. Coworkers used wallboard and paint to "erase" the door.

During a 1998 trip with friends, Gates and his party stopped at a small, exclusive restaurant in Carmel, California. The manager pulled Gates aside and said there was a problem with their reservation. A Colorado couple that had been married there twenty years previously had vowed to return on their twentieth anniversary. The manager had forgotten all about it. The couple showed up, and the proprietor didn't have the heart to turn them away.

Gates said it was no problem. He invited the couple to share a table with his party of high-ranking executives.

This turned out to be a mistake. The anniversary couple was thoroughly obnoxious. The man got drunk and asked where everyone was from. Microsoft vice president of sales and marketing Jeff Raikes said "Nebraska."

"Oh, that's where they have the convicts playing football!" the man said. He went off on how terrible Nebraska's football coach, Tom Osborne, was. (Raikes, as it happened, idolized Osborne, who had been a surprise guest at Raikes's fortieth birthday party.) The executives were about ready to punch the guy when the anniversary couple dropped the pretense. They admitted they were actors, hired by Gates as a practical joke.

The Redmond campus is itself an amazing place, likened to Disneyland with some justice. Like the theme park, it is a large, clean, master-planned community, a micromanaged utopia purportedly representing the best that America has to offer, and everywhere permeated by the personality of its purportedly benign founder. Unlike Disneyland, at Microsoft, the soft drinks and candy are free, and all the arcade games are set to free play.

The campus has eighty-two buildings with just over 6 million square feet of floor space. That is nine times that of the Louvre, and nearly the size of the Pentagon. There are twenty-four cafeterias at Microsoft headquarters, seven of which serve breakfast, lunch, and dinner. There is a Microsoft transit service, library, TV studio, museum, company store, soccer field, and art collection.

Employees are given a great deal of freedom, assuming they get their jobs done. What might be considered affectations elsewhere are fairly normal here. One software tester comes to work in Victorian outfits. Developer J Allard (just J, with no period) goes by quasi-official titles such as "Minister of Soul" for Xbox. One male executive reportedly has a massive cache of digitized pornography. The porn figures into another long-running practical joke. People would turn on their computers and find one of the porn images installed as wallpaper. The perpetrator was not the porn enthusiast but a female manager.

Stay Hungry

That kind of pseudobohemianism is endemic to the entire software industry, not only to Microsoft. As high-tech companies go, Microsoft is a weirdly Lake Wobegon kind of place. Its people fly coach and stay in nice, not-too-expensive chain hotels. There are no executive dining rooms. Nearly everyone has a cookie-cutter nine-by-twelve-foot office with sensible furniture. Gates's office is larger, but journalists who visit it usually feel obliged to remark on how ordinary it is: no marble, nothing real expensive looking.

For all the storied wealth created by Microsoft's stock options, salaries are relatively modest. A beginning software developer makes about $80,000 a year. Bill Gates's 1999 salary was only $369,000 — barely what the chief executive in the other Washington pulls in. Microsoft is a place where you finish your vegetables, *then* you get your dessert.

Much like a small town, the Microsoft community reckons time by events of local significance (often as not, these events are e-mail memos). Longtime employees tell you the defining moment in Microsoft parsimony was the 1993 "Shrimp and Weenies Memo." After chief technology officer Nathan Myhrvold commented about seeing "a lot more shrimp than weenies around here these days," human resources director Mike Murray issued a memo against the profligate folly embodied in that moderately expensive finger food. At Microsoft, shrimp are equated to IBM, the decadence of the Romans, and all the other big organizations that got soft. *Inside Out,* a coffee-table book issued to commemorate Microsoft's twenty-fifth anniversary, captures this aspect of the corporate value system perfectly:

> Just in case anyone is in danger of forgetting this, the secret to remaining ahead of the pack is not "Get Fat." It's "Stay Hungry." Creativity doesn't happen without a few constraints. That's why wise use of resources has been a business tradition at Microsoft since the early days, when, to be perfectly honest, there wasn't much choice in the matter. But it remains our practice today, for the simple reason that when you start leaning on your wealth instead of living by your wits, you're in real danger of losing your edge.

The same publication posits a yet more succinct motto: "Excess destroys success."

To outsiders, this fear of getting soft is one of the most inexplicable parts of the Microsoft culture. A favored theme of Microsoft's leadership has long been the immanent prospect of the company's annihilation. "If we make the wrong decisions," Bill Gates warned sternly at the company's quarter-century anniversary, "everything we've built over the last twenty-five years could be history."

"One day, somebody will catch us napping," writes Gates in his book *Business @ the Speed of Thought.* "One day, an eager upstart will put Microsoft out of business."

This is not just a personal obsession of Gates's. Try Steve Ballmer: "Our next competitor could come out of nowhere and put us out of business virtually overnight." Or

Jeff Raikes: "If we don't continue to innovate to keep up with consumer needs and technology advances, we can be unseated at any time, by anyone." Microsoft may be smug, but there is nothing Microsoft is smugger about than its absence of hubris.

Outsiders scoff at this rhetoric. Microsoft is a pretty big balloon. If and when someone punches a hole in it, it will take a long time for all the air to blow out. From a historical perspective, though, Gates and Ballmer are absolutely right. Companies' tenures at the top of the corporate heap are short. A company that lives by innovation dies by innovation.

In the Microsoft culture, the Harvard Business School's Clayton M. Christensen is practically the equivalent of a rock star. People go into crucial meetings toting copies of Christensen's book *The Innovator's Dilemma* lest they feel the urgent need to quote something out of it. Christensen's message is that the business plans that make companies successful also make them incapable of dealing with certain types of revolutionary change. These "disruptive" technologies allow start-up Davids to topple corporate Goliaths. In short, the book plays perfectly into Microsoft paranoia.

The Innovator's Dilemma cites the disk-drive business as its archetype. Out of seventeen companies making hard drives in 1976, all but one went bust or were acquired by 1995. (The sole survivor was IBM.) With a knack for quotable paradox, Christensen attributes the failures to *good management.* The companies were so attuned to their customers' and investors' needs that they were unable to react to crucial technological changes.

Christensen's is a gospel of *cluelessness.* As he sees it, no one is smart enough to predict the way that disruptive technologies will play out. Companies have to learn along with their customers how disruptive technologies will be used. The process is, in computer jargon, massively parallel. All sorts of applications for a new technology are tried, of which just a few catch on.

The Innovator's Dilemma recounts a telling anecdote. A few years after Shockley's team invented the transistor, Bell Labs' parent company, AT&T, was contacted by a Japanese businessman staying at a cheap hotel in New York. The businessman wanted to license the transistor. AT&T kept putting him off. The man persisted and finally negotiated a deal. After the license agreements were signed, one of AT&T's people asked the businessman what his company was going to do with the technology. The man said they were going to build small radios.

"Why would anyone care about small radios?" the AT&T executive asked.

"We'll see," said the businessman. His name was Akio Morita, and his company was Sony. Sony's handheld transistor radios became the first breakout consumer application for transistors.

Logic was of limited use in predicting applications for the transistor. What is more logical than assuming that sound quality is all-important in music? The first transistor radios had *terrible* sound quality. Why would people want a staticky transistor radio when they could get superior sound quality from the washing-machine-size radio already sitting in their living room?

As Christensen wrote, "Markets that do not exist cannot be analyzed. Suppliers and customers must discover them together. Not only are the market applications for disruptive technologies *unknown* at the time of their development, they are *unknowable*."

Following Taillights

Christensen's point is not, of course, that business-people should reject logic. His message is akin to the advice offered to solvers of puzzles: You have to recognize that the type of reasoning that works so well most of the time may not work in certain situations. In those situations, logic can be misleading. It's necessary to step back, consider all the options, and proceed methodically. You need to combine logic with creativity and mental flexibility. It will be necessary to brainstorm a number of possible approaches, try them out without committing too many resources (for most of the approaches will fail), and then devise a game plan from what you learn. This is how both business innovation and puzzle solving work.

Words such as "creativity" and "innovation" are loaded terms at Microsoft. We've all heard the rap: "Microsoft cannot make great products" (James Gleick writing in the *New York Times*). "It has no spark of genius; it does not know how to innovate; it lets bugs live forever; it eradicates all traces of personality from its software." An adage goes, "Microsoft just needs a set of taillights to follow."

Naturally, Microsoft's people cringe at these perceptions. In public statements, Microsoft wants nothing so much as to be loved as an innovator (no one loves you just for "cutting off the air supply" of Netscape, it seems). People "don't always realize all the innovative things we've got going on here because we don't often talk about them in the press" — so recruiting head David Pritchard complained to *Fortune* magazine.

Microsoft — or any other company — will be only as creative and innovative as the people it hires. Microsoft has particularly focused ideas about the personnel it wants to attract, and it is a company with the money to recruit them.

Developers, Program Managers, Testers

Like New York City, Microsoft has had the dubious honor of confronting problems of scale before its smaller rivals. At Microsoft, programmers — called "developers" or "software design engineers" (SDEs) — have always been the heart of the company. For a long time they *were* the company. In the earliest days, everyone wrote code. Bill Gates handled the hiring personally. He held "recruiting parties" at his own house. He interviewed every prospective employee. He believed that one of the best ways to evaluate a programmer was to read the code he had written.

Gates was loath to hire nonprogrammers. He felt that the company's core competencies were programming and hiring good programmers. Paul Allen wanted to expand into making hardware. Gates vetoed it. Steve Ballmer wanted to hire nonprogrammers — you know, like salespeople. *What, are you trying to bankrupt me?!?* Gates wanted to know.

Hiring developers was and is a dicey business. Microsoft's first product was a version of BASIC for the Altair 8800, a computer that hobbyists built from a kit. Microsoft soon had its first monopoly — on the Altair 8800 platform — and it did not last long. Soon the Altair was left in the dust by the next big thing — namely, computers that came fully assembled.

Meanwhile, processors and their machine instructions were changing every few years. So were the higher-level languages used for software development. There was limited value in testing a developer for competence in one programming language when the company might soon switch to a different language. In that kind of environment, the important attribute was flexibility.

A primary goal of Microsoft hiring is to find "Bill clones." That is company jargon for a young person of Gates-like intelligence and competitive edge, though often of little or no experience. Microsoft's hirers pride themselves on being able to identify people who can achieve great things rather than those who already have.

It is this hiring philosophy that creates an impermeable membrane between Microsoft employees and everyone else. Microsoft considers itself to be an exclusive club of very smart people. Two badges of that club are the brainteaser interviews and the stock options. For the record, not everyone who works at the Redmond campus is a Microsoft employee. Groundskeeping, reception, security, the mailroom and cafeteria, and CD manufacturing are all outsourced. These people are not expected to answer riddles such as "How many times a day do a clock's hands overlap." Neither do they get stock options.

Microsoft's hiring has always been cautious, like Gates himself. Gates wanted to be sure that everyone hired was very good at what he or she was supposed to do. Programming candidates were expected to write code during the interview. They were also expected to prove themselves more informally by solving puzzles.

That was once as outré as Shockley's intelligence tests. Many applicants have felt (and do feel) that the coding and puzzle solving asked of them are demeaning. As anyone who's watched a game show knows, people will do amazingly demeaning things when you dangle enough money in front of them. Microsoft's candidates are willing to put up with its grueling interviews because they know how many Microsoft employees become multimillionaires well before middle age. Due to Microsoft's influence, coding and puzzle solving during interviews are now common throughout the software industry.

From Microsoft's viewpoint, puzzles test competitive edge as well as intelligence. Like business or football, a logic puzzle divides the world into winners and losers. You either get the answer, or you don't. As a coach will tell you, winning is more than ability. You have to be hungry. Winning has to matter.

The situations in puzzles are almost always silly and irrelevant. All a puzzle has to offer is a challenge. For some people that is enough. Like mountain climbers, they search for a solution because it's there. The feeling is that good puzzle solvers are not only intellectually capable of problem solving but motivated to tackle whatever challenge may be assigned to them.

A crisis came when software products got too big for one person to handle. MS-DOS 1.0 was largely designed, coded, compiled, and debugged by one auteur, Tim Paterson. As software products became more complex, dividing the labor between two or more developers became necessary. That was easier said than done. Chunks of code written by different people cannot be melded together unless the chunks are written with that aim in mind every step of the way. There has to be an ongoing dialog between developers and an efficient way of resolving the inevitable differences of opinion about the "right" way to do things. "Communicative" and "easygoing" are not words often used to describe the personalities of developers. Instead of communicating, developers wrote their code alone, in the middle of the night. This was a big problem.

One of the people called upon to tackle this problem was Charles Simonyi. Simonyi is a renowned computer scientist who has chosen to work in a corporate world that is sometimes suspicious of academics. At Xerox PARC, Simonyi wrote the first what-you-see-is-what-you-get word processor. He chafed at Xerox's profound lack of interest in marketing the windows and mouse interface its own research lab had invented. During a business trip to Seattle, Simonyi dropped in at Microsoft without an appointment. The hiring was a little looser back then. An underling (Steve Ballmer) looked at Simonyi's portfolio and decided that Bill should see it. Gates was in a meeting. By the time he was free, Simonyi had to catch his flight home. Gates rode with him to the airport. Their personalities clicked. Simonyi soon accepted an offer to come to Microsoft.

Simonyi's solution to the multiple developer problem was to create a new job description called master programmer. Somewhat like a medieval craftsman, the master programmer would have full responsibility for laying out the program and writing the code. Working underneath the master would be a team of assistants. They would have the responsibility for debugging and optimizing the code.

The idea made a lot of sense. It too hit a brick wall, however, because of the unique personality of the typical developer. Everyone wanted to be a master programmer. No one wanted to be a code serf, as the assistants were called. Since there could be only one master programmer on a project (that was the point), the majority of developers were doing grunt work.

Thanks to Microsoft's famous feature bloat, the master programmer concept was itself quickly stretched to the breaking point. Software products became too big for even one master programmer. Another problem was more fundamental. The master programmers weren't always good at designing software. As software became more sophisticated, consumer-end design issues became ever more distinct from the nuts-and-bolt coding. Asking the same person to handle both was asking a lot. There may be great linebackers who are also great playwrights — still, if you hire someone for one thing and expect him to handle the other, you're likely to be disappointed.

The term "master programmer" was never used much. It sounded too patriarchal even for a place full of screaming alpha males. They toned it down to the non–gender-specific program manager. That job title is now used throughout the software industry. But the program manager as we know it is largely the creation of Excel developer Jabe Blumenthal.

Like many Microsoft employees, after making a suitably large fortune, Blumenthal left the company to devote himself to suitably eclectic post-Microsoft careers. Blumenthal runs a paragliding school in the Cascade Range and teaches high school math and physics at his (and Gates's) alma mater, Lakeside School. Blumenthal's great inspiration was that a program manager doesn't need to know how to program. He decided that the program manager should envision what a product is going to do and establish its look and feel. The program manager writes not code but a product specification ("spec") detailing that vision. Thereafter the program manager's job is to run herd on the developers, making sure they implement the spec and do it on time.

The relationship of program managers to developers is strange. As developers see it, they do the real, hard, productive work. The program manager is a "lower life-form," an overpaid, buzzword-spouting goof, the pointy-haired boss in the *Dilbert* cartoons.

As program managers see it, they do the creative work and the developers supply the plumbing. The program manager is Frank Gehry; the developers are the guys riveting titanium panels on *his* Guggenheim.

With this perception gap, it's no wonder that the program manager's authority is tenuous. Program managers diplomatically compare what they do to herding cats. Developers (who outnumber program managers) are more open in their scorn. The running joke is "Call a program manager" any time a task demands their level of technical skill — like maybe ordering a pizza. Developer Adam David Barr recalls a Microsoft meeting in which the speaker was having trouble getting slides to display on a big projection screen. "Is there a program manager in the house?" someone yelled out. *Peals of laughter.* "Why, is there a game of golf that needs to be played?" someone else asked. The house went wild.

Another important job at Microsoft is tester. The tester is also a reflection of the complexity of today's software. It used to be that developers tested their own software for bugs and usability. They were aided by beta testers, ordinary people outside the company who were willing to try prerelease software and report bugs in exchange for a break on the price of the finished product. Today, debugging software is such a monumental task that it demands its own experts. Microsoft employs hundreds of people who do nothing all day but try to find bugs in software that other people have written.

Testers torture-test software — say by adding columns to a spreadsheet until it crashes, or opening window after window after window until something goes wrong, or simulating the effects of viruses and hackers. Unlike program managers, testers are expected to know programming. They often write special-purpose code to help test a software product. Of course, nothing they write is marketed.

Here is one point on which program managers and developers can agree: They both look down on testers. Being a tester is like being a dentist when everyone else in the room is a doctor. It's all "couldn't get into med school" smirks. There is at any rate not much glory in the clean-up work that testers do. Testers don't fix the bugs they find. They report the bugs so that developers can fix them.

Okay, so testing just possibly isn't as intellectually demanding as some other jobs. What of it? At Microsoft, the competitive atmosphere makes it difficult for anyone to admit to being less smart, or less *anything*. Testers are sensitive about their status, and officially, Microsoft soft-pedals the differences between these three extremely different job titles. "If you ever say anything even vaguely implying that testers don't require the same technical ability as developers or program managers, you will get shouted down," says Adam David Barr. Management and human resources insist that developers, program managers, and testers are all equally smart, equally creative, and equally ambitious. They have evolved a mythology to explain away those inequalities that can't flatly be denied. The gist of this mythology is that all three groups have special talents. These talents are "different," but by a mystic coincidence they are all "equally important." This is the company line, says Barr, who calls it "totally bogus."

The tester mythology is the most ingenious. How would *you* characterize an innate gift for crashing Excel? Grant George, vice president of Office Test, puts it this way: "The most successful testers just think differently than developers or program managers. We walk around criticizing or at least having an opinion about the quality of everything we see, touch, come in contact with, or use in our daily lives. We live to criticize and make better. . . . Thank goodness for this industry and Microsoft. What a great way to use that passion we have for quality to tangibly improve products that are used by millions of people."

George is not alone in this view, which might be summarized as "Testers have opinions, and other people don't."

This evolving division of labor forced (or accelerated) changes in Microsoft's hiring. Not many people go to college intending to become program managers or testers. Not all the people who occupy these positions majored in computer science. You can't always ask a potential program manager to code in an interview. Some program managers are English majors.

So how do you tell whether a nonprogrammer is a "Bill clone"? One way is to use puzzles, riddles, and hypothetical problems. For potential program managers and testers — as well as for the legions of salespeople, documentation writers, and others who were being hired — brainteasers became an important means of assessing talent.

Many of these are classic logic puzzles. Other interview questions are intended to help assign candidates to specific positions. Some of the questions that outsiders find most eccentric (*Which of the fifty states would you remove? Which way should a key turn in a car door?*) fall into this category. They test mainly whether the candidate can come to a decision and articulate it.

Jabe Blumenthal liked to ask program manager candidates to design a house. Sometimes the candidate would go to the white board and draw a square.

This is about the worst possible thing to do, in Blumenthal's estimation. A house can be anything. You never build a house without asking who's paying for it and how much money, space, and time are available. A candidate who started to draw a house without addressing these issues was usually out of the running.

In such questions, the important thing is the "algorithm." An algorithm is the exacting, step-by-step method underlying any computer program. Here, it's interview-speak for the way a candidate addresses a complex, open-ended question. On questions such as this, a good algorithm begins with the candidate eliciting the details from the interviewer.

Those who fail to do this can expect to be penalized. One of Blumenthal's colleagues, Joel Spolsky, took to interrupting the square-drawers. "Actually, you forgot to ask this," he'd say, as they were putting the finishing touches on their floor plan, "but this is a house for a family of forty-eight-foot-tall blind giraffes."

Smart People Who Don't Get Things Done

One of Spolsky's more minor accomplishments was inventing the Microsoft interview question "How would you make an M&M?" Now the CEO of Fog Creek Software in New York, Spolsky is both a thoughtful proponent and a critic of Microsoft's interviewing techniques.

As Spolsky sees it, two of the biggest challenges in technical hiring are identifying *people who are smart but don't get things done* and *people who get things done but aren't smart.* A company in a competitive industry needs to avoid hiring both classes of people.

"People who are smart but don't get things done often have Ph.D.s and work in big companies where nobody listens to them because they are completely impractical," explains Spolsky. "People who get things done but are not smart will do stupid things, seemingly without thinking about them, and somebody else will have to come clean up their mess later."

These two groups of people can be hard to distinguish from those you do want to hire, *people who are smart and get things done.* (Not so problematic are *people who aren't smart and don't get things done* because they are usually easy to identify.)

Logic puzzles and design questions can be useful because they present mini-allegories of the issues that any company in the business of innovation confronts. In the software business, you have to generate a lot of ideas, decide which ideas are good enough to keep, work on those ideas, and finally, get the product out the door.

What Spolsky looks for in interview responses is closure. "Sometimes candidates will drift back and forth, unable to make a decision, or they will try to avoid hard questions. Sometimes they will leave difficult decisions unanswered and try to move on. Not good."

After brainstorming on an interview question, a candidate should select the strongest idea. That is itself a test of critical judgment. The candidate should then add any further details or elaborations needed to make the chosen idea a complete answer. It is important to conclude with all significant gaps filled and all important contradictions resolved.

"Good candidates have a tendency to try to naturally keep things moving forward," says Spolsky, "even when you try to hold them back. If the conversation ever starts going around in circles, and the candidate says something like

'Well, we can talk about this all day, but we've got to do something, so let's go with decision X,' that's a really good sign."

Dead Man Walking

It was a rainy Thursday in Seattle when Carl Tashian arrived. When he made his way to the front of a long check-in line at the Bellevue Courtyard by Marriot, the clerk crossed his name off a list and handed him a key. As he was walking away, he heard another person give a name and the scrunch of the pencil crossing it off the same list.

The next morning, Tashian had to wait half an hour in the lobby of Microsoft Building 19. The waiting area had a computer kiosk with a big sign saying EXPLORE! The screen was blank. A Post-it note stuck on the monitor said OUT OF ORDER.

A TV, turned to MSNBC, had another Post-it note: PLEASE DO NOT CHANGE THE CHANNEL.

Tashian's recruiter told him there would be four interviewers. The first was an eastern European man, unshaven, dressed in nylon athletic gear. Wasting no company time on social niceties, the man handed Tashian a dry-erase marker and announced: "I'll start you out with a simple problem. You have b boxes and n dollars. If I want *any* amount of money, from zero to n dollars, you must be able to hand me zero to b boxes so that I get *exactly* what I request."

Tashian was asked how he would distribute the money among the boxes in order to achieve this aim, and then what the "restrictions" were on b and n.

Tashian thought a bit and gave a good answer.

The interviewer demanded a "mathematical proof" that it was the right answer. "Is that an algebraic or geometric progression?" he wanted to know.

Tashian asked the interviewer if he would define his terms.

"No."

By the time the interviewer had run out of nits to pick, Tashian felt he had flubbed the question badly — even though his answer was *correct*. He was also sure the interviewer didn't like him.

Compared to that, the second and third interviews were a breeze. Interviewer number two was friendlier and spent a long time explaining the purpose of the team's current project. The third interviewer's questions were so easy that Tashian wondered if they'd been dumbed down for him. This interview ended with instructions to wait in the lobby for the final interview.

A bit later, the third interviewer reappeared to inform Tashian that his manager — who was supposed to conduct the final interview — didn't come into work that day. There would be no fourth interview. Tashian could go.

The peculiar structure of a Microsoft interview has been called a three-act play. Act one is often a screening interview. A human resources person calls the applicant for a thirty-minute conversation. The phone-interview questions are mostly traditional and rarely include a difficult brainteaser. Sometimes they feature a question such as "How would you test a saltshaker?" The applicant's answers to the phone questions determine whether he or she will get a fly back, the all-expense-paid trip to Redmond or another Microsoft campus. Notwithstanding a cozy deal with the local Marriott, these fly backs represent a considerable investment in view of the number of people Microsoft flies in.

A full day is set aside for interviews. At the beginning of the day, Microsoft's interviewers receive a list of the people who are supposed to interview a particular candidate. The candidate never sees this list. There are typically six interviewers listed. Much of the time, the last couple of interviews never happen. The last name on the list is marked "as appropriate." The as-appropriate interview takes place *only* when the previous evaluations have been so positive that the candidate is almost certain to be hired. The as-appropriate interviewer — often the person who would be the new hire's manager — makes the final decision.

Microsoft's interviewers covertly compare notes, by e-mail and otherwise, throughout the process. They usually walk the candidate to the next interviewer's office. It's customary to signal a thumbs-up or -down during the handoff. In any case, each interviewer must write "feedback." That's a quick e-mail assessment of the candidate, sent to each of the other scheduled interviewers. Feedback e-mails often arrive in the middle of an interview.

There are rules governing these assessments. One is that the header is supposed to read either "hire" or "no hire." The assessment is to be strictly digital, 0 or 1.

Interviewers' impressions are often a bit more analog than that. As Adam David Barr recalls it, what the interviewers really want to say — in a large portion of cases — is "No hire, unless everyone else thinks hire, in which case don't let me be the person who stops him from being hired."

Weasel words such as these are frowned upon. Interviewers are expected to justify their decision in the body of the e-mail. The explanation should tell what questions and puzzles were asked (in this way, up to half a dozen interviewers "magically" avoid repeating popular questions) and how well the candidate answered them. The assessment should also be written as if it were going to be subpoenaed by someone miffed at not being hired. Microsoft is sensitive about e-mail these days.

The guiding principle of the Microsoft interview is similar to that attributed to Hippocrates: "Do no harm." Microsoft seeks to avoid hiring the wrong person, even if this occasionally means missing out on some good people. The justification is that never before has it cost so much to recruit, maintain, and — heaven forbid — discharge an employee.

"A false negative is bad," explains Joel Spolsky, "but it's not going to hurt the company. A false positive will hurt the company and will take a long time to clean up." Lest that jargon not be entirely clear, a "false negative" is when the interviewing process rejects someone who would actually be a good employee. A "false positive" is when it results in hiring someone who's not capable.

Discussions of the false-positive issue sometimes take on a paranoid stance. "The best thing we can do for our competitors is hire poorly," said David Pritchard, director of recruiting. "If I hire a bunch of bozos, it will hurt us, because it takes time to get rid of them. They start infiltrating the organization and then they themselves start hiring people of lower quality."

Consequently, just one strongly negative opinion can capsize a candidate's chances. To play it safe, a candidate who gets a no hire is usually *not* hired. On top of that, bad reviews are self-perpetuating. After one really bad review is e-mailed to the list, the other interviewers feel like Hawaiian voters going to the polls after the networks have already projected the winner. It gives the fence-sitters license to say no hire with a clear conscience. After *two* no hires, there's almost no point in saying hire (and who wants to get a reputation for being "soft" on bozo infiltration?).

* * *

"There's always a problem: How do you avoid wasting people's time?" Spolsky explained. "Because at Microsoft, you're going to hire probably one out of six of the people who actually make it all the way to campus. You don't want to waste too much time of too many people. On the other hand, you don't want to fly candidates out to Redmond and give them one interview and then immediately tell them 'Bye!' So I think everyone got at least three interviews."

After that, the whole afternoon of interviewing falls out. This is presented to the candidate as a freak combination of traffic, missed planes, absenteeism, or personal emergencies. Like social excuses generally, the reasons often seem peculiar in retrospect. (Tashian's third interviewer was unaware that his manager had not come into work until well into the afternoon?)

The most excruciating situation is the one that Tashian evidently found himself in. For whatever reason, the very first interviewer disliked him. As soon as his e-mail went out, Tashian was a dead man walking.

What follows, then, is the Blind Date from Hell. The disappointed partner prolongs things just to the point where it is not *too* apparent that the other is being dumped. Oddly enough, that point is usually a meal (buy them a cheeseburger, offer the social excuses, and then it's "We've got your number").

The typical Microsoft interviewee is unaware how frequently this scenario plays out. A cheery list of interview tips on Microsoft's website aims to keep it that way:

> As the day goes on it's tempting to try to evaluate how things are going each step of the way. Try not to. Resist

getting stressed out if you feel like a particular question didn't seem to go well. . . . there might not be a correlation between how it actually went and how you perceived it went. (Like when you took that exam you thought you'd totally tanked on — and you actually did well, or vice versa?) Just be yourself — that's who we're interested in meeting and talking with.

The opposite of Tashian's predicament is possible too. One candidate, characterized as a "frat boy," breezed his way through the interviews and made it to his as-appropriate interviewer, Karen Fries. Fries is an important person at Microsoft. She invented both the "wizards" that walk users through tasks and, less successfully, "Bob," the now-discontinued cartoon helper that impressed focus groups and Bill Gates, if no one else. Fries is a strikingly attractive woman. Frat Boy suddenly got the idea that the *real* interviews were over and that, as a "reward" for doing so well, they had handed him off to this babette/receptionist/whatever for small talk. Fries's e-mail assessment of the candidate was so vitriolic that it is still revered as a classic in a place that has never lacked for venomous e-mail. Frat Boy was not hired.

As a rule, Microsoft's candor about one's chances of being hired is in direct proportion to those chances. People who are destined to get a job offer leave Redmond with a good idea that an offer will be forthcoming. People who leave without a clear expression of interest on Microsoft's part generally do not get an offer.

There is a mystique to being a "hard" interviewer. This is (almost always) a male who shuns chitchat, does nothing to put the candidate at ease, asks unusually hard questions, and rates an anomalously high percentage of candidates as no hires. "It's sort of a status thing," says Barr. "It means you're not just letting anyone in the door. But it can backfire."

As a Stanford student, Noah Suojanen was flown to Redmond and subjected to a full day of challenging interviews. After the sixth, he was again told to wait in the lobby of Building 19 for another interview.

The final interviewer came up to him and said "Hey." That was all he said; he did not introduce himself then or ever. They went into another windowless room with another white board. The interviewer posed a complex problem. Suojanen dutifully took up the marker and began working.

In the middle of this, the interviewer abruptly excused himself. He got up and left the room.

He did not return to the room. Suojanen never saw him again.

As the minutes passed, Suojanen pondered what to do. He couldn't ask where so-and-so was because he didn't know so-and-so's name. Could he even give a physical description? The only thing that had impressed Suojanen about the interviewer's appearance was that he had managed to find a shirt color (royal blue) that clashed with blue jeans.

Finally, Suojanen put down his marker, got up, and walked out of the building.

In this way Microsoft lost out on a potential employee who had evidently been favorably reviewed by half a dozen people. No doubt Microsoft's human resources department deplores such slipups, but they are to some extent inevitable.

The Microsoft practice of having "regular" employees — rather than human resources experts — interview candidates for their own teams has generally been praised in the business press. There is little question that peer interviewing boosts morale and has evident advantages in technical fields.

Microsoft's human resources department conducts periodic seminars instructing employees on interview protocol. For the most part, these are concerned only with the basics, such as avoiding questions that would leave the company open to a discrimination suit. They do not instruct people on what questions to ask, or how to tell who is "good enough" to hire. These seminars can do little to address the issue of the hard interviewer, who is by definition a rogue, albeit often an admired one within the Microsoft culture.

Four
___

The Microsoft Interview Puzzles

Microsoft's interview questions are intended to be secret. I soon learned that the secrecy of Microsoft's questions has never been absolute. "Honey, how did the interview go?" Well, if they ask you how many piano tuners there are in the world, you're probably going to mention that to your significant other and anyone else who asks.

Microsoft's interviewers ask many types of questions besides those that are the subject of this book. Traditional and behavioral questions are used, just as they are practically everywhere else. "What gives you joy?" is one that Steve Ballmer likes to ask. Other traditional questions reported from Microsoft interviews include "If you saw a coworker doing something dishonest, would you tell your boss?"; "How many projects can you handle at once?"; and "Is it more important to you to complete tasks quickly or perfectly?"

Developers are asked a variety of programming questions and are required to write code. Two of the best-known examples are "Reverse a linked list" and "Write a backspace function that works with both ASCII and Kanji characters."

Interviewers also toss in softer hypothetical questions that are specific to the computer industry ("How would you explain Excel to your grandmother?"; "If Microsoft told you we were willing to invest five million dollars in a start-up of your choice, what business would you start?"). Because these questions are not "portable" outside of programming, I don't include them here. Anyone interested in seeing more of Microsoft's programming questions can find them on the websites listed in the bibliography.

I include here only the brainteasers, trick questions, tests of ingenuity, and ambiguous, open-ended hypothetical questions — in other words, the types of questions that are most distinctive and provocative in Microsoft's interviews. Most of these questions have been widely adopted at other companies.

Where Does Microsoft Get Its Puzzles?

Microsoft's brainteasers might be described as mitochondrial, not nuclear, DNA. There is no official list imposed from above. Microsoft's people are free to ask whatever interview questions they want.

About half of the questions listed here are "logic puzzles." Traditionally, a logic puzzle is almost any recreational problem that is stated in words and involves little or no math. Interview puzzles are popular lunchtime talk at the Building 16 cafeteria. In Microsoft's spirit of competition, it is considered cool to come up with a "new" and presumably effective question. "New" to Microsoft does not necessarily mean "original."

A few of Microsoft's puzzles have founding myths. It's said that Steve Ballmer was jogging with another Microsoft executive when he saw a manhole cover. "Why are manhole covers round?" Ballmer asked. "Hey, that would be a good question to ask in interviews."

This story may be true as far as it goes. Nevertheless, Ballmer almost certainly was not the first human being to pose the manhole-cover question. It appeared in a 1983 book by Martin Gardner that collected *Scientific American* columns dating back to the early 1970s. Gardner did not claim to have invented the manhole-cover riddle and probably didn't. Tracing the authorship of a puzzle is about as hopeless as trying to find out who invented a joke.

Like jokes, puzzles evolve in the retelling. People supply new anecdotes, forget a detail, or toss out most of the puzzle and replace it with something different. Since puzzles are transmitted largely by word of mouth, there is a premium on those that are easy to remember. The person who cleverly simplifies a puzzle may have as much to do with perpetuating it as the one who invented the original. Most puzzles bear the polish of many hands.

For this reason it is very hard to sit down and invent a truly good and original logic puzzle. Microsoft's people probably don't have the time to try. Virtually all of Microsoft's logic puzzles have appeared, give or take cosmetic variations, in puzzle books and Internet sites devoted to puzzles.

Impossible questions and open-ended posers testing imagination are a lot easier to invent. Many of these appear to be original to Microsoft. (Answers start on page 147)

QUESTIONS

? How would you weigh a jet plane without using scales?

? Why are manhole covers round rather than square?

? Why do mirrors reverse right and left instead of up and down?

? Which way should the key turn in a car door to unlock it?

? Why is it that, when you turn on the hot water in a hotel, the hot water comes out instantly?

? How do they make M&Ms?

? If you are on a boat and toss a suitcase overboard, will the water level rise or fall?

? How many piano tuners are there in the world?

? How many gas stations are there in the United States?

? How much Mississippi River water flows past New Orleans each hour?

? What does all the ice in a hockey rink weigh?

? If you could remove any of the fifty U.S. states, which would it be?

? How many points are there on the globe where, by walking one mile south, one mile east, and one mile north, you reach the place where you started?

? How many times a day do a clock's hands overlap?

? Mike and Todd have $21 between them. Mike has $20 more than Todd. How much does each have? You can't use fractions in the answer.

? On the average, how many times would you have to flip open the Manhattan phone book to find a specific name?

? How do you cut a rectangular cake into two equal pieces when someone has already removed a rectangular piece from it? The removed piece can be of any size or orientation. You are allowed just one straight cut.

? How would you design Bill Gates's bathroom?

? How would you design a microwave oven controlled by a computer?

? How would you design the controls for a VCR?

? Design a remote control for a venetian blind.

? Design a spice rack for a blind person.

? How would you test a saltshaker? [A toaster? A teakettle? An elevator?]

? How would you locate a specific book in a big library? There's no cataloging system and no librarian to help you.

? Suppose you're hired as an IRS agent. Your first job is to find out whether a nanny agency is cheating on its taxes. How would you do it?

? You have eight billiard balls. One of them is "defective," meaning that it weighs more than the others. How do you tell, using a balance, which ball is defective in two weighings?

? You have five jars of pills. All the pills in one jar only are "contaminated." The only way to tell which pills are contaminated is by weight. A regular pill weighs 10 grams; a contaminated pill is 9 grams. You are given a scale and allowed to make just one measurement with it. How do you tell which jar is contaminated?

? There are three ants at the three corners of a regular triangle. Each ant starts moving on a straight line toward another, randomly chosen corner. What is the probability that none of the ants collide?

? There are four dogs, each at a corner of a large square. Each of the dogs begins chasing the dog clockwise from it. All of the dogs run at the same speed. All continuously adjust their direction so that they are always heading straight toward their clockwise neighbor. How long does it take for the dogs to catch each other? Where does this happen?

? A train leaves Los Angeles for New York at a constant speed of 15 miles an hour. At the same moment, a train leaves New York for Los Angeles on the same track. It travels at a constant 20 miles an hour. At still the same moment, a bird leaves the Los Angeles train station and flies toward New York, following the track, at a speed of 25 miles an hour. When it reaches the train from New York, it instantly reverses direction. It travels at the same speed until it reaches the train from Los Angeles, when it reverses again, and so forth. The bird flies back and forth between the two trains until the very moment they collide. How far will the bird have traveled?

? You have 26 constants, labeled A through Z. Let A equal 1. The other constants have values equal to the letter's position in the alphabet, raised to the power of the previous constant. That means that B (the second letter) = $2^A = 2^1 = 2$. $C = 3^B = 3^2 = 9$, and so on. Find the exact numerical value for this expression:

$$(X–A) * (X–B) * (X–C) * \ldots (X–Y) * (X–Z)$$

? Count in base *negative* 2.

? You have two jars and 100 marbles. Fifty of the marbles are red, and 50 are blue. One of the jars will be chosen at random; then 1 marble will be withdrawn from that jar at random. How do you maximize the chance that a red marble will be chosen? (You must place all 100 marbles in the jars.) What is the chance of selecting a red marble when using your scheme?

? You have a 3-quart bucket, a 5-quart bucket, and an infinite supply of water. How can you measure out exactly 4 quarts?

? One of your employees insists on being paid daily in gold. You have a gold bar whose value is that of seven days' salary for this employee. The bar is already segmented into seven equal pieces. If you are allowed to make just two cuts in the bar, and must settle with the employee at the end of each day, how do you do it?

? You have b boxes and n dollar bills. Seal the money in the boxes so that, without thereafter opening any box, you can give someone any requested whole amount of dollars, from 0 to n. What are the restrictions on b and n?

? You have a bucket of jelly beans in three colors — red, green, and blue. With your eyes closed, you have to reach in the bucket and take out two jelly beans of the same color. How many jelly beans do you have to take to be *certain* of getting two the same color?

? You have three picnic baskets filled with fruit. One has apples, one has oranges, and the third has a mixture of apples and oranges. You cannot see the fruit inside the baskets. Each basket is clearly labeled. Each label is wrong. You are permitted to close your eyes and pick one fruit from one basket, then examine it. How can you determine what is in each basket?

? Every man in a village of fifty couples has been unfaithful to his wife. Every woman in the village instantly knows when a man other than her husband has philandered (you know how small towns are) but not when her own husband has ("always the last to know"). The village's no-tolerance adultery statute requires that a woman who can prove her husband is unfaithful must kill him that very day. No woman would dream of disobeying this law. One day, the queen, who is known to be infallible, visits the village. She announces that at least one husband has been unfaithful. What happens?

? An evil demon captures a large, unspecified number of dwarfs. At each dwarf's entry interview, the demon plants a red or green gem in the dwarf's forehead. The demon informs the new recruit that he, the dwarf, has an unremovable red or green jewel in his forehead; that he, the demon, is not going to tell him which color, nor will anyone else (the dwarfs are strictly forbidden to speak); that one of the colors denotes sniveling company spies and the other color denotes those particularly luckless captives who are not even sniveling company spies; that the demon does not choose to tell him which color denotes which, nor will he tell him, ever. End of entry interview.

Every day the dwarfs line up in formation so that the demon can count them, just to make sure no one has escaped.

One day the demon gets tired of the dwarfs and decides to get rid of them. He announces that he will set the dwarfs free, provided they all deduce the color of their gems. As a hint, he tells them that there is at least one dwarf with a red gem, and at least one with a green gem.

To earn their collective freedom, the dwarfs must signal wordlessly at the daily lineup. All of the dwarfs with red gems are to step one pace forward, while the dwarfs with green gems remain behind. If they are correct, then all the dwarfs are free to go back to their homes in the coal mines. If they are not correct, all the dwarfs will be slaughtered on the spot.

The dwarfs are free to take as long as they want to determine the colors of their gems. They are all perfectly logical, and all are dying to get back to their homes. What should they do?

? Four people must cross a rickety footbridge at night. Many planks are missing, and the bridge can hold only two people at a time (any more than two, and the bridge collapses). The travelers must use a flashlight to guide their steps; otherwise they're sure to step through a missing space and fall to their death. There is only one flashlight. The four people each travel at different speeds. Adam can cross the bridge in one minute; Larry in two minutes; Edge takes five minutes; and the slowest person, Bono, needs ten minutes. The bridge is going to collapse in exactly seventeen minutes. How can all four people cross the bridge?

The Challenge

There is a covert "test" used in interviews at Microsoft and many other companies as well. It is often known as the Challenge. "A friend of mine was not hired at Microsoft, and after the interview I went out to dinner with him," says Spol-sky. "He said, 'God, I hated that guy [the interviewer]! He was so stupid, he didn't know the first thing about Peano numbers! I did my senior thesis on this, and I know all about it. He kept saying wrong things about it.' He was mad about this and thought the interview had gone badly because the interviewer had unfairly been wrong about a particular topic.

"It turns out, the position he was applying for was program manager, and that is a person who designs software but does not program. So that person needs to do an awful lot of convincing. They need to convince programmers who are very logical people but are also apt to be lacking in social skills. It's a very particular talent. One of the things you look for in a program manager very specifically is 'Do you have the ability to convince people of a fact when you know it's right?' Because you're going to have to do this all day long. And not in an aggressive way, not in an angry way, but just in a sort of patient and friendly way. That was one of the things we looked for in that particular job."

A version of the Challenge occurs on the original, orally administered Stanford-Binet IQ test. The test-giver was supposed to pose the following puzzle:

You know, of course, that water holds up a fish that is placed in it. Well, here is a problem. Suppose we have a bucket which is partly full of water. We place the bucket on the scales and find that with the water in it, it weighs exactly 45 pounds. Then we put a 5-pound fish into the bucket of water. Now, what will the whole thing weigh?

Most adults answered that 45 pounds plus 5 pounds is 50 pounds. The person giving the test was then supposed to ask "How can this be correct, since the water itself holds up the fish?" Wrote Terman, "If the subject keeps changing his answer or says that he *thinks* the weight would be 50 pounds, but is not certain, the score is failure." Only if the subject logically defended his correct answer to two successive challenges from the test-giver was the answer marked correct.

Whether this measures intelligence or something more along the lines of chutzpah is an open question. Not in doubt is the importance of chutzpah at the companies that use this trick in interviews. According to Spolsky, at Microsoft, it works like this: "Throughout the interview, you look for the candidate to say something that is absolutely, positively, unarguably correct. Then you say, 'Wait a minute, wait a minute,' and spend about two minutes playing devil's advocate. Argue with them when you are sure they are right.

"Weak candidates will give in. *No hire.* Strong candidates will find a way to persuade you. They will have a whole laundry list of Dale Carnegie techniques to win you over. 'Perhaps I'm misunderstanding you,' they will say. But they will stand their ground. *Hire.*"

Exposés

Microsoft has evolved an uneasy détente with exposés of its interview questions. This book is only a belated example of something that has been going on at least since the Web took off. Several people "collect" Microsoft interview puzzles and post them on the Web.

In the early 1990s, Chris Sells was interviewing at a company called DevelopMentor. At the end of the interview, one of the company's founders announced: "Okay, you've got the job. But I want to ask you one of the questions that Microsoft asks." The question was, naturally: "Why are manhole covers round?"

"No problem," said Sells. "I'll answer that question if you answer *this* question: 'Why do firemen wear red suspenders?'"

The company founder hadn't a clue.

This experience inspired Sells to begin collecting puzzles with the hazy idea that he might interview at Microsoft one day. In May 1996 he started a website, posting the Microsoft questions he'd heard through friends and friends of friends.

Several of USC student Kiran Bondalapati's friends interviewed at Microsoft at the same time. Bondalapati assembled his own set of questions and started a Microsoft "Interview Question Bank." Other sites listing Microsoft interview questions include 4guysfromRolla.com's "Microsoft Interview Questions" and Michael Pryor's "Technical Interview Questions" (which features a wide range of puzzles, not all used at Microsoft). All seem to be popular sites.

You might think that Microsoft would be incensed at people giving away its questions. The reality is more nuanced. Both Bondalapati and Sells have heard that Microsoft HR people steer new employees to their sites when they don't know what questions to ask candidates. It is the unauthorized, outside compilations that provide the only fixed record of the questions asked at Microsoft.

Of course, interviewees can and do use these sites to prepare. Both Sells's and Bondalapati's sites are relatively benign in that they give few or no answers. Bondalapati once fielded a frantic call from a friend of a friend. She was in the Marriott the night before her interview. She had in front of her a printout of his site. It didn't give a certain answer, and she needed to know it.

Less predictable are reactions from other companies.

Sells receives a stream of e-mail from other companies' interviewers who want to "hire like Microsoft." The problem? They need the *answers* that Sells's site omits. "I always reply that if they don't know the answers, then they shouldn't be asking the questions," says Sells. "This often pisses them off."

Five

Embracing Cluelessness

Maybe you're stumped by some of the puzzles in the previous chapter. What are you *supposed* to do when confronted with a problem you don't know how to solve?

People have been trying to answer that question for a long time. In a way, it's the core issue of the field of artificial intelligence (AI).

Bill Gates and almost everyone else at Microsoft grew up with the dream of artificial intelligence, of machines programmed to think, make judgments, and solve problems much like humans. One traditional approach to AI is to study how people solve problems. If you could understand, in rich step-by-step detail, how humans solve problems, then maybe you could program a computer to do the same thing.

How do people who are good at solving problems do it? Anecdotal accounts are not always illuminating. Geniuses often find what they do mysterious. In his Caltech classes, physicist Murray Gell-Mann used to demonstrate the problem-solving method of colleague Richard Feynman. Gell-Mann would write a complex problem on the board, stare at it in silence a few minutes — and then write the correct answer. Gell-Mann's half-serious point was that the genius of Feynman, and the creative process generally, resists being put into words. As Louis Armstrong said, "Man, if you have to ask 'What is it?' you ain't never goin' to know."

What is particularly troubling is how little "logic" seems to be involved in some phases of problem solving. Difficult problems are often solved via a sudden, intuitive insight. One moment you're stuck; the next moment this insight has popped into your head, though not by any step-by-step logic that can be recounted.

The problems used in AI research have often been puzzles or games. These are simpler and more clearly defined than the complex problems of the real world. They too involve the elements of logic, insight, and intuition that pertain to real problems. Many of the people at Microsoft follow AI work closely, of course, and this may help to explain what must strike some readers as peculiar — their supreme confidence that silly little puzzles have a bearing on the real world.

Solution Spaces, Clueless Plateaus

A godfather of the modern study of problem solving is economist and polymath Herbert Simon (1916–2001). Simon, recipient of the 1978 Nobel prize in economics, spent most of his career at Carnegie Mellon University, a school with strong computer and robotics programs. He was one of many economists of his day making use of computer models.

Simon was so taken with the computer that he examined how people solve problems as a means of exploring how computers might be programmed for similar tasks. In *Human Problem Solving* (1972), Simon and colleague Alan Newell published results of studies in which volunteers performed a variety of number or word puzzles. A later publication, *Scientific Discovery* (1987), attempted to reconstruct, through historic accounts, the individual reasoning behind a number of celebrated scientific breakthroughs.

In both humble puzzle solving and great scientific advances, Simon found nothing fundamentally mysterious. People parlayed justifiable hunches into testable hypotheses, negotiated a few false turns, and ultimately arrived at a "right answer." Never did a puzzle's solution or a scientific advance depend on a totally out-of-left-field "inspiration."

Simon and colleagues popularized a number of terms that are now in wide use. One is "solution space." This means roughly the set of all potential solutions to a problem. When a computer program plays chess, it "searches a solution space." It examines all possible moves (and countermoves, and counter-countermoves, as far ahead as is practical) in order to find the most advantageous ones.

Simon believed that searching a solution space was a model for how people solve puzzles or even for how scientists such as Kepler and Planck achieved great breakthroughs. The notion of a solution space has been hugely influential. When you are trying to program a computer to solve a problem, identifying a solution space is extremely desirable. Then the software can search the set of solutions, using the impressive speed advantages that computers have.

There are a number of limitations to this approach. Many problems have solution spaces that are too astronomically large for even the fastest computers to run a brute-force search. (Computers can't play "perfect" chess for this reason, even though they can beat human grand masters.) Equally vexing is the possibility that the solution space may be hard to define and/or irrelevant. Solution spaces often seem to have little to do with the way that people actually solve problems.

"Which way should a key turn in a car door?" In a narrow sense, you might say the solution space consists of two possible answers: "clockwise" and "counterclockwise." That's missing the spirit of this question. Microsoft's little riddle is really asking you to give a good reason for your answer. The number of possible *reasons* for turning a key clockwise or counterclockwise is bigger than two! It's more realistic to say that the ensemble of possible reasons is the real solution space (and this ensemble defies accounting).

In general, puzzles and riddles have solution spaces that are difficult to define. It is not immediately clear what the scope of the problem is or what types of solutions might be legitimate, much less right. This is what makes AI such a formidably difficult enterprise. On a much more modest level, it is what makes certain questions so difficult to answer in job interviews.

Much recent work in cognitive psychology has pulled back a bit from Simon's optimistic view of rational problem solving. Some recent analyses send the message that *no one knows how to solve a problem until he or she solves it.* In contrast to Simon's solution space, Harvard psychologist David Perkins speaks of a "clueless plateau." If the space of possible solutions is a landscape, and the right solution is somewhere on a big plateau over there, then you've got to search the whole plateau (and are clueless about where to start).

Perkins likens the solvers of puzzles to prospectors looking for gold in the Klondike. There is not much rhyme or reason to where the gold is. You might say that prospecting is pure luck ("the luck of the Klondike"). At a deeper level of analysis, some prospectors are better at finding gold than others. That is because they accept the "randomness" and deal with it. Their *search* for gold is not random; it is a methodical survey in which they are sensitive to such geologic clues as do exist.

This view of problem solving is neatly captured in Microsoft's weird puzzle (or *anti*puzzle?) that asks how you would find a book in a library. Zen master Shin'ichi Hisamatsu said that all koans (Zen riddles) really boil down to "Nothing will do. What do you do?" This is Microsoft's version of that. There's no way of locating a book — how do you locate the book? People are baffled, not because this is a *hard* question but because it offers so little purchase to logic.

Obviously, the answer can't be something such as "I've memorized the Dewey decimal system, and the book is on the nineteenth shelf, three aisles over to the left." You haven't been told what the book is, the library may not use the Dewey decimal system, and even if it did, the books could be laid out any which way on a floor plan that could be anything. There is no way of *deducing* the book's location. All you can really do is "search the solution space" — the library itself — as efficiently as possible.

Uncertainty and Disjunction

Puzzles are not just difficult because they have big, "clueless" solution spaces. Most good puzzles contain booby traps, psychological tricks that penalize the would-be solver. These tricks help explain why many seemingly simple problems (including many asked in job interviews) are difficult.

People aren't good at dealing with the uncertainties or missing information in a puzzle. Here's a neat little example that's been tested in psychological studies and widely discussed. You've got four cards on the table. Each card has a letter on one side and a number on the other side. Naturally, you can only see the side that's faceup:

The puzzle is this: "Identify which card(s) you need to turn over in order to test the rule 'If there is a vowel on one side of the card, there is an even number on the other side.'"

I'll give you two hints (which aren't normally given). Hint number one is that this *isn't* a trick question. There's nothing underhanded going on. The puzzle is as simple as it looks.

Hint number two is that your answer is probably going to be wrong.

Most people say either the A card or the A and 2 cards. Well, A is a vowel, and we don't know what number is on the other side. There could be an odd number on the back of the A card. That would disprove the rule. You have to turn the A card over to test it. Fair enough.

What about the 2 card? Two is an even number, and the rule says that if there's a vowel on one side, then there's got to be an even number on the other side. It doesn't say that *only* vowel cards have even numbers. Say there's a C on the other side of the 2. It wouldn't disprove the rule. Whether there's a vowel or consonant, it makes no difference. The 2 card is irrelevant.

So the answer's just turn over the A card, right? Wrong. You need to turn over the 7 card too. For all we know, there could be a vowel on the other side of the 7. That would disprove the rule.

The correct answer, then, is that you have to turn over

the A and the 7. This type of puzzle is known as the Wason selection task, after Peter Wason, the psychologist who described it in 1966. In studies using this type of puzzle, the reported success rate has ranged from about 20 percent all the way down to *0*.

Why is this so hard? You might think it's hard because people don't get the exacting, Boolean logic use of the word "if" in the puzzle. Studies have addressed this point and found that it's not the problem. When researchers point out that there could be a vowel on the other side of the 7 card, nearly all would-be solvers understand, *then,* why they should have turned the 7 over and why they don't have to turn over the 2.

As a "logic puzzle," this is as simple and clear-cut as it could be. It hardly deserves to be called a puzzle — it's not clever enough for that. Yet at least four out of five people give the wrong answer.

The difficulty appears to be this: People prefer to reason from sure things, from cards that are already faceup on the table. People shy away from reasoning about things that are unknown or uncertain.

The A is right in front of your face, no ifs, ands, or buts about it. It is straightforward to draw the relevant logical conclusions. You see the 2 as well, and it is easy for some people to jump to the faulty conclusion that they should turn over the 2.

What's hard is reasoning from uncertainty. You know there's a letter behind the 7, but you can't see it. It could be a consonant or a vowel. In logic, the term for this is "disjunction." A disjunction is an either-or situation where exactly one of two or more mutually exclusive possibilities is true.

When a problem presents a disjunction, you need to list all the possibilities and reason from each of them. You say, "Suppose the unseen letter is a vowel. . . . What then?" And "Suppose the unseen letter is a consonant. . . . What then?"

This is what you ought to do. With real people, what is out of sight is often out of mind. In this puzzle particularly, getting the mind to think the right way is like getting an un-ruly horse to accept a saddle. There's a deep-seated resistance that cannot easily be overcome. The mind's resistance to dis-junctions has been called a cognitive illusion. Like an optical illusion, it's a quirk you may come to understand intellectu-ally but never really free yourself from.

A wide range of studies documents the disjunction ef-fect. Psychologists Amos Tversky and Eldar Shafir polled Stanford students on the following hypothetical situation: You've taken an important exam and don't know whether you've passed or flunked. You have the opportunity to lock in a great deal on an upcoming trip to Hawaii. The deal expires tomorrow. You won't know your grade until the day after that. Do you buy the Hawaiian trip or not?

Most of the students said they'd refuse the trip. They didn't want to commit to a frivolous fling while awaiting cru-cial exam results. The researchers also posed the following questions: Suppose you *knew* you passed — would you take the trip then? Suppose you *knew* you failed — would you take the trip then?

When put this way, most of the students admitted that they would take the trip in either case. If they knew that they had passed, sure, they would take the trip to celebrate. If they knew that they had failed, they'd take the trip to console them-selves. But when faced with uncertainty, they were like deer in the headlights, unable to act, unable, even, to reason that the exam results should not make any difference in the decision.

The same researchers claimed a similar effect in the stock markets. The markets are usually in the doldrums in the days leading up to a presidential election. Many investors put off making financial decisions until they know the election's outcome. After the election, there is often a big move in the market. Oddly, its direction does not necessarily depend on who got elected. In the 1988 election, big investors largely favored Republican George Bush. As soon as Bush was elected, the markets plunged. "When I walked in and looked at the screen," said one trader quoted in the *New York Times*, "I thought Dukakis had won."

That statement reflects the view that the market would have been down at least as much had Dukakis won. Prior to the election, investors were unable to "think past" a still-uncertain outcome. They had to wait until the uncertainty was resolved in order to act.

The disjunction effect probably figures in most logic puzzles. The ants are moving clockwise or counterclockwise . . . *but you don't know which;* the picnic basket may have apples, or oranges, or a mixture . . . *but you don't know which;* there may be one red gem, or two, or three, or ten thousand . . . *but you don't know which;* the slow traveler may cross the rickety bridge first or second or last . . . *but you don't know which.*

It is human nature to say "Let's just forge ahead, see what happens, and *then* decide what to do." In a logic puzzle, no one's going to supply the missing information. You have to say "Okay, there's some missing information here; I'm going to have to lay out the possible scenarios and hope that I can come to a definite conclusion even though the information is missing."

Impossible questions are a particularly concentrated

case of disjunction. When asked how many piano tuners there are in the world, you may well feel that *all* the necessary information is missing. The successful approach is to reason that "I don't know A, but I could figure it out if only I knew B and C, and I could figure B if I knew D. . . ." Answering these questions well is a matter of charting the most direct route from what you know to what you don't know. It's a little like the way that Yahoo! generates road maps between any two points.

Why do people resist reasoning from uncertain premises? One guess is that we fear it will be a waste of time and effort. How do you know that looking past one uncertainty won't just reveal another uncertainty, and another, and another?

The answer is that you don't, not in real life. *Logic puzzles are different.* They are toy problems that are designed to have solutions you can find.

A puzzle is a puzzle because of two things: One, it's difficult, and two, it has a right answer. You have to be willing to explore beyond the first disjunction. (No guts, no glory!) This is what separates the people who solve puzzles from those who don't. Once you look past the disjunction, you almost always find that the situation is a lot simpler than it could be. The tree of possibilities does not branch endlessly; all roads lead to the solution. This is how nearly all logic puzzles work.

The disjunctive reasoning that is so difficult for most people is something that computers excel at. There are efficient algorithms for "tree searching" and "path finding" (think of how quickly Yahoo! shoots back route maps). Good software makes the most of such algorithms. Therefore software developers need to be comfortable with this type of reasoning.

Why Is It So Easy to Kill a Robot?

You've probably seen robot battles on television. People build robots whose only purpose is to destroy other robots. Then they put a bunch of these robots in an arena to see what happens. These competitions prove at least one thing: It's easy to kill a robot.

It's easy because robots have such rigid behaviors. They don't "look at the big picture" and they never "think outside the box." Say you've got a robot that protects itself with a flamethrower. Whenever another robot comes within 10 feet of it — BOOM — it torches it.

All the next guy has to do is build a robot that sprays gasoline on your robot from 11 feet away — and then backs away fast. Pretty soon your robot will use its flamethrower and incinerate itself. A human being would be smart enough to say "Hey, I'm covered in a flammable liquid. I'd better not use the flamethrower right now." Robots aren't that smart.

This is an example of what AI researchers call the framing problem. The framing problem is the problem of knowing what exactly the problem is. How is a robot, or any would-be sentient being, supposed to know what is relevant to the current situation? How does it know what it can safely ignore?

This is one of the thorniest problems of AI. Some would say it is *the* problem of AI.

The obvious fixes are unavailing. When your prize robot has just self-immolated, the knee-jerk response is to vow to build a new and better robot that *pays attention to more things* in its environment and *contemplates more logical consequences* of actions or inactions. These are fine goals. In the world of chips and code, they are a devil to implement. Broadening the scope of the robot's "attention" involves exponential increases in the computation the robot brain must do. The more consequences a robot ponders, the slower it is going to react. There's nothing more vulnerable than a slow robot.

Humans are a lot better than today's AI systems at framing problems. We have good instincts about what is and isn't relevant in most of the problems we encounter. These instincts aren't infallible, though. Many logic puzzles exploit this fallibility. You start the problem with a set of natural assumptions about what is relevant and what is not. In many cases the puzzle has been designed so that some of these natural assumptions are wrong.

To deal effectively with puzzles (and with the bigger problems for which they may be a model), you must operate on two or more levels simultaneously. One thread of consciousness tackles the problem while another, higher-level thread monitors the progress. You need to keep asking yourself "Is this approach working? How much time have I spent on this approach, and how likely is it to produce an answer soon? Is there something else I should be trying?"

This self-awareness is characteristic of good problem solvers. It is also something you find in people who are good at job interviews of any kind, where it's important not only to answer questions but to be aware of the body language of the interviewer — and, for that matter, whether your hair looks okay. Should one approach not work, you need to step back, take a look at the big picture, and question some of the assumptions you have been making.

The process of stepping back can involve several stages. There are many assumptions at work in almost any situation. Rarely if ever are all of these assumptions wrong. A trick some people use when stumped by a puzzle is to list their assumptions and then try to imagine how the problem would be different if each assumption was in fact known to be wrong.

Take the contaminated-pills puzzle. There are five jars of pills, one contaminated. You have to find which jar is contaminated in one weighing. You're stumped and can go no farther. What assumptions are you using?

For most people, the problematic assumptions are one or more of these:

1. You're not allowed to open a jar.
2. The pills you weigh must come from the same jar.
3. A weighing can tell you just *one of two things:* that what you test is the *normal* weight, or that it's *less* than it should be.

All three of these assumptions lead you astray. You need to reject them all to come to the intended solution. In general, how are you supposed to decide which assumption(s) to toss out? It's a difficult question, because the above assumptions are not the only ones people make when thinking about this puzzle. Here are some more:

4. You're not allowed to break apart a pill and weigh just a fraction of it.
5. You're not allowed to heft the jars in your hands to tell which is suspiciously light.
6. You're not allowed to chemically analyze the pills for contamination (in which case you may not need the weighing at all).
7. You're not allowed to ask someone which jar is contaminated (or bribe someone to tell you).

All of these assumptions happen to be reasonable ones for this particular puzzle. They keep you from straying off into directions that don't lead to the intended solution. Unfortunately, you don't know that at the outset. There are puzzles, riddles, trick questions, and real-world situations where the solution might take exactly the forms proscribed in the second list. These too are more or less reasonable assumptions that you should be willing to surrender if and when circumstances demand.

A key to solving any puzzle is to be sensitive to clues as to what kind of puzzle it is. These clues come in many forms. They range from the wording of the puzzle to the tone of voice of the person posing it to your own reasoning about the assumptions themselves.

When on a sinking ship, you first throw off the cargo that weighs the most and is valued the least. Similarly, the usual way of dealing with possibly faulty assumptions is to go from least to most essential. The very first assumption listed (that you're not able to open a jar) bothers relatively few people. Nothing in the puzzle explicitly gives you permission to open the bottles. Nothing says you can't open the bottles, either. The question asks which *jar* is contaminated, not which pills are. Timid folks, as well as perfectionists looking for the most elegant answer, might start off searching for a solution in which jars are weighed whole. There's nothing wrong with that, as a first stab at the problem.

Give it a little more thought, and this assumption self-destructs. Let's say you pick jar number two and it tips the scales at 1,027 grams. How much of that is the weight of the jar? You don't know. There's been no talk of how much the jars weigh. How many pills are in the jar? There's been no talk of that, either. Conceivably there are few enough pills to count. Otherwise you're like a kid trying to win a bicycle by guessing the number of marbles in a jar. You don't even know whether there is the same number of pills in each jar.

This is consequently an assumption you should question right off. It's not strongly justified by the wording of the puzzle. Should you adopt it, you find that you don't have enough information to solve the puzzle. It's evident that you must weigh pills, not jars.

Much of the above goes for assumption number two, that the pills weighed must be from the same jar. There is a sometimes treacherous tendency to simplify problems. It is easier to think about the situation when all the pills are from the same bottle. But should you accept that restriction (which again is not stated in the problem), the puzzle is impossible to solve.

You can quickly convince yourself that this assumption is dubious. When the weighed pills come from one jar, there are only two possibilities — that you weigh contaminated pills or normal pills. Should you choose to weigh ten pills from jar number three, and the scale registers the contaminated weight of 90 grams, you're in luck. Jar number three has the ringers. The trouble is, you might just as well have picked one of the other four jars. Then you would have gotten the normal weight of 100 grams for ten pills. You would be left uncertain of which of the four jars you didn't weigh had the lighter pills. You are going to have this problem under any scheme where you sample a single jar. This strongly suggests that the right answer will involve weighing pills from more than one jar.

The third assumption is a killer for some of Microsoft's interviewees. (It rarely troubles nonprogrammers.) Anyone used to thinking in terms of information is liable to reason that a single weighing, whether of one pill or a group of identical pills, can return only a yes-or-no result. The weight will be either the normal weight or the contaminated weight.

That is a single bit of information. Every programmer knows it's impossible to identify one of five things with a single bit. You need three bits.

This analysis is junk, of course. It folds in the second assumption. You will get a yes-or-no result only if all the pills are known to be identical — that is, taken from the same jar.

Preliminary thinking about puzzles often leads to "proofs" of impossibility. A good puzzle should make you bang your head against the wall. Looked at another way, impossibility can be helpful. When an assumption leads to a proof that the puzzle is impossible to solve, then there is something wrong, either in the assumption or in the reasoning.

One of the best routes to a solution of this puzzle is to accept assumption number three, turn it over in your mind, and see how it leads to impossibility. This impossibility should lead you to repudiate the third assumption. Somehow, you must get more than a yes-or-no result from a single weighing. The problem then becomes "How can you design a weighing so that the result encodes enough information to point to one of five bottles?" Depending on your skills and background, you may or may not find this to be a challenge. For nearly everyone, the biggest challenge is getting to the point where the problem is framed so clearly.

Logic puzzles are not the only way of testing skill in reframing problems. "How many gas stations are there in Los Angeles?" Confronted with such a question on a job interview, you must first decide what kind of response is expected. Some possible reactions are

- ◆ *Oh, God! I'm supposed to know this and I don't.*
- ◆ *This is a joke. No job applicant is expected to know this. I should laugh now.*

◆ *This is a "test." They want to see how I react when asked something I don't know. I should say "I really don't know" rather than trying to fake them out.*

◆ *It's another kind of test. They want me to estimate it. The answer doesn't have to be exact.*

Not until you've rejected the first three ideas and settled on the fourth can you begin to answer the way that interviewers expect. Not everyone finds that easy. "Not-so-smart candidates will get flustered and upset," says Joel Spolsky. "They will just stare at you like you landed from Mars. You have to coach them. 'Well, if you were building a new city the size of Los Angeles, how many gas stations would you put in it?' You can give them little hints. 'How long does it take to fill up a tank of gas?' Still, with not-smart candidates, you will have to drag them along while they sit there stupidly and wait for you to rescue them. These people are not problem solvers and we don't want them working for us."

In some regards, questions "with no right answer" are the most perilous of all. "If you could remove any of the fifty U.S. states, which would it be?" This is a silly question, sure. That does not mean that all answers to it are equally good. In answering, you may end up reframing the question itself several times. Should it be understood as "What state is most 'expendable' politically?" or "What state don't you like personally?" or "What state looks like it doesn't fit on the map?" The only criterion for deciding is how good an answer you can supply. If there's a compelling story about why you dislike Delaware — and you can tell it without coming off as a self-absorbed, Delaware-hating loser — then maybe that's a good approach. Otherwise, it may be best to try something else.

One important difference between this type of question and a logic puzzle is that there is no right answer to click into place. Stumble across the right answer to a puzzle, and it's normally obvious that it *is* the right answer and you can stop looking for a better one. A less-structured question is like a badly designed keyboard. There is no feedback — you never know if you've punched the keys hard enough. Unstructured questions encourage the answerer to explore a number of different paradigms before settling on one.

Paradigm Shifts

"Paradigm" is a popular word in the Microsoft vocabulary. Bill Gates claims that no corporation has ever managed to maintain its position of dominance through a paradigm shift in technology. (Therefore, big, successful Microsoft is in constant peril from every upstart start-up.) Gates has said that his goal is for Microsoft to break that rule and find a way of prospering through paradigm shifts.

"Paradigm shift" is one of those terms that everyone uses and no one understands. It was coined by historian of science Thomas Kuhn in *The Structure of Scientific Revolutions* (1962). There Kuhn contended that academic science is a form of puzzle solving. Kuhn compared what scientists do to working on riddles, crossword puzzles, and jigsaw puzzles. Occasionally there is a scientific problem so difficult that it transcends the usual sort of puzzle solving. It requires scientists to question basic assumptions and assume a new perspective. This is what Kuhn called a paradigm shift.

Critics charged, and Kuhn admitted, that even he didn't use the word "paradigm" in an entirely consistent way. Kuhn in turn seems to have borrowed "paradigm" from the title of a 1949 scientific paper by J. S. Bruner and Leo Postman, "On the Perception of Incongruity: A Paradigm."

The latter recounted a marvelously simple psychological experiment. A group of people were shown brief glimpses of playing cards and asked to identify them. Most of the cards were normal ones. The experimenters also threw in some special cards printed with the wrong color. They'd use, for instance, a *red* six of spades or a *black* four of hearts.

The participants didn't notice anything unusual when the cards were presented quickly. Shown a red six of spades for a split second, people would identify it confidently — and wrongly — as either the "six of spades" or the "six of hearts."

When people were permitted longer glimpses of the anomalous cards, hesitation crept in. They commented that something was wrong. They offered explanations, not necessarily correct ones, saying something such as "It's the six of spades, only there's a red border around the black."

Finally, with longer exposure to the anomalous cards, people would realize the trick. They would be able to call a red spade a red spade. Once someone understood that wrong-color cards were a possibility, responses to later anomalous cards were much improved. At a brief glimpse of a black four of hearts, they would identify the card *and* its "wrong" color.

A similar psychological effect is at work in many puzzles and real-world problems. The solution is "right in front of your face" and still you can't see it. That's because reality is too richly complex to store in your head. It must be broken down for easy packing into a set of established concepts and assumptions. Thinking about a problem really means manipulating this mental model. But should an experiment or puzzle challenge expectations, this mental model will likely be wrong. A struggle ensues. Denial is followed by recognition of the situation's novel elements, sometimes in stages and sometimes in a leap of insight.

Reactions to the Bruner-Postman experiment were just as individual as reactions to puzzles are. There were a few participants who just couldn't shift mental gears. Even when they were shown the wrong-color cards for forty times the interval normally sufficient to identify the card, these people were unable to supply a correct description of what they had seen. "I can't make the suit out, whatever it is," one subject complained. "It didn't even look like a card that time. I don't know what color it is now or whether it's a spade or a heart. I'm not even sure now what a spade looks like. My God!"

Six

Wall Street and the Stress Interview

By about 1990, Microsoft's way of interviewing had metastasized. Puzzles, trick questions, deceptions, and just plain odd tasks began showing up in interviews well outside the Seattle–Silicon Valley axis. A major nexus for interview puzzles was the New York financial community.

The puzzle interview was tailor-made for the culture of Wall Street. There too, competition is intense and market share tenuous. High finance is becoming more and more like the software business. Derivatives and other sophisticated financial instruments are "software" that must be devised and implemented by math-savvy wonks working long hours. Quite aside from that, the investment banking community has long been known for some of the toughest job interviews in the East.

The "stress interview" strives to make the candidate uncomfortable in order to provoke a reaction. In the time-honored "silent treatment," you're ushered into someone's Wall Street office for an interview. They don't say a thing for five or ten minutes. *Nothing.* You introduce yourself, extend your hand — no reaction. The interviewer may read the newspaper or your résumé. And doesn't say a word.

Or the interviewer pretends to fall asleep. This sounds like a joke, but it's a common enough tactic that WetFeet.com, a website for job seekers, has felt it necessary to debate possible responses. The site recommends writing a note saying "I enjoyed meeting you," putting it on the snoozing interviewer's desk, and getting up to leave. You *hope* the interviewer will stop you before you get to the door.

In another stress-interview technique, you're ushered into a conference room and told to "sit anywhere." Once you do, the interviewer demands, "Why did you sit there?" Tables in most conference rooms are rectangular or oblong. Do you choose to sit at the "head of the table" — or not at the head of the table? The implication is that *wolves* sit at the head of the table and *sheep* along the sides. The job opening is for a wolf.

Michael Lewis's 1990 Wall Street memoir, *Liar's Poker,* reports that Lehman Brothers interviewers were known for asking the applicant to open a window. This was a casual request made just as the interviewer excused himself to take a call in another room. Lehman Brothers interviewed in a skyscraper office where the windows didn't open. Lewis mentions the tale that one interviewee "opened" the forty-third-floor window by tossing a chair through it.

Many of the same questions that Microsoft asks are now common in Wall Street interviews. Possibly some of the analysts studying tech firms heard of the puzzle interviews and brought the idea back east. Goldman Sachs (which handled Microsoft's 1986 initial public offering) asks the puzzle about weighing eight balls to find the heavier one. Smith Barney asks how to measure 4 gallons of water with 3- and 5-gallon containers. The manhole-cover riddle and impossible questions are common too.

Beam Me Up

Another early adopter of puzzle interviews was the management consulting industry. A good consultant must be a "quick study"; thus, puzzles and riddles are seen as a way of judging "non–context-specific" intelligence. A favorite question dusts off one of the oldest logic puzzles in the book (many books).

? In front of you are two doors. One leads to your interview, the other to an exit. Next to the door is a consultant. He may be from our firm or from a rival. The consultants from our company always tell the truth. The consultants from the other company always lie. You are allowed to ask the consultant one question to find out which is the door to your interview. What would you ask? (Answer on page 223)

Questions such as this are often subsumed under the label of "case questions," usually known simply as cases. That most properly refers to the hypothetical management questions familiar to any M.B.A. "Company ABC is thinking about expanding into the Korean market, where it will compete with a government-supported Company XYZ. . . ." Traditionally, case questions are realistic and relevant. More and more, they grade freely into brainteasers. "The *Star Trek* transporter has just been invented. How will it affect the transportation industry?" The career website vault.com gives a transcript of such an interview.

Applicant: How common are these devices? Are they going to be readily available to the average consumer? How much do they cost?

Interviewer: For the time being, the transporters are expensive. They would cost about one hundred thousand dollars each.

Applicant: That clearly takes them out of the range of most home users. How much does it cost to use them?

Interviewer: Assume that the marginal cost of a transport is near zero. The only cost is for the transport-operator time, which is relatively small.

Applicant: Are they safe? You said they were just invented.

Interviewer: Except for the occasional freak accident, yes, they are safe.

The applicant ended by concluding that transporters were too expensive to dent the car market but would affect air travel. He recommended that Fed Ex buy some transporters and charge a stiff premium for beaming packages.

The Immersive Interview

Stress interviews are not unique to Wall Street. Admiral Hyman G. Rickover insisted on personally interviewing candidates for service on the Navy's nuclear submarine fleet. These officers would have their hands on the nuclear button, so to speak, and it was vital that they be up to the responsibility and stress of the job. Rickover made sure the stress started with the interview. He sawed two of a chair's legs short so that the chair would not sit flat. The candidate had to sit in that seat during the interview. "It was difficult because it was a shiny chair and they kept sliding off," Rickover told *60 Minutes*'s Diane Sawyer shortly before his death.

When a candidate gave an unsatisfactory answer, Rickover ordered him to stand in the broom closet. "I'd put them in there for a couple of hours, three hours, and it gave them plenty of time to think." The purpose of all this, claimed Rickover, was "to draw out of them what they had potentially in them."

Today, the military's most famous — and most Microsoftlike — interview is probably that at the U.S. Marines' Officer Candidate School in Quantico, Virginia. "School" is not really the word for it. The ten-week "course" is not designed to teach anybody anything. Its purpose is to weed out recruits who don't have what it takes. In other words, it's a job interview that lasts ten weeks, 24/7. Quantico's officer candidates perform physically demanding tasks that also require brainteaserlike logic. Instead of just analyzing how four people might cross a bridge, the Marines have to physically carry a "wounded" soldier across a "mined" stream using just a board and rope. Another puzzle is to scale a wall that seems to be unscalable. Instructors observe from catwalks.

You might call this the immersive interview. In the private sector too, companies have adopted the tactic of immersing people in artificial, self-contained environments to see how they perform. Because of the expense, the immersive interview is usually restricted to people who are already employees. Presented under the guise of training, its hidden agenda is generally to help decide whom to promote.

Microsoft sends its managers to retreats that fall somewhere in the gray area between a role-playing game and a "reality show." Once, fourteen Microsoft managers were sent to a remote village on Cape Cod. They were split randomly into three teams: Elites, Managers, and Immigrants. The Immigrants immediately had to surrender their wallets and cell phones. They were allowed to carry around just a paper bag containing a single change of underwear. The Immigrants were packed in a dormitory and ate franks and beans. The Managers shared a home and got better food while the Elites got spacious accommodations and dined on lobster and wine. Participants were rated on how well they pulled together to achieve common goals, despite the disparity in perks.

These immersive interviews have grown into a mini-industry. Pittsburgh-based Development Dimensions International (DDI) claims to have assisted in hiring 15 million people through what it calls, with a straight face, "competency-based recruitment." One of the companies that has made use of DDI's services is Unisys. People applying for a managerial job at Unisys are required to spend a day managing a fictional company called Pilot, Inc. The candidate is sealed in a fake office (actually a set at DDI) on the pretense that he or she has already been hired as manager and is reporting for the first day of work. The candidate sits down to a quickly increasing pile of e-mail and phone messages that must be dealt with ASAP. DDI's psychologists watch on a bank of TV monitors to determine how well the applicant performs. Explained DDI founder William Byham, "We take all the crises a manager might experience in a year and cram them into one day."

The Absurdist Interview

For hirers on a budget, the most cost-effective form of "competency-based hiring" remains puzzles and riddles. Interview puzzles are like a pop tune you don't like but can't get out of your head. Catchy and easy to remember, they continue to insinuate themselves into hiring in an ever-wider range of industries. Chris Sells likens the puzzle-interview phenomenon to "a fad diet — 'well, the last six diets I tried didn't work, but this sounds like it will.'"

And like people on diets, companies have a tendency to overdo, then binge. People generally take away one of two impressions from Microsoft's interviews: The interviews are *crazy* — or the interviews are *hard.* Consequently, interviews elsewhere have gotten crazier and/or harder. The puzzle interview keeps mutating along the way, not always for the better.

Some see puzzle interviews as the human-resources equivalent of Dada. *Anything goes — we are all merry pranksters here.* A hirer at Blair Television (a New York company selling television ads) spices up interviews by reaching in her desk and tossing out a hand grenade. "If you're so good," she says to prospective salespeople, "sell me *this.*"

Other companies pose obtuse riddles such as "Define the color green." Superficially that has the flavor of some of Microsoft's wackier questions. Wacky or not, every well-known Microsoft question has at least one good reasonable answer. How do they expect you to "define the color green" without sounding as tiresomely self-important as the question itself?

For interview zaniness, a defunct Boston firm takes the cake. Zefer Corp. was a dot-com consulting firm that crashed and burned in 2001. Its most lasting claim to fame may be its job interviews. The candidate was given a set of Lego blocks. He or she had five minutes in which to build something. That was part A of the interview. Part B was "Justify what you built." Susan Perry, Zefer's "vice president of talent," insisted that the Lego test "sparked some great conversations and insights that challenged and intrigued people."

Seven

The Hardest Interview Puzzles

Most or all of the Microsoft questions in chapter four are in wide use at other companies. As puzzle interviews have proliferated, many other questions have been added to the canon. Some are amazingly hard to expect someone to solve under time pressure. Maybe there's an element of one-upmanship (if Microsoft asks *that,* we'll ask an even harder question and get smarter people). Below are several of the most difficult interview puzzles in reasonably wide use. (Answers start on page 226)

? Why are beer cans tapered at the top and bottom?

? How long would it take to move Mount Fuji?

? There are three switches in a hallway. One switch controls a light fixture in a room at the far end of the hall. The door to the room is closed, and you can't see whether the light is on or off. You need to find out which of the three switches controls the light. How can you be certain of finding that out, making just one trip to the room?

? You play this game with one other player: Starting with an empty rectangular table like this one, and an unlimited supply of quarters, each person takes a turn by putting a quarter anywhere on the table. The rules say only that you must place your quarter so that it doesn't touch any quarter already on the table. You and your opponent take turns placing quarters in succession, until the table is nearly full of quarters. The first player who is unable to add a quarter without touching a quarter already placed loses.

   You move first. What strategy would you use to play this game?

? Five pirates on an island have one hundred gold coins to split among themselves. They divide the loot as follows: The senior pirate proposes a division, and everyone votes on it. Provided at least half the pirates vote for the proposal, they split the coins that way. If not, they kill the senior pirate and start over. The most senior (surviving) pirate proposes his own division plan, and they vote by the same rules and either divide the loot or kill the senior pirate, as the case may be. The process continues until one plan is accepted. Suppose you are the senior pirate. What division do you propose? (The pirates are all extremely logical and greedy, and all want to live.)

? A high school has this ritual on the last day of school: The students go into the hall and stand by their closed lockers. At the first blow of a whistle, the students open every locker. At the second whistle, the students close every second locker (lockers 2, 4, 6, etc., are slammed shut). At the third whistle, the students toggle every third locker. To "toggle" means to close it if it's open, and to open it if it's closed. They toggle lockers 3, 6, 9, etc. At whistle four, they toggle every fourth locker. At whistle five, they toggle every fifth locker, and so on.

Let's make things easy and say it's a small school with only 100 lockers. At the one hundredth whistle, the student standing next to locker 100 (and only that student) toggles his locker. How many lockers are then open?

? You have two lengths of fuse. Each will burn for exactly one hour. But the fuses are not necessarily identical and do not burn at a constant rate. There are fast-burning sections and slow-burning sections. How do you measure forty-five minutes using only the fuses and a lighter?

? You are in a boat in the exact center of a perfectly circular lake. There is a goblin on the shore of the lake. The goblin wants to do bad things to you. The goblin can't swim and doesn't have a boat. Provided you can make it to the shore — and the goblin isn't there, waiting to grab you — you can always outrun him on land and get away.

The problem is this: The goblin can run four times as fast as the maximum speed of your boat. He has perfect eyesight, never sleeps, and is extremely logical. He will do everything in his power to catch you. How would you escape the goblin?

Eight

How to Outsmart the Puzzle Interview

It is tough to answer tricky, loaded, or "not exactly fair" questions under pressure. Aggressive questioning at a March 1998 news conference had Bill Gates himself "roaring with indignation and disdain for those who question his business practices," reported the *Washington Post*. "He dismissed one question as 'unfair,' another as 'dishonest.' 'Come on!' he said impatiently to one questioner. 'Give me a break!' he said a few moments later to another."

A lot of job seekers feel the same way. Like it or not, you may be confronted with tough and tricky questions on your next interview. What can you do to prepare? *Can* you do anything to prepare?

As we've noted, critics of Microsoft-style interviewing often charge that solving puzzles demonstrates nothing except the ability to solve puzzles and/or prior exposure to same. This is partly true. As a genre, logic puzzles are as stylized as the Kabuki theater. Unless you understand the idiom, you're going to be at a serious disadvantage. The same goes for impossible questions, design questions, and so forth. Like most other abilities we care about, puzzle-solving ability is surely a combination of innate talent and learned skills. The less prior experience you have with puzzles, the more you have to gain by learning how puzzles work.

Articles and websites on interviewing often suggest strategies for solving interview puzzles. Much of the advice is too broad to be of much use. Other tips involve risky subterfuges. One goes like this: Upon being given a particularly difficult puzzle, say "To be perfectly honest, I've heard that before." With luck, the interviewer gives another, easier question (while crediting you for your "honesty")!

Like most tricks, this one does not bear repeating. The odds are stacked against anyone who tries it. Most interviewers see a lot more candidates than candidates see interviewers. Chances are, the average interviewer learns this trick before the average candidate does. And if the interviewer is wise, you're in trouble. You may be asked to recount the answer anyway.

It is much more productive, as well as honest, to learn to recognize the "tricks" in the interview questions themselves. On the surface, these questions show bewildering variety. Look inside, and you find that most puzzles repackage the same small set of cognitive "tricks," especially the aforementioned disjunction effect and framing problem. Knowing this can give you a leg up.

1. First decide what kind of answer is expected (monologue or dialogue).

Most difficult interview questions require a verbal performance in which you explain how you approach the problem and end with a right or suitable answer. Questions need to be categorized by whether they demand a monologue or a dialogue.

Logic puzzles normally call for a monologue. You're given an intentionally limited amount of information and expected to arrive at a solution on your own. It's bad form to keep pressing the interviewer for information that has been purposely excluded.

That's reasonable enough, but then interviewers often use an entirely different set of rules for other questions. With many design and case questions, interviewers expect you to ask for more information. You may be penalized if you try to go it alone. The personality of the interviewer is a factor too. "Hard interviewers" pose a question and sit there, stone-faced. Other interviewers like to engage the candidate in conversation.

Design questions ("Design a spice rack") have no single right answer. That does not mean that everything is a right answer. "Not-so-smart candidates think that design is like painting: you get a blank slate, and you can do whatever you want," says Joel Spolsky. "Smart candidates understand that design is a difficult series of trade-offs."

Good answers show awareness that trade-offs exist. The candidate should try to elicit as much relevant information as the interviewer is willing to give. "What will happen is that people will launch into drawing a picture of the spice rack they remember from when they were a child," says Spolsky, who has posed this question many times. "And you say 'No, no, I didn't ask you to draw your mother's spice rack, I asked how you would *design* a spice rack.' Then you look for certain things like, do they start to look for who's going to be using it and where it's going to be placed? If they do, you say 'Aha! I'm glad you asked. It's going to be used in a cooking school,' And that tells them all kinds of things like, if it's going to be used in a cooking school, you need lots of different types of spices. You can have a conversation that goes on for an awful long time."

Some open-ended questions ("Which of the fifty U.S. states would you remove?") are almost like Rorschach blots. They are intentionally unstructured. With all types of questions, but especially with these, "the point of the question is to generate a half hour of conversation," says Spolsky. "You tell how smart the person is based on the conversation you have."

A good plan is to assume a dialogue is called for unless it's clear that the question is a conventional logic puzzle. By "dialogue" I mean that you'll probably do most of the talking but you're free to ask intelligent questions of the interviewer.

2. Whatever you think of first is wrong.

With puzzles and riddles, the first potential answer that pops into the mind of a reasonable person is usually *not* the right answer. If it were, there wouldn't be much of a puzzle.

These questions are supposed to be difficult. That is what makes them "puzzling." Like optical illusions or magic tricks or con games, puzzles depend on your basic, everyday mental competence to deceive you. Children are the most skeptical audience for magic tricks, people with some brain lesions don't experience optical illusions, and you can't cheat an honest man. Your failure to solve a puzzle right off the bat simply means that your mind is working the way it's supposed to. So is the puzzle.

Many people get nervous when they can't think of

something to say right off. The best place to start the running narration you're expected to supply is with an explanation of why the "obvious" solution is wrong. It not only fills dead air but also is an excellent way of understanding the problem.

3. Forget you ever learned calculus.

In logic puzzles, that is. No commonly used corporate interview puzzle requires calculus. If you think a puzzle requires a greater-than-TV-quiz-show level of knowledge in a field not related to the position you're interviewing for, then you're probably making a mistake.

There is a genre of faux calculus problems that have simple, noncalculus solutions. Always give the simple answer. Even if you do the higher math and get the right solution, you may be faulted for not seeing the forest for the trees.

(Needless to say, if you're interviewing at an investment bank and they ask you to compute a Black-Scholes PDE, you'll be using calculus. This rule applies only to logic puzzles.)

4. Big, complicated questions usually have simple answers.

Call it the *Jeopardy!* effect. When a quiz-show host asks what country Voltaire described as "neither holy, nor Roman, nor an empire," it's a safe bet that the answer is the Holy Roman Empire. You know this even if you know nothing about Voltaire or the Holy Roman Empire. Quiz shows write the questions so that the largest fraction of the viewing audience can say "I should have gotten that!"

Puzzles and riddles often work the same way. A logic puzzle is neither a typical problem nor even a typical hard problem. It is usually a difficult problem with a simple answer. This is particularly true of questions with big, complicated set-ups (the evil demon and dwarfs, the 100 slamming lockers).

5. Simple questions often demand complicated answers.

One-liners such as "Why do mirrors reflect right and left?" or "Why are beer cans tapered at the top and bottom?" often call for relatively long, involved answers. Make sure you think these questions through. You may be penalized if the interviewer thinks you missed an important part of the answer.

When a very short question is about design or testing ("Design a bathroom for Bill Gates"; "How would you test an elevator?"), it often means you're expected to ask the interviewer for more information.

6. "Perfectly logical beings" are not like you and me.

Many logic puzzles speak of "perfectly logical beings" (PLBs). Examples include the puzzles about the adulterous village or the pirates splitting the gold coins. "Perfectly logical" is a code word, almost, whose meaning is clear to puzzle fans but opaque to everyone else. When you hear a phrase such as this, the puzzle is telling you to forget practically everything you know about human psychology. It means you are supposed to make these assumptions:

◆ PLBs have simple, one-dimensional motivations. The PLB is concerned *only* with getting the most money, or escaping the demon, or obeying a silly law, etc. Nothing else matters. As a corollary, PLBs never do favors for "friends." It's every PLB for himself.

- ◆ PLBs think quickly. The being is promptly aware of the logical consequences of everything. Never does his mind wander, never does he make a mistake, never does he forget.

- ◆ PLBs understand the psychology (such as it is) of other PLBs and draw precise conclusions about their actions in utter confidence. More than anything else, this is what throws non–puzzle fans. Human actions are always somewhat uncertain. PLBs' actions never are. The intended solutions of these puzzles are therefore wildly unrealistic. They generally take the form of A concluding that B will conclude that C will conclude that D will conclude . . . and so on. No way would that work in the real world. Small uncertainties about real people's motivations would bubble up chaotically and render that kind of convoluted reasoning worthless. But not in these puzzles.

You can take this as a hint. When you hear about a perfectly logical being, the solution will almost always involve that being's reasoning about other PLBs (or about yourself, in puzzles that ask "What would you do in this situation?").

7. When you hit a brick wall, try to list the assumptions you're making. See what happens when you reject each of these assumptions in succession.

As mentioned, this old trick is often easier said than done. In the cleverest puzzles, the problem assumption(s) may be so natural that you're hardly aware of them as "assumptions." But it's worth a try. Go down the list and assume the *opposite* of each assumption in turn. Does that lead you anywhere promising? With luck, you'll find that one of the assumptions, when tossed out, leads to a solution.

Even when this doesn't work, it may win you points from the interviewer. It will show that you understand reframing is an important part of problem solving.

8. When crucial information is missing in a logic puzzle, lay out the possible scenarios. You'll almost always find that you don't need the missing information to solve the problem.

Virtually everything we call a logic puzzle uses the same trick, namely that most people stop cold when they come to missing information.

When a puzzle has a disjunction — an unknown that might be one thing or another, and you don't know which — you have to be prepared to reason methodically from each of the possible contingencies. Pretend it's X, and see what conclusions you can draw. Pretend it's Y, and see what conclusions are possible. You will almost always find that this sort of reasoning leads to a breakthrough. It will turn out that you didn't need the missing information to solve the puzzle.

Think of it this way: When the bridge is out, you have to swim. Fortunately, you never have to swim very far (they build bridges only at the narrowest parts of the river).

9. Where possible, give a good answer that the interviewer has never heard before.

This applies especially to open-ended questions "with no right answer." Interviewers have heard every *common* answer many times. When Spolsky asked one Microsoft candidate to "design a spice rack for a blind person," the candidate decided that a blind person would prefer a counter-level spice drawer to a spice rack hung on the wall at chest or face level. Which is easier: to reach up, locate by feel a rack you know is *somewhere* over there, and then, with your arm still uncomfortably extended, read the braille that's probably on the tops of the jars — or simply to slide your hand across the counter to a drawer with braille labels on top? These ergonomic issues never occurred to any other candidate. Just as impressive, the candidate effectively redefined the problem. A "spice rack" doesn't have to be a spice rack if there's a good enough reason for it to be something else. Said Spolsky, "On the strength of that answer alone, and no negatives, I hired the candidate, who went on to be one of the best program managers on the Excel team."

There is enough anecdotal evidence that I am inclined to think interviewers not only value but possibly overvalue good, original answers. There may be a boredom factor. You know the way that some poor saps try to send out a really jazzy résumé to get hirers' attention? That hardly ever works, but in these interviews, a creative but good answer does stand out. Just make sure it's *good*.

Nine

How Innovative Companies Ought to Interview

Some good ideas underlie the puzzle interview. They are too often mixed in with tricks, traps, power games, and hazing stunts. The goal of hiring the most capable people is frequently compromised by the interviewer.

Let's start with the good ideas. The puzzle interview recognizes two discomforting facts of life. They are

- When the technology is changing beneath your feet daily, there is not much point in hiring for a specific, soon-to-be-obsolete set of skills. You have to try to hire for a general problem-solving capacity, however difficult that may be.
- A bad hiring decision is likely to hurt the company more than a good hiring decision will help it. Above all, you want to avoid bad hires.

The first condition exists in any company undergoing rapid change. That is not *every* company or organization, of course. There is little point in posing brainteasers to a wedding planner, surgeon, taxi driver, or counterperson at Starbucks. The skills these people are being hired for will still be valid tomorrow, and ten years from now. It is when the profession changes fast, relative to the average tenure of an employee, that conventional interviewing techniques fail.

The second point, about bad hires being costly, is true almost anywhere. Lose out on hiring a good employee and there will always be another to come along and fill the position — assuming the position hasn't already been filled with a not-so-good employee. In any field, putting up with and terminating an unqualified employee is excruciating.

Interview puzzles are most realistically conceived as a *negative* screen. They are a way of making sure you don't hire the wrong people rather than a way of identifying "geniuses." That conservative approach makes sense when bad hires are so costly.

At a lot of companies today, hiring is as centerless as the Internet. Microsoft-style peer interviewing is most often used in companies with flat organization structures ("pancakes," not "pyramids"). This places a lot of responsibility on the shoulders of people who are not hiring experts.

In evaluating interview questions and practices, you should focus on what you hope to achieve. "You're going in there with absolutely no information," says Joel Spolsky. "You're not going to get very much information because you don't have very much time."

The overriding goal has to be *information you can use.* Does the question, and the answers you are likely to get, tell you something that helps you make a hiring decision? Few interviewers bother to ask themselves this.

Some think that a good puzzle is a good interview question. This is not necessarily the case. Here are two examples, both used in job interviews.

? Does the sun always rise in the east?

? You've got six matchsticks. Arrange them so they form four equilateral triangles. (Answers on page 243)

The first is a "trick question." It has a simple, clever answer. That's the problem. Once you hear the clever answer, you'll remember it for a long time. This riddle has been making the rounds, by word of mouth, print, and the Net, for years. There are many places a job candidate could have heard this puzzle and its solution. How do you know whether the candidate has heard it before? You don't, of course, and this isn't the sort of riddle where thinking out loud is especially informative.

Much the same goes for the matchstick puzzle. It has a further problem: *It's too hard to ask on a hiring interview.* That will strike some interviewers as a peculiar objection when the goal is to hire extremely bright people for a demanding technical job. But this is not the Mensa Quiz for Super-IQ Brains. There is not time to ask everything that *might* tell you something worthwhile. Not enough people solve this puzzle within a reasonable time to make it worth your while to ask it.

The matchstick question hinges on a paradigm shift. When you make the reasonable assumption that you are going to lay the six matchsticks out on the table and arrange them in the many ways possible, you can continue, logically and efficiently, for some time *without* solving the problem, and *without* exhausting the possibilities of the paradigm. Because there

are so many possibilities to play around with, you do not necessarily find yourself backed into a corner (which might
prompt the paradigm shift needed to get the right answer).

This is considered an especially successful puzzle because the solution is simple and audacious. But since the
puzzle is hard, and the answer simple, it may well be that
more candidates "solve" it by remembering the answer than
by truly figuring it out in the interview. That renders the
question useless for hiring purposes.

Before you pose any question to a job applicant, you
ought to ask yourself two questions:

◆ Am I willing to hire someone because of a good answer to this question?
◆ Am I willing to reject someone because of a bad answer?

Unless your response to (at least) one of the two questions is yes, *there's no point in asking the question*. The question may tell you something about the candidate, but what it
tells you is not information you can act on. You don't have
time to ask a question like that.

In this chapter I will propose a way that companies in
the business of innovation *ought* to interview. Let's suppose
you find yourself interviewing candidates for a demanding
job in a competitive industry. Most likely you are a regular
employee, not a human resources expert, and you are conducting one of several interviews of the job candidate. No
matter how many or how few questions you ask, you are ultimately required to render a "hire" or "no hire" verdict. Here
are a few guidelines to make sure you get the most information you can act on.

1. The value of puzzles is in inverse proportion to the candidate's experience.

"To college kids, this way of interviewing is kind of cool," says Adam David Barr. "It's a good recruiting device to have these interviews where they can say 'Wow, I really was able to be clever and strut my stuff in this interview.' With an experienced person, it's harder, unfair in a way, to ask them puzzles. 'Okay, we're going to judge you on whether you know why manhole covers are round and not talk about your fifteen-year career at Oracle.'"

Microsoft does not use logic puzzles in interviewing senior management. This fact often gets lost in the translation as other companies rush to jump on the bandwagon. When a candidate has a track record, it's almost always more informative and relevant to discuss that than to pose puzzles.

A goal of any interviewing technique should be that it be perceived as fair. But candidates' perceptions of how fair interview questions are tend to be "based on one thing — how well they are able to answer them," notes Chris Sells. "New college grads consider questions about their experience unfair simply because they don't have any. Geezers like me *love* these kinds of questions."

One of the best reasons for using interview puzzles is that many bright college kids with little or no experience actually prefer these questions. They would rather demonstrate their problem-solving abilities with puzzles (which they "respect," in a way) than struggle to answer traditional human resources questions (which they often believe to be meaningless). Used with these applicants, interview puzzles make for good public relations. For more experienced candidates, however, who may judge interview puzzles insulting, the opposite is likely true.

2. Have an interview plan.

Hiring experts often recommend "structured interviewing." That means you settle on a fixed set of questions and a fixed way of posing them. You ask every candidate the same questions in the same way. This is an attempt to minimize the variables. It's easier to evaluate a candidate's responses when you've heard a wide range of answers to the same questions.

In the real world, it is tough to stick to structured interviewing. You may do interviews for different positions with different requirements. You may want to try different questions or change them from time to time lest they become too well known.

It is nonetheless worthwhile to be as consistent as practical. You will probably be asking questions other than the "tricky" ones that are the subject of this book. They will likely include general inquiries about experience and goals, and others specifically addressing job skills. It is easy to get distracted in an interview, so it's a good idea to make a list beforehand of the questions you intend to ask.

3. An interview is not an IQ test.

There are interviewers who bombard the candidate with half a dozen tough brainteasers in an hour interview. The rationale is that this provides a crude measure of problem-solving ability. "Barbara solved three of the killer puzzles while Ed solved two. Hire Barbara."

This amounts to an IQ test with way too few items to

offer even the dubious reliability that IQ tests offer. You can't ask enough puzzles in an interview to get a statistically valid sample. There's too great a chance of someone lucking out or remembering an answer, or of someone missing one because of nervousness.

A related practice is the "sword in the stone" technique. Some interviewers like to toss out a puzzle they know is hard. They don't really expect the candidate to solve it. But if, one day, a candidate *does* solve the superhard puzzle, make an offer immediately! The candidate is a genius.

Once again, the issue is "information you can act on." Maybe the person who solves the superhard puzzle *is* a genius. Are you so certain of that that you're willing to hire this person solely on the basis of solving one hard puzzle? That's putting a lot of faith in puzzles. Are you sure, for that matter, that a "genius" would contribute more to the company than someone merely very competent? That's putting a lot of faith in genius.

When things are put this way, most everyone will concede that, no, they wouldn't hire someone *just* for solving a puzzle. They would look at the résumé, the other things said in the interview, and everything else. In short, they wouldn't hire someone for solving a hard puzzle unless "everything else" was practically just as encouraging. In that case, why do you need to ask the puzzle?

So what are puzzles good for (assuming they're good for anything)? The answer follows.

4. An interview puzzle is a filter to prevent bad hires.

The sword in the stone idea has got it backward. The main agenda with an interview puzzle should be to identify the people you *don't* want to hire.

A good interview puzzle should be easy enough that you're willing to reject anyone who doesn't solve it. That's probably the best way of describing the optimal difficulty level for a question with a definite right answer. You want a puzzle such that many people will fail to solve it, but practically all "acceptable" candidates will get the answer. Not solving the puzzle should raise a red flag.

There is a trade-off. People's reactions to puzzles are personal. You should expect that there will be capable candidates who fail to solve the puzzle and who will be rejected unnecessarily. Remember, the guiding principle should be that it's better to lose some good people in order to avoid hiring unsuitable people.

One weakness of interviewing is that smart people generally come off well. Selective companies tend to hire smart people and then are baffled when some turn out to be disastrous employees. Just like everyone else, smart people can lack motivation.

Puzzles, design questions, and impossible questions are miniprojects. It is not enough to have good, intelligent insights. You also have to weave them together and bring things to a conclusion. Now, sure, it's a lot easier to solve a puzzle than to ship a new product at a big company. For that very reason, leaving puzzles and questions unresolved should raise a red flag.

Fog Creek Software president Michael Pryor reports that everyone hired at the company has correctly solved the five-pirates puzzle. This will probably astonish some people. It is a hard puzzle by usual standards. But it is kind of like those climbing walls that are used to train rock climbers. There are handholds at just the places you need them. There is a way of building incrementally on that first handhold to arrive at a complete solution. The puzzle is thus not so much a test of fantastic insight as one of determination to follow something through. Solving the puzzle does not identify a candidate as a "genius." A good explanation of the solution does, however, increase the interviewer's comfort level that the candidate has the sort of skills necessary to succeed at the company. Conversely, being unable to solve the problem raises such a red flag that it would be hard to justify hiring the candidate. Asking this question provides information that the company's hirers are comfortable acting on.

5. Interview questions are only as fair as you make them.

The history of intelligence testing demonstrates that the easiest thing in the world for a well-meaning tester to do is to assemble a "fair" set of questions that is biased in subtle, or not-so-subtle, ways "invisible" to the tester. Interview puzzles and riddles raise the same issue. That would be a good reason for not using them, were it not for the likelihood that traditional interview questions are equally or more biased.

As interviewer, you have an awesome responsibility. The interview can only be as fair as you make it. Not everyone grew up reading the books or playing the video games that you did. You can't assume that every talented person you interview will "get" the arcane conventions of puzzles (such as how perfectly logical beings operate). Be prepared to explain the ground rules. Avoid faulting people for not approaching a question exactly the way you would.

The fairness issue is often intentionally skirted in the name of "finding people who will fit into the corporate culture." We hire "[Bill] clones" (fill in the name of your own company's figurehead), and as long as we find them in all genders and colors, what does it matter?

Look at it this way: The more narrowly you choose to define the corporate culture, the greater the chance the most capable person for the job is going to lie outside that culture. Being an off-hours puzzle fan is way too narrow a prerequisite for employment. It's your responsibility to make sure the candidate understands the questions, including any unspoken assumptions.

6. Choose questions so that it doesn't matter (much) whether the candidate has heard them before.

There is no keeping interview questions secret in the age of the Web. Prudent interviewers have to assume that many applicants will have prior exposure to the puzzles they're posing. Some candidates will have heard the puzzle from a friend ten years ago. Some will have pulled it off the Web the night before the interview. Many (most?) are not going to be so candid as to inform you of that fact.

"You want a question that's not just right or wrong and can't be ruined if they've heard the answer," says Barr. "Not to be too pretentious about coding, but it's like being an artist. You hire an artist, and you might have them draw something while you're watching. They may have practiced it beforehand but they still have to *do* it. You can't fake that."

That means you want questions where the candidate can walk you through the reasoning he or she used. There may be one right answer, but the ways of arriving at it, and the ways of verbalizing how one arrives at it, are often highly personal. By listening to *how* a candidate deals with a question, you learn a lot about his or her problem-solving personality.

Avoid trick questions. By definition, trick questions have a "trick," and tricks are easy to remember. When a question depends on a clever insight (like the two examples cited above), people usually have difficulty articulating how they got the insight. That means the answer is not very informative.

A good strategy is to introduce variations. "How many Ping-Pong balls will fit in a 747?" is a fine question. Take a coffee break sometime and see how many off-the-wall variations you can come up with. Ask one of your original variations instead. It will help level the playing field between those who have and haven't heard the original question.

Many logic puzzles allow you to change the numbers or other details too (make sure you've still got a satisfying puzzle of reasonable difficulty level). The five-pirates puzzle is good because you can change the number of pirates and coins at will. Make it four pirates splitting eighty-three coins. While the reasoning is analogous to the original (and yes, that still gives someone exposed to the puzzle an advantage), the "right answer" is totally different. This helps to distinguish someone who truly "gets" the concept from someone who has memorized an answer. A good verbal performance is hard to fake.

7. Challenge your first impression.

There are jobs where first impressions should count. A salesperson is going to be meeting people all day. Whatever combination of charisma, appearance, and body language makes a good first impression is a legitimate factor in a hiring decision. For most other jobs, first impressions are less important. For someone who is going to be sitting in a cubicle writing code, they may be irrelevant.

Just as substance abusers need to admit their problem before they can get help, interviewers should recognize their first-impression problem. It really does appear that many interviewers make an unconscious decision within the first seconds of the interview. They then ask wishy-washy questions whose answers may be interpreted as they please.

It is important to ask questions where the answers may challenge the first impression. For many types of jobs, logic puzzles are one way of doing that. It's also a good idea to *always* make a mental note of your first impression of a candidate. At the end of the interview, compare your opinion to that first impression. *If it's the same, make sure that you can justify why it's the same.* If your opinion of the candidate has changed, make sure you know why that is too.

8. Avoid "questions with no right answer."

"Define the color green." "If a spaceship landed outside right now, would you get in it and where would you ask it to take you?" These may be fun party games. Or not. They're definitely not worth the time they take up in a hiring interview. The intent of these questions, apparently, is to gauge "creativity." It's anyone's guess whether they do that. Many creative people think these questions are just stupid. Worse, no one really knows how to "grade" answers to these questions. They give interviewers license to go with their first impression, and that defeats the purpose of an interview.

9. Don't do a "stress interview."

Stress interviews are adolescent power games that do little to identify the most suitable people for a job. In order for answers to be informative, the candidate must be comfortable enough to verbalize thoughts freely. Anything that puts the candidate on edge defeats that. This includes the practice of pointedly avoiding all small talk. *People are supposed to introduce themselves, and anything else is just weird.* This sends the message that "my time is so valuable it's not worth introducing myself to someone who may or may not be hired." Remember, you want successful candidates to choose to join the company.

The apparent justification for the stress interview — "There will be stress on the job, so let's see how the candidate deals with stress in this interview" — is dubious. The "stress" created in a stress interview is artificial. It is more informative to see the candidate at his or her best. If hired, the candidate will be mostly working under conditions less stressful than a job interview.

10. Don't pass notes.

Having interviewers e-mail each other during the interview process skews the results. No one would think of conducting an opinion poll where subjects are told the running tallies before answering. Why do it with job interviews?

Evaluations should go to human resources or some neutral party who is not interviewing. Interviewers should not be permitted to see other people's evaluations until after they have sent their own.

11. Avoid deception, even the common "white lies" about as-appropriate interviews.

Employment is a relationship of trust. The worst way to begin that relationship is by telling lies. A company hopes that candidates will speak truthfully about themselves. In return, the company should not make it a practice to deceive candidates about the interview process. Saying someone got stuck in traffic when they didn't sends the message that the company does not care about honesty or courtesy.

The deception is unnecessary. It seems to be founded on the fear that anyone who surmises a rejection will go postal. Such extreme unlikelihoods are a matter for campus security, not human resources. Instead of telling people they will have five interviews and then offering excuses for why two of them fall out, the recruiter should simply say that the company blocks out a full day for interviews, and the actual number of interviews will vary.

Honesty is important whether the job candidate will end up working for your company or not. Today's rejected candidate may be tomorrow's customer, stockholder, or lawmaker. No one should leave an interview feeling ill-used, ill-treated, or deceived.

Paradigms and Puzzles

In Lewis Terman's time, employee competence was a simple matter. It was all about intelligence, all-purpose and monolithic. Though folks such as Bill Gates sometimes sound alarmingly similar, the practice of assessing this intelligence is different today. The longevity of the often-venerable logic puzzles used in interviews owes something to the stories in which they are framed. Today we add a new layer of narrative about what these puzzles mean and what they might tell us about human beings.

The software industry itself is in large measure responsible for the new perspective. As an old saying goes, "The man with a hammer sees every problem as a nail." Our age's great hammer is the algorithm.

The problem-solving methods we call algorithms are surely the apotheosis of logic. When you turn out algorithms on an industrial scale, you find that devising algorithms is a lot more mysterious, and a lot less obviously "logical," than the algorithms themselves. How people devise good algorithms is a mystery.

The same dichotomy is apparent in puzzles. Solutions to "logic puzzles" are logical, all right. How you come up with those solutions is something else entirely. There is much trial and error, much following of instincts, and often much learning to *avoid* following instincts where they fail you (as they many times do in puzzles). The metalogic of solving puzzles is a good deal more complex than the logic of their solutions.

Puzzles, programming, Christensen's disruptive technologies, Kuhn's paradigm shifts, psychological studies of disjunction, and the still-modest progress of AI all share a common element: the *failure* of logic in what appears to be a logical enterprise. These divergent ideas and fields (puzzles were the only such concept known to the first generations of intelligence testers) remind us that logic and intelligence get you only so far.

Today we all live in a software world, not a hardware one. Change comes faster and is more pervasive. The assets that matter are the human ones. Hiring is therefore no longer a matter of finding a few executives to manage a team of interchangeable worker-drones. A start-up mentality prevails at Fortune 500 companies. Businesses feel that their survival depends on filling every position with the most talented and mentally nimble people.

Puzzle interviews are the most visible reflection of this climate of uncertainty (desperation?). Today's hirers are looking for something that resists being put into words. It is not intelligence, not solely. Confidence and motivation figure into it. The ability to accept uncertainty, question assumptions, and bring projects to completion is one way of putting it. There is a strong element of critical judgment too. "Question assumptions" is as much a platitude as the IBM THINK sign, unless you also have the knack of knowing *which* assumptions to question *when*. No one really knows how talented people manage to do all this so well. We are left, for the time being, with more provisional assessments. The road ahead forks, and there's not even one of those helpful truthtellers or liars to give you directions. How do you find your destination?

Answers

It is easy enough to verify the right answer to a logic or math puzzle. It is trickier to divine the intended or optimal responses to questions that have "no right answer." For these I have made use of reports from both interviewers and interviewees. Be warned that interviewers' ratings of answers to the "softer" questions are subjective and often idiosyncratic. The "right" way to test a saltshaker is apt to be whatever pet idea the person asking the question has in mind.

In supplying answers, I have given more attention than usual to the reasoning behind them. For the purposes of a job interview, the reasoning *is* the "answer."

? Let's play a game of Russian roulette . . .

The spin-the-barrel option is the simpler of the two to analyze. There are two bullets in six chambers, or, to put it more optimistically, four empty chambers out of six. Spin the barrel, and you've got a four-in-six, or two-in-three, chance of survival.

For the other option, look at it this way. The four

empty chambers are all contiguous. One of them just spared your life. For three of these four empty chambers, the "next" chamber in succession will also be empty. The remaining empty chamber is right before one of the two bullets. That means you have a three-in-four chance of survival when you don't spin.

Three-fourths is better than two-thirds, so you definitely *don't* want the barrel spun again.

? How would you weigh a jet plane without using scales?

Some candidates propose to look up the specs from Boeing's website. They're crushed when the interviewer brushes this aside (not allowed to use the Internet!?!). A traditional version of the puzzle asks you to weigh an *elephant* without scales. Elephant or jet, you aren't allowed to cut it into manageable pieces.

The intended answer is that you taxi or fly the jet onto an aircraft carrier, ferry, or other ship big enough to hold it. Paint a mark on the hull of the ship showing the water level. Then remove the jet. The ship will rise in the water.

Now load the ship with items of known weight (100-pound bales of cotton, whatever) until it sinks to exactly the line you painted on the hull. The total weight of the items will equal the weight of the jet.

If you're more work-phobic than math-phobic, you can save effort by computing the volume of the ship between the two water levels, and multiplying that by the density of water. That too will give you the jet's weight.

? Why are manhole covers round rather than square?

The answer interviewers consider the best is that a square cover could fall into its hole, injuring someone or getting lost underwater. This is because the diagonal of a square is $\sqrt{2}$ (1.414 ...) times its side. Should you hold a square manhole cover near-vertically and turn it a little, it falls easily into its hole. In contrast, a circle has the same diameter in all directions. The slight recess in the lower part of the cover prevents it from ever falling in, no matter how it's held.

A more flippant answer (not that this question merits any other kind) is "because the holes are round." Maybe that's *not* so flippant: Holes are round, you might claim, because it's easier to dig a round hole than a square one.

Another answer is that a person can *roll* a circular cover when it needs to be transported a short distance. A square cover would require a dolly or two persons. Perhaps a lesser reason is that a round cover need not be rotated to fit the hole.

This is probably the most famous of all Microsoft questions — so much so that Microsoft has stopped using it because of overexposure. Magazines long cited it as an example of how wacky those Microsoft interview questions are. "Candidates showed up in the lobby yelling 'So they won't fall in the hole!' before they had been asked anything," said Adam David Barr.

When this question appeared in one of Martin Gardner's *Scientific American* columns, it brought a reply from a Brooklyn man, John Bush, who reported that some of Consolidated Edison's manhole covers are square. Bush said that an explosion had recently blown off one of these square covers. The cover was later found, naturally, at the bottom of the manhole.

In 2000 author and NPR commentator Andrei Codrescu gave a talk at Microsoft. During the question-and-answer period, someone asked him, "Why are manhole covers round?" "That's easy," Codrescu said. "In a fight, a round shield is better than a square one. The circle is also a symbol of infinity, which is why church domes are also round. The principle of 'as above as below' reminds pedestrians that they live in a divine world."

? Why do mirrors reverse right and left instead of up and down?

When you first start thinking about this question, you may feel cut adrift from everything you learned in school. You can't apply arithmetic, physics, or psychology. It is not even a logic puzzle in the usual sense.

In outline the two most popular responses are the following:

(a) denying that a mirror *does* reverse right and left
(b) insisting that mirrors *can* reverse up and down (as for instance when the mirror is on the ceiling or floor)

Start with (a). When you hold the front page of a newspaper up to a mirror, the reflection is reversed and hard to read. Imagine the text is printed on a transparent plastic sheet. You can press the sheet up against the mirror and see that the text exactly coincides with its reflection. The mirror is not "flipping" the image underneath the sheet.

This is even clearer when you hold an arrow up to the mirror. Hold the arrow horizontally and point it toward the left. The arrow's reflection also points left. Nothing is reversed. Point the arrow right, and the reflected arrow points right.

These are valid points, as far as they go. We still know that some kind of quote-unquote reversal *is* going on, even if this reversal is not quite what people imagine. Your interviewer will come back with "Yes, but if there's no reversal, why can't you *read* a newspaper's mirror image? Why do you have to flip the transparent plastic sheet left for right, and not up for down, in order to read its reflection?"

Answer (b) takes the opposite tack. Mirrors reverse in *every* direction. When the mirror is on the floor — pointing "up" you might say — it reverses up and down. A mirror pointed north by northeast reverses north by northeast and south by southwest. A mirror pointed left reverses left and right. There are no "favored" directions. Nothing in the physics of mirrors tells them to reverse left and right.

The interviewer will probably then want to know why we have this popular misconception that mirrors reverse right and left. You might argue that it all comes down to culture, to conventions of architecture and interior design. Mirrors are not positioned at random orientations in space. They almost always hang on vertical walls of rectilinear rooms. They consequently almost always reverse horizontally (north and south or east and west), not vertically (up and down). This horizontal reversal is conventionally described as a reversal right and left. It makes more sense than saying that a particular mirror reverses north and south, for these are geographic absolutes, and there is nothing absolute about a mirror's reversal. It is all relative to the way the mirror is pointed.

Explanation (b) makes some good points. It still skirts the main issue. In a Las Vegas hotel suite with mirrors on the ceiling; in an igloo, a yurt, or a carnival hall of mirrors; in the most unconventional or un-Western environment you can devise — you *still* can't read a newspaper in a mirror because it's "reversed right and left." Why is that?

Let's go back to square one. Which way *do* mirrors reverse? This time, let's be careful about language and decide what is the best, most general description of how mirrors reverse.

Explanation (a) is accurate in maintaining that mirrors do not (necessarily) reverse right and left. It would be an odd thing if they did. "Right" and "left" are defined relative to a human observer's body. How can a dumb piece of glass know that someone's looking at it and from what orientation? It would have to "know" that in order to reverse right and left *consistently*.

It is much more plausible, and correct, to think that a mirror's direction of reversal depends on its own orientation in space. This is what explanation (b) is driving at. By pointing a mirror in any direction, you can cause it to reverse in any direction.

How does this work, exactly? The arrow experiment demonstrates that an arrow parallel to the mirror's surface is not reversed at all. Is there any way of holding an arrow so that its reflection points in a different direction? There is. Just point the arrow straight at the mirror (away from you). The reflected arrow points in the *opposite* direction, out of the mirror (toward you). Or point the arrow toward you / away from the mirror. Then the reflection points away from you / deeper "into" the mirror.

A wordy but accurate way to describe what a mirror does is to say that it reverses the directions "into the mirror" and "out of the mirror." When you look into a mirror, some things that appear to be in front of you — behind the glass of the mirror — are really behind you. Directions parallel to the mirror's surface, such as left and right or up and down, are not reversed.

This fact is so totally obvious that we almost always ignore it. For the most part, you don't perceive a mirror image as a looking-glass world behind the mirror. You know you are seeing your own face in your own room. The brain filters out the into-the-mirror / out-of-the-mirror reversal and interprets the mirror's reversed image as the real world.

This normally useful deception fails only with certain asymmetrical objects and actions. Screw threads, snail shells, knots, and scissors can exist in one of two otherwise identical forms. The most familiar of all such asymmetrical objects are our hands. A right hand is similar to a left hand in all details, yet it is also completely different.

Your right and left hands are "mirror images" of each other. Touch the tips of your fingers together, as if there were an invisible pane of glass between them. It seems like the right hand has undergone an into-the-glass / out-of-the-glass reversal to become the left hand.

Here is where the great confusion comes in. It is conventional in English and many other languages to describe the two mirror-image forms of asymmetric objects as "right-handed" and "left-handed." This is a figure of speech. *It has nothing to do with right and left as directions.* We could just as well call the two forms of a screw thread "A" and "B" or "plus" and "minus" or "normal" and "reversed."

One consequence of a mirror's reversal is that the reflection of any of these asymmetrical objects is transformed into the object's "other" form. Evidently, the brain is not very good at filtering out *this* difference. Because most text is strongly asymmetrical, its mirror image becomes strange and unreadable. Asymmetrical actions, such as using scissors, can be frustratingly difficult when working from a mirror image.

We struggle also to put these difficulties into words. A careful speaker could say that the mirror reverses the so-called right- or left-handedness of asymmetric objects. That is usually shortened to the statement that a mirror "reverses right and left" — a statement that is actually quite different, and actually quite wrong. We all accept and pass on a lot of statements we've heard without thinking them through. This is one of those statements.

The fifteen-second version of all this: A mirror doesn't necessarily reverse left and right *or* up and down. It reverses only in the directions into and out of the mirror. This changes the so-called handedness of asymmetric objects, so that a right hand's reflection looks like a left hand, and reflected text is unreadable.

Answering this question well demands a paradigm shift. You are asked to explain why mirrors reverse right and left, *when really, they don't.* Many interviewees never dig themselves out of that hole. The question tests a willingness to challenge assumptions, including those that come from a "superior."

Martin Gardner mentioned this question in the 1950s and probably deserves credit for framing it as a logic puzzle. He wrote a whole book *(The Ambidextrous Universe)* addressing this question and its far-flung implications.

? Which way should the key turn in a car door to unlock it?

The riddles of Zen pose absurd dilemmas in order to annihilate the binary distinctions of the world. Has a dog Buddha nature or not? Do you call a short staff a short staff or do you not call it a short staff? Microsoft's car-key riddle has something of the same flavor.

There is a school of thought among interviewees that it doesn't matter whether you pick right or left. The real agenda is to see whether you can make a *fundamentally meaningless*

A or B decision without getting hung up over it. (Insignificant decisions are part of the software business too. If they hire you, you'll have to go to meetings and give explanations for your own meaningless decisions.)

Actually, there is a preferred answer. Here's why: Hold your right hand out, pretending you're holding a key. (Also pretend you're right-handed if necessary.) Your hand is a fist, palm side down, with the imaginary key between your thumb and the curled side of your index finger.

Turn your hand clockwise, as far as it can go without discomfort. You can probably turn your fist a full 180 degrees, easily. The palm side is now up.

Try it again, turning the hand counterclockwise. It's tough to turn it just 90 degrees. You have less strength near the limit of the turn.

The design of the hand, wrist, and arm thus makes it easier for a right-handed person to turn a key *clockwise* (so that the top of the key turns to the *right*). It is the opposite with left-handed people. There are fewer left-handed people, though, creating a true asymmetry. That provides a basis for saying that the key should turn one way or the other.

Now we're getting somewhere. Or are we? In the long run, you lock and unlock your car door exactly the same number of times. One of these motions is going to be "easy," and the other one "awkward." It's six of one or half a dozen of the other. The asymmetry keeps slipping away.

Microsoft's interviewers consistently ask about *unlock*ing the door. They never, as far as I can tell, ask which way the key should turn to *lock* it. Given that the clockwise turn is easier for most people, there are several reasons for making a door unlock when the key is turned in the easy direction:

◆ Faced with an unfamiliar car, you probably try the more natural movement first. For the greatest number of people, that's clockwise. It's more user-friendly to have the first thing that most people try be right.

◆ Unattended cars are normally left locked. A spin in the car normally starts by unlocking the door. Making the *initial* unlocking action "easy" is a subtle way of making the car seem more inviting. Software designers know the importance of making programs and features load as quickly as possible. When start-up is cumbersome, people are less apt to use a certain program or feature.

◆ With remote-control locks, people turn the key mainly when the battery is dead or the electrical system has failed. Most likely, a lot of people use the key so infrequently that they forget which way it turns. In that case the initial reason above applies — the first thing they try should be correct. You most often discover a dead battery when you try to get into a locked car. There, the second point applies — it's best to have the easier motion for getting into the car, especially when there's a problem.

◆ There are life-or-death situations where it's vital to get *into* a car. When you're in a blizzard in the Cascades, getting into the car can save your life. If a maniac with a hook is after you, you need to get in that car. Locks jam, and some people have arthritis or injuries that make it difficult to turn a key. You can imagine a situation where a life depends on opening the car door, and someone has barely enough strength to turn the key. That's when you want a lock that turns in the easier direction. In comparison, locking a car from the outside (the only time you need the key) is simply a matter of protecting property.

None of these reasons are overwhelming. They are either far-fetched scenarios or minor grace notes. Like the direction in which water drains out of a circular tub, some design questions are decided by a miniscule impetus one way or another.

In practice, most car doors do unlock by turning the key clockwise *on the driver's side.* On the passenger side, a counterclockwise turn usually unlocks the door. In other words, you unlock by turning the top of the key toward the nearest edge of the door. This is the usual convention with household door locks too. Most people unconsciously learn this convention, even if they can't explain it. That provides another reason to think that the driver unlocking a car for the first time is likely to try clockwise first.

In short, both convention and ergonomics say that the key should turn clockwise (to the right) to unlock a driver's side car door. Microsoft people are crazy about ergonomics. They are even crazier about getting everyone to obey a single standard.

? Why is it that, when you turn on the hot water in a hotel, the hot water comes out instantly?

In most people's homes, the hot water heater is dozens of feet from the hot water taps. "Hot water" pipes themselves are not actually heated, of course. When no water is flowing, the water in the pipes cools to ambient temperature. When you turn on the hot water tap, the line pressure has to flush a volume of now-cool water out of the pipes before you get hot water.

It's possible to brainstorm several ways of getting instant hot water. You could have a mini–hot water heater for each tap, as close to the tap as possible. You could have a system for heating the hot water pipes. These are acceptable (though wrong) guesses in an interview.

The real answer is this: Hotels and some homes have a hot water recirculating system. It consists of a pump attached to an extra line that runs "backward." This line goes from near the hot water tap farthest from the hot water heater, all the way back to the heater. The pump slowly circulates hot water through the hot water lines so that the water in the lines never gets cold. When you turn on the tap, the line water is already hot.

One advantage of this system over the two wrong guesses above is that it's easy to retrofit. The "backward" line does not have to be high capacity. It is usually just a thin, flexible plastic tube, easily attached with a minimum of plumbing.

? How do they make M&Ms?

The main issue is how they get a perfectly smooth, layered candy shell on a mass-produced product that never knows the touch of a human hand until the bag is opened. Dipping the chocolate in a liquid candy that hardens seems unsatisfactory. You would have to place the candy somewhere while waiting for the shell to harden. If you did that, you'd expect the candy to have a flat bottom, like hand-dipped chocolates do. One ingenious (wrong) answer: "There's a sheet of hot boiling chocolate, and they freeze the peanuts and fire them through it so it instantly freezes and the chocolate is hard by the time it hits the ground."

The actual method used by the Mars Company is both clever and simple. Unfortunately, it's hard to guess, and no one expects you to be a candy-trivia buff. The chocolate centers of "plain" M&Ms are cast in little molds. The chocolate ellipsoids are then put in a big rotating drum, something like a cement mixer. While jostling in the drum, they are sprayed with a sugary liquid that hardens into a white candy shell. The constant movement prevents the candies from congealing into a big lump. The motion also smoothes out any rough edges. In concept, the rotating drum is like that used to polish gemstones.

The candies are then squirted with a second, colored sugar liquid. This hardens into the colored coating on top of the white shell.

A distinct enigma is how they print the little "m"s without human intervention. The "m" is always in the middle of one of the two flattened sides. That means that each candy must be aligned with the die imprinting it. This is achieved by pouring the candies onto a conveyor belt with thousands of tiny M&M-shaped depressions. Each candy fits flat in a depression. The candies are then gently imprinted with a bank of rubber dies carrying the letter "m" in a white edible ink.

This is one of the few Microsoft riddles for which I was able to establish a time and place of origin. Joel Spolsky, who worked for the Excel team, invented it around 1990. "All I remember is having a sort of bullshit session, with a bunch of other program managers at Microsoft. We were saying, 'What questions do you use?' I said, 'You know, I've been wondering about M&Ms. I'm going to use the M&M question.' And the others said, 'Oh that's no good, too much of a key insight thing. You have to know about chocolate.'"

Spolsky reports that he used the question only a few times. He now feels there are better questions to ask. Like the manhole question, this one has been widely reported and is apparently used elsewhere.

They're not kidding when they say you don't have to know the "right answer." Spolsky admitted that even he didn't know how M&Ms were made. He didn't have to know to judge the answers. Like most of these questions, the point is to see if the candidate can say something reasonably convincing — and/or avoid saying anything stupid.

? If you are on a boat and toss a suitcase overboard, will the water level rise or fall?

This question is easy, provided you know the rule that floating objects displace a weight of water equal to their own. That's the catch. Probably, most technically trained people interviewing at Microsoft have heard of that rule somewhere along the line. Most are shaky on how well they remember it (Uh, was it the *weight* or the *volume* that objects displace?). It's not a rule you use in writing code.

Here's a virtually math-free way of working it out for yourself. Start with the basics. Any time you throw weight out of a floating boat, the boat gets lighter and therefore rises. Okay?

Unfortunately, that's not what this question asks. It asks whether the *water level* rises or falls, not the boat.

Normally you don't pay attention to the water level in a body of water large enough to permit boating. Tossing a suitcase out of a boat is not going to change the water level of a lake or ocean perceptibly. The question is whether it changes the level in principle.

The only thing that will change the water level is a change in the volume of submerged objects. The fancy term for that is "displacement." Picture a toy boat in a bathtub. The submerged hull of the boat occupies a certain volume that, consequently, isn't occupied by water. That volume is called the boat's displacement. It is not the total volume of the boat but only the part that is below the waterline.

The tub's water level depends on the total displacement of all the toy boats, rubber ducks, and other objects that are floating or submerged in it. Add more toy boats, and that increases the displacement. The displaced water has to go somewhere, so the water level rises. Take toy boats out, decreasing the displacement, and the water level falls.

All this applies to a lake or ocean too. It's just that the irregular shape of a lake bed or ocean basin makes it harder to visualize the effect. Any water-level changes in the ocean are going to be microscopic anyway.

The question becomes "How does tossing a suitcase out of a boat change the displacement?" We know that tossing the suitcase out makes the boat lighter. That in turn makes the boat sit a little higher in the water, decreasing the boat's displacement. But once the suitcase splashes back into the water, it displaces water too. Is the net effect positive, negative, or zero?

To answer that, we need to establish a relationship between displacement and weight. Here's a "mental physics" experiment to do so.

Picture an inflated beach ball floating in a bathtub. A beach ball normally does not have much weight, being mostly air and thin plastic. In your mind's eye, it sits practically on top of the water surface, barely displacing *any* water — right? Conclusion: Near-zero weight means near-zero displacement.

Now imagine you've got a beach ball in which you've somehow managed to seal a 5-pound brick. The added weight means it will sit lower in the water and have greater displacement. Five pounds of weight means — well, some unknown, greater-than-zero amount of displacement.

Now picture a third beach ball in which you've sealed exactly 5 pounds of water. It too sits lower in the water. Your mental simulation of physics is probably accurate enough to tell you that the ball would sink until the water level *inside* was just about on a level with the water level *outside*. (Were the beach ball made of infinitely thin, infinitely strong nanotechnological plastic, the inner and outer water levels would be identical. The ball would be a bubble intersecting the water surface.)

What this means is that 5 pounds of water displaces exactly 5 pounds of water. And there is nothing special about the 5 pounds of water. We could have used 12 pounds, or 2 ounces, or any amount that would fit in the ball. The beach ball would displace just that amount of water, so that the inner and outer water levels were equal.

It doesn't even matter what shape the beach ball is. It could be an inflated ring with a horse's head on it. Put 5 pounds of water in the ring, and it too will sink to displace 5 pounds of water. Or imagine it's the shape of a boat — or the shape of a suitcase — it makes no real difference. All that matters is the weight of water inside.

Back to the beach balls: We've got one that contains 5 pounds of water, and one that contains a 5-pound brick. Is there any difference in their displacement? You'll probably agree that the answer is no. If you'll excuse the anthropomorphism, Dame Gravity is blind. She can't see that there's a brick in one ball and water in the other. She merely *feels* 5 pounds of weight inside an object of a certain shape. That alone determines the physics of floating.

Conclusion: For floating objects, displacement depends on weight, period. In case things aren't already clear, do another mental experiment. You've got an inflatable pool toy shaped like a boat, containing 5 pounds of water. Transfer 1 pound of water from the boat into another pool toy shaped like a Samsonite suitcase. The displacement was 5 pounds of water before the transfer, and 4 + 1 = 5 pounds after. It makes no difference.

Tossing a suitcase out of a boat makes no difference in the total displacement (or water level), *assuming the suitcase floats.*

The latter is an all-important detail. As any baggage handler knows, the density of suitcases varies amazingly. While an average suitcase, with folded clothes and lots of air, will probably float, a suitcase packed with lead weights or imported crystal will sink.

Pretend you throw a heavy suitcase overboard, having first secured it to the boat with fishing line. The boat briefly rises, then the line draws taut as the suitcase sinks as far as the line permits. The boat is thereafter dragged down somewhat by the suspended weight of the heavy suitcase. The displacement of boat plus suitcase is identical to what it was originally. The total weight is the same, and thus the displacement is the same, just as long as the boat and suitcase are floating as a unit. If you snip the fishing line, though, the suitcase will sink to the bottom while the boat's hull will rise upward. Obviously, this will decrease the total displacement and lower the overall water level slightly.

The answer to the question is that tossing off a suitcase makes no difference in overall water level *provided the suitcase floats.* If the suitcase sinks, the water level will fall.

? How many piano tuners are there in the world?

In the 1940s and 1950s, Nobel laureate physicist Enrico Fermi used to challenge his University of Chicago students to estimate absurd quantities without looking anything up. Still used in some physics classes, "Fermi questions" are now probably better known from job interviews. Maybe the best-known Fermi question, if only because it was the silliest, was to estimate the number of piano tuners in Chicago.

Microsoft's version of Fermi's original asks how many piano tuners there are in the world (rather than Chicago). You aren't expected to know any statistics about piano tuners, or about pianos for that matter. Professional pianists don't know how many pianos there are in the world. You *are* expected to have some idea of the population of the United States and the world. You are also allowed to favor round numbers in estimates, since you're usually doing the math in your head. (But there are exceptions. Accounting, banking, and consulting firms often allow you to have pencil and paper and expect more precision than software and dot-com companies do.)

A typical analysis goes like this: The number of piano tuners must be related to the amount of work for piano tuners. That in turn depends on how many pianos there are and how often they are tuned.

How many pianos are there? In the United States there are pianos in schools, philharmonic societies, churches, piano bars, recording studios, museums, and a lot of other places. Still, most pianos are probably in people's homes.

Pianos are expensive and cannot easily be wedged into a studio apartment, dorm, or trailer home. Piano ownership is pretty much limited to middle- or upper-class homes.

The U.S. population is nearly 300 million. Assume the average household is three people. Then there are about 100 million households. It is the wealthier half of that — 50 million households — that is the primary market for pianos. Not all of these have pianos, of course. The proportion of wealthier households having a piano is much less than 100 percent but probably greater than 1 percent. Let's say it's 10 percent. Then there may be 5 million U.S. households with pianos. We'll take that as the total number of pianos in the country.

How many piano tuners does it take to service those 5 million pianos? Say that the average piano tuner works 40 hours a week (it's not the software business!). How long does it take to tune a piano? An offhand guess is an hour. Pianos are not something customers bring into the shop. Allow another hour for travel time. That means a piano tuner might tune 40/2 = 20 pianos a week. In a year of 50 workweeks, that amounts to a nice round figure of 1,000 piano tunings.

How often does a piano *need* tuning? That may be a stumper for those who know nothing about pianos. The most likely shrug of a guess (once a year?) is probably close to the mark. (An Internet search turned up the recommendation that new pianos be tuned four times the first year and at least twice a year thereafter. Just from the sound of it, this is one of those rules, like chewing twenty-six times before swallowing, that hardly anyone save piano tuners takes seriously. There must be plenty of hardly ever used pianos, sitting in living rooms, that haven't been tuned in *years*.)

If pianos are tuned once a year, and piano tuners can do 1,000 tunings a year, you would expect there to be 1 piano tuner for every 1,000 pianos. With 5 million pianos in the United States, there must be something like 5,000 piano tuners.

America is not typical of the world in many ways, piano tuners among them. Because of its wealth and its Eurocentric musical traditions, the United States probably has more than its share of the world's piano tuners. The world population of over 6 billion is more than twenty times the

U.S. population. You would expect the total number of piano tuners to be several times the U.S. figure, but certainly less than twenty times. A reasonable guess is that Europe might have twice as many piano tuners as the United States, and the rest of the world might have about as many as the United States does. That would mean that the United States has about 1 in 4 of the world's piano tuners. The number of piano tuners in the world is estimated, then, at 4 times 5,000, or 20,000.

The above is the sort of answer interviewers look for. How accurate is it? The Piano Technicians Guild, the major trade group, has more than 3,500 members throughout the world. Not all piano tuners are members, though, and not all members work exclusively as piano tuners. The U.S. Bureau of Labor Statistics reports that there were about 13,000 "musical instrument repairers and tuners" in the United States in 1998, of which "most" worked on pianos.

Trade statistics found on the Web suggest that the United States produces about 23 percent of the world's pianos and buys 27 percent of the world piano production. Assuming that America's 10,000 or so piano tuners constitute a quarter of the world's total, that would scale up to 40,000 piano technicians in the world. It looks like the 20,000 figure is off by a factor of two (which is pretty *good* for a Fermi question). The underestimate might be due to the fact that most so-called piano tuners perform repairs, restoration, and other services as well as tuning. That means there is more work than estimated, and hence more "piano tuners."

? How many gas stations are there in the United States?

Microsoft's interviewers also ask how many cars there are in the United States. Estimating cars is usually the first part of the gas-station question, so let's lump the two together.

Children, people who live in cities with good public transportation, homeless people, the Amish, etc., don't have cars. On the other hand, some people have more than one car: rich people, vintage-car collectors, the taxi driver who owns a taxi and also has a car for personal use.

Is there a car for every person? No. For every two people? Sounds more reasonable. In that case the U.S. population of 300 million would imply that there are about 150 million cars in the United States.

An average car is refueled once a week, maybe. In a week's time, the nation's gas stations service the equivalent of all the nation's cars.

How many cars can a single gas station handle in a week? There are 24×7 hours in a week, but not all stations are open around the clock. Say that the average station is open one hundred hours a week. If we say it takes six minutes to fill up, a given pump can handle ten cars an hour. Now a big, busy gas station may have many pumps and many cars fueling at one time. Balance that against all the one-pump stations out in the middle of nowhere that go hours without a customer. Let's say that ten cars an hour is about average. Then our average station fuels something like 100×10, or 1,000, cars a week.

That means there are about 150 million/1000 = 150,000 gas stations in the United States.

Both the car and gas-station estimates are good, as these things go. The U.S. Department of Transportation reported 129,748,704 "registered passenger vehicles" in the United States in 1997. The June 1998 issue of the *Journal of Petroleum Marketing* claims there were 187,097 retail sites selling motor fuel in the United States.

? How much Mississippi River water flows past New Orleans each hour?

There are at least two approaches. The more direct is to estimate the width of the Mississippi at New Orleans, its average depth, and the water's velocity. As long as the estimates are in feet and feet per hour, all you've got to do is to multiply the three figures to get the answer (in cubic feet per hour). Most people outside of the delta haven't a clue about *any* of those figures.

The second approach is to work from the drainage area. You may know, or can estimate by picturing a map, that the Mississippi and its tributaries drain something like half of the area of the conterminous United States (and a little of Canada). Guesstimate that area, and multiply it by the average annual rainfall for the region. This gives the volume of water that falls as rain each year. Practically all of that ultimately drains into the Mississippi, with one big exception: evaporation. You'd have to make some allowance for that, and most people don't have any idea how much.

Now the first approach doesn't look so bad. At least there are only three figures to worry about.

How wide is the Mississippi at New Orleans? On detailed maps, the lower Mississippi is not just a blue line. It's shown more like a squiggly lake, as a palpable area of light blue. Let's say it's two miles across. That gives us the nice round figure of about 10,000 feet.

The Mississippi carries huge amounts of silt that it deposits to form the delta. That probably prevents its channel from being very deep. Besides, the lower Mississippi has meandered over historic times. It could hardly do that if the channel were deep.

So okay, it's shallow. How shallow: One foot deep? Ten feet? One hundred feet? One foot deep would be ridiculous.

Were it *that* shallow you could wade across it. You would have heard about the "amazing fact" that the Mighty Mississippi was only a foot deep.

Ten feet is still remarkably shallow, all things considered, but credible. English majors up for a program manager job may recall that "mark twain" was riverboat slang for two fathoms, or 12 feet, of water. "Mark twain" meant smooth sailing for riverboats. It was significant because there were many places in the river that were *shallower* than that. Ten feet is definitely in the ballpark.

The final estimate is the river's flow velocity. Once again, think of the riverboats. Even with their steam engines, they were a leisurely means of transportation, significantly slower than a car on an interstate. A reasonable guess for the river's speed is 10 miles an hour. That is about 50,000 feet an hour. The answer, then, is $10,000 \times 10 \times 50,000 = 5$ billion cubic feet of water an hour.

The "real" discharge rate of the Mississippi is difficult to measure and varies greatly with season and rainfall. Microsoft's *Encarta* encyclopedia gives a confident, three-significant-figure estimate of 593,000 cubic feet per second. Another, seemingly authoritative Web page gave 14,000 cubic meters per second. That's about 490,000 cubic feet per second. Still other sources cite a round 1 million cubic feet per second. The latter would come to 3.6 billion cubic feet per hour.

? What does all the ice in a hockey rink weigh?

A hockey rink is maybe 100 by 200 feet. The ice is about an inch thick. Let's put everything in inches: around 1,000 by 2,000 by 1, or 2 million cubic inches of ice.

How much does a cubic inch of ice weigh? A little less than what a cubic inch of water does. It's probably easier to fall back on the metric system. A cubic centimeter of water weighs a gram. An inch is about 2.5 centimeters, so a cubic inch is about (simplifying it for mental math) $2 \times 3 \times 2.5$, or 3×5, or 15 cubic centimeters. That means a hockey rink's ice comes to 15×2 million = 30 million cubic centimeters and weighs as many grams. Or 30,000 kilograms. Or about 60,000 pounds.

An NHL regulation rink is an oval, 85 by 200 feet, with a corner radius of 28 feet. One inch is a common ice thickness in rinks. Use these accurate figures, and the weight of that volume of *liquid* water would be 38,500 kilograms. Allowing for the lower density of ice, the weight should be about 35,200 kilograms. The guesstimate above is close.

? If you could remove any of the fifty U.S. states, which would it be?

Popular answers: *Alaska, Hawaii, North Dakota.*

Bad answer: *Washington.*

Worse answer: *I'd remove all of them.*

This is Microsoft's most notorious example of an ill-structured problem. It is not like asking for your favorite color. They want you to reframe the question so that it has a "right answer" you can determine by logic.

You don't have to name the state up front. You can walk the interviewer through your reasoning and decide the state at the end of it. Here is a composite and elaboration of approaches that have met with approval:

The central issue is, what happens to the *people* in the "removed" state? Are we nuking the state? Let case (a) be that when you "remove" a state, you are killing all the people in it. Then there is a moral obligation to minimize casualties.

Case (b) is that the state's people just disappear. They're not actually killed; they're just gone. Maybe it's like

going back in time and stepping on a butterfly . . . then returning to the present to find that the state and its people
don't exist and *never did.* All the flags have forty-nine stars,
and there is no mention of the removed state in any encyclopedia.

Case (c) is that only the real estate vanishes. The people
are left behind — as homeless refugees sitting next to a gap-
ing hole in the ground and wondering where they're going to
sleep tonight. The people will be relocated at a staggering
cost (to Microsoft? to the federal government?).

Case (d) is that the people are "magically" relocated, at
no emotional or financial cost to anyone. Push the button,
and the ex-state's ex-residents all have homes and jobs (assuming they had them before) somewhere in the remaining
forty-nine states, without displacing anyone in those forty-
nine states.

Case (e) is that no one, and no real estate, vanishes. The
"removal" is purely political. The removed state becomes
part of Canada or Mexico. Or it becomes an independent
nation.

The choice in case (a) is clear enough. People are being
killed, so you have to pick the state with the smallest population. In the 2000 census, that was Wyoming.

Case (b) is a tough call. People just vanishing is an entirely hypothetical situation without any moral precedents.
Still, the people are living, breathing souls until you hit the
history-eraser button. That seems tantamount to killing
them. Again, the choice should probably be Wyoming.

The dilemma in case (c) is whether to *consider* removing a more populous state than Wyoming, in view of
Wyoming's natural attributes. Wyoming is a big state with
beautiful scenery and Yellowstone National Park. To save all

that, you might be willing to pay for the higher relocation costs involved in removing a more populous (but smaller and/or less scenic) state.

By the 2000 census, the five least populous states are Wyoming, Vermont, Alaska, North Dakota, and South Dakota. Vermont and Alaska also have spectacular scenery, and Alaska is huge. South Dakota has Mount Rushmore. North Dakota — well, North Dakota *doesn't* have Mount Rushmore. It stands out as the only state where it's hard to imagine *anyone* from another state intentionally taking a vacation there. (The joke is that the state tree of North Dakota is the telephone pole.) While other plains states are flat and treeless, North Dakota has the harshest winter climate — harsher than the main population centers of Alaska.

Now in case (c), no one's killed but we have to pay for relocating the people from the removed state. Surely it's worth springing for somewhat higher relocation costs in order to save Yellowstone, or the Vermont ski resorts, or all of Alaska, or Mount Rushmore. North Dakota is dispensable.

In case (d) the relocation is magical and free. That's all the more reason to remove North Dakota.

Finally, in case (e), neither people nor real estate is lost. We just redraw the political map. There is something to be said for removing Alaska or Hawaii. Each is outside the contiguous United States. Some would say that having them as states savors of colonialism. If you are concerned mainly about *the way countries look on the map,* it's probably a toss-up between Alaska and Hawaii.

Face it: Were Congress to debate which state to remove, maps would be the least of it. Alaska has oil and minerals. Hawaii is a place mainlanders like to vacation. Both states have strategic importance. That would nix any talk of ceding them.

The debate would focus, as in (c) and (d), on the states with the smallest population and least natural resources. That would again lead to North Dakota, which is helpfully on the Canadian border. Offer it to Canada. If they don't want it, set it up as a country.

? How many points are there on the globe where, by walking one mile south, one mile east, and one mile north, you reach the place where you started?

Microsoft's grading system for each answer is roughly as follows:

0 points:	No hire
1 point:	No hire
$\infty + 1$ points:	Fair
$\infty * \infty + 1$ points:	The "right" answer

Start by drawing a mental map: One mile south, one mile east, and one mile north covers three sides of a square. You ought to end up a mile east of where you started. The situation seems impossible, and you might think the answer is zero points.

Try again. The only way to make sense of the situation is to remember that the compass directions are relative ones applied to the surface of a sphere. At the North Pole, *every* horizontal direction is south. As long as you start precisely at the North Pole, you can walk a mile in *any* direction and that will count as walking south. Not only that, but a subsequent one-mile-east leg will curve in a circle centered on the North Pole. At any rate, it will if you interpret the puzzle to mean that you not only point yourself due east but constantly adjust your direction so that your bearing remains due east throughout the second mile. That then allows a final, straight, one-mile-north leg returning to the pole. The journey looks like a wedge of pie rather than an open square.

So the North Pole is one point where this could happen. Notice that it *couldn't* happen at the South Pole. At the South Pole, every direction is north. You can't go a mile south from the South Pole.

You might therefore think the answer is one point, and again you're wrong. You're wrong because you can manage such a journey *near* the South Pole. Imagine starting out from a point a little more than a mile from the South Pole. You travel a mile due south, make a 90-degree turn east, and execute a complete circle about the South Pole of one mile circumference — at every point traveling due east, of course — and then backtrack north a mile to the starting point.

There is not just one point from which you can do this but an infinity of them. You can start from any point that is the correct distance from the South Pole. There is a complete circle, centered on the South Pole, of possible starting points.

What is the "correct distance"? The one-mile circumference circle must have a radius of $1/2\pi$ miles. The starting point of the journey must be a mile farther from the pole than that, or $1 + 1/2\pi$ miles, which comes to about 1.159 miles.

We're still not done. Suppose you started a little closer to the pole. You go a mile south, then travel continuously due east in a smaller circle, centered on the pole, of 1/2 mile circumference. You will go full circle twice. Then backtrack a mile north. This scheme nets another infinity of possible starting points, each $1 + 1/4\pi$ miles from the pole.

You can also manage a route in which you circle the pole three times, four times, or any whole number n of times. Each yields a new circle of starting points $1 + 1/2n\pi$ miles from the pole. There is an infinite ensemble of ever-closer circles, each with an infinity of starting points.

* * *

This question is adapted from one of the best known of all brainteasers: An explorer made the above journey and shot a bear along the way. What color was the bear? The answer was white because only polar bears live near the North Pole. In the late 1950s, Martin Gardner wrote that "not so long ago someone made the discovery that the North Pole is not the only starting point" for this "old riddle." The "new" answers don't spoil the old riddle, for there are no land mammals native to Antarctica.

? How many times a day do a clock's hands overlap?

Most people quickly realize that the answer has to be twenty-four, *give or take.* The issue is nailing down that "give or take" part.

Recognize, first of all, that there is nothing capricious about the overlaps. Both hands move at fixed speeds. Therefore, the time interval between overlaps is a constant.

This constant interval is a little more than an hour. At midnight, the hour and minute hands are exactly superimposed. It takes an hour for the minute hand to make a complete circuit. In that same time, the hour hand has moved 1/12 of a circuit to the numeral 1. It then takes another five minutes for the minute hand to catch up to where the hour hand *was,* in which time the hour hand has crept a bit farther. . . .

Before getting sucked into a Zeno's Paradox, let's settle for the moment by saying that the interval is a little more than sixty-five minutes. We also know that the *exact* interval has to divide evenly into twenty-four hours, since the day ends as it started, with both hands up and overlapping. In fact, it has to divide evenly into twelve hours. The way the hands move in the P.M. is an exact replay of the way they move in the A.M.

Focus on the twelve-hour period from midnight to

noon. The hands cannot overlap twelve times in that period, for if they did, it would mean that the interval between overlaps was 12/12, or exactly one hour — and we know it's a bit more than sixty-five minutes. No, there must be eleven overlaps in a twelve-hour period. That means the interval between overlaps is 12/11 hour, which comes to 65.45 minutes. This must be the precise interval that we balked at calculating a moment ago.

Doubling eleven gives twenty-two overlaps in a twenty-four-hour period. Twenty-two is the answer — unless you want to split hairs. Should you count the overlap at the midnight that begins the day, and also at the midnight that ends the day, the answer is twenty-three.

? Mike and Todd have $21 between them. Mike has $20 more than Todd. How much does each have? You can't use fractions in the answer.

A trick question incorporating a challenge. The basic problem is straightforward. You may be tempted to say that Mike has $21 and Todd has $1. But no, that adds up to $22. The real answer has to be that Mike has $20.50 and Todd has $0.50. If that's not obvious, you can write out the equations and use algebra. You can also prove that this is the only answer. But the interviewer insists that there can be no fractions in the answer.

The interviewer is wrong (or hiding behind the technicality that whole cents aren't "fractions"). You're supposed to stand your ground and defend the $20.50 / $0.50 answer. That's life in a big organization.

? On the average, how many times would you have to flip open the Manhattan phone book to find a specific name?

By "flip open," the interviewer means that you open the book to a *random* two-page spread. (You don't try to open it to the right place based on the letter of the alphabet.) Should the desired name be *anywhere* on the two visible pages, you've found it.

There is a simple answer and a more sophisticated one. The simple answer is this: Say the Manhattan white-page directory has one thousand pages. (That's close: The 2001 edition has 1,138 directory pages. You can ignore the complication that there are pages without listings in the front and back of the book.) That means the book has five hundred openings. The chance of flipping the book open to any specific name on your first (or any subsequent) try is therefore about one in five hundred. On the average, it takes about five hundred random flips to a particular name.

This quick answer is adequate, considering that the weakest link is your offhand guess at the number of pages in the phone book.

Now for the math-camp answer. In a realistic situation where this mattered, you would probably want to know how many times you would have to flip open the book to achieve a given confidence level that at least one flip will be to the right page. Suppose you want to be 90 percent sure of finding the name. How many times would you have to flip the pages?

Since this is a random procedure, there are no guarantees. You could get lucky and flip to the right page your first time out. You could flip the book open a million times and *never* come to the right page. If you want to be 100 percent sure of flipping to the right page, the answer is simple: No matter how times you plan to flip the pages, you can never be 100 percent sure of flipping to the right page.

In general, you are going to keep flipping the pages as

long, and only as long, as you *fail* to find the right page. We should be looking at the chance of flipping repeatedly to a *wrong* page, really.

Say that you know there are exactly 1,000 pages in the phone book and exactly 500 openings to flip to. The chance of flipping to the *wrong* opening on any given attempt is 499 out of 500 because all but one of 500 possible openings are wrong. The chance that the first n flips will all fail to open to the right listing is then $(499/500)^n$.

The chance you'll flip to the *right* opening in n flips or less is $1 - (499/500)^n$.

This formula lets you see how many times you have to flip to get a given probability of hitting the right opening. If you try this in a spreadsheet, you will find that the odds of flipping to the right page just tops 50 percent on the 347th flip. Half the time you'll hit the right page in 347 flips or less, and half the time you won't. That might be called an average value.

On the other hand, it might be considered an optimistic value. Three hundred forty-seven flips gives you *only a fifty-fifty chance* of finding the name. The original, simple-minded estimate of five hundred flips would give you about a 63 percent chance of finding the name. To achieve 90 percent confidence, you would need 1,150 flips.

? How do you cut a rectangular cake into two equal pieces when someone has already removed a rectangular piece from it? . . .

There are two answers, and it's best to get both. The *simpler* solution is often overlooked.

It's easy to cut a rectangle into halves. All you have to do is make sure that the cut passes through the precise center of the rectangle. The cut can be at any angle.

Here we have two rectangles, a positive one (the cake) and a negative one (the missing piece). Decide where the centers of the two rectangles are. These two points determine a line. Make a cut along that line, and the cake will be split evenly.

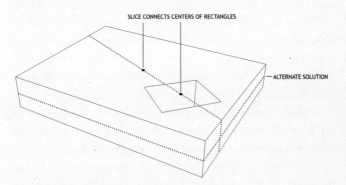

Because this slice halves *both* rectangles, the two resulting pieces are each guaranteed to have an area equal to half the original cake *minus* half the area of the missing piece. In other words, both of the resulting pieces have the *same* area. This is true even though they aren't necessarily the same shape.

In the unlikely event that both rectangles share the same center, you can make a cut at any angle, going through that center of course.

The alternate solution is to slice the cake horizontally to get two slices, each half as thick as the original, and each missing a rectangle. This doesn't work so well when the cake has icing.

? How would you design Bill Gates's bathroom?

There are two key points in answering this question. One is that Bill Gates gets what Bill Gates wants. The other is that you're supposed to come up with at least some ideas that

Gates wants but wouldn't have thought of on his own (otherwise, what's the point of hiring you to design his bathroom?).

You're supposed to start off saying that you'd sit down with Gates and listen to what he wants his bathroom to be like. You'd get the budget and deadlines up front. You'd suggest a lot of ideas and see which ones he likes. Then you'd make a plan and show it to Gates for feedback. The plan would go through many cycles of revision. Meanwhile, you'd make sure the project came in on time and within budget. This much applies to any design question.

As to the ideas you come up with, be warned that it's tough to top the reality. Gates's bathtub has a feature that lets him fill it to desired temperature from his car. For real.

Putting computer technology throughout the home, bathroom included, is something that Microsoft people take seriously. Microsoft's research divisions are pursuing things such as "smart" medicine cabinets and cupboards that tell you when your prescription needs refilling or you're out of toilet paper. "Some of these future scenarios can get pretty weird," admitted Ted Kummert, vice president, MSN Internet Access. "You know, the toilet monitors the family's general health by chemical sampling, the medicine cabinet checks dad into Betty Ford and locks the car in the garage."

So if you want to impress Microsoft's interviewers, you're not going to get much mileage out of talk of electrically warmed toilets. Here are a few ideas of the slant they're looking for ("futuristic" but possible for today's money's-no-object consumer):

♦ A feature that automatically locks medicine cabinets or cupboards containing household chemicals when an unaccompanied child enters the bathroom. Gates's house already has rudimentary ways of "knowing" when someone is in a room, and who that someone is. There's talk of iris scanners and such that would monitor people's identities more accurately and unobtrusively. Locking medicine cabinets against children is right in line with that, and "if it saves just one child's life," etc., etc.

♦ A hands-free notepad. Everyone gets great ideas in the bathroom. You don't want to use a PDA when your hands are wet, and if there's one room in the house that isn't going to have a PC in it, it's the bathroom. All you need is a voice-recognition device that can record a spoken message after you say a code phrase such as "Memo for Bill." The device automatically e-mails the message to your mailbox so it's ready for you at work.

♦ A mirror that *doesn't* reverse left and right. It's a video screen with a hidden camera, showing your own image the way other people see you. It makes it much easier to use scissors to trim a stray hair. If you think these modest advantages don't justify replacing a low-tech solution that never crashes, never needs a software update, and never fails during a power blackout . . . well, are you *sure* you want to work for Microsoft? (Gates originally had the idea that his home's ubiquitous flat-screen reproductions of artworks should, when not in use, blend invisibly into the woodwork by displaying a woodgrain image. They couldn't get it to work. Gates ended up having carpenters make sliding wood panels to cover the video screens.)

Other software companies sometimes ask essentially the same question. They often toss in a free sex- and girth-change for its protagonist: "How would you design a toilet for a wealthy three-hundred-pound aunt?"

? How would you design a microwave oven controlled by a computer?

It is easy to feel that microwave plus computer is not the greatest pairing since Fred and Ginger. A lot of design questions work that way: Given an iffy concept, come up with something that's not totally stupid.

Microwave ovens are pretty simple to operate now. Consumers probably don't want something that makes them more complicated (but say you'd do consumer studies to evaluate this — that's almost always expected in a design question). Based on the hints that Microsoft's interviewers drop, they are thinking along the lines of *smart packaging*. Household appliances and cupboards could have sensors that detect and read special labels or codes on consumable products. In the case of a microwave, you'd pop in a frozen lasagna, and it would read the code and the heating instructions (or download them). It would automatically customize the instructions for its power and the altitude. You'd never have to key in a time or power level.

Smart packaging would allow the microwave to keep a log of all the food prepared. This is probably worth mentioning, because mining usage logs for marketable information is now an important idea at Microsoft. From the consumer's standpoint, the log could be helpful in preparing shopping lists, or it could tally calories consumed for dieters.

Another decent answer is to say that voice-recognition software might replace a microwave's keypad. Instead of tapping keys, you'd *tell* the microwave how long to cook something (maybe vegetables or fish — products that don't have a code), or tell it what you're cooking and let the microwave decide the heating time.

? How would you design the controls for a VCR?

Scores of talented industrial designers have grappled with this problem. You're not likely to do much better, off the top of your head, in fifteen minutes. The interviewer doesn't expect you to. The best way to begin is to show that you understand the important trade-offs. There are at least two major ones:

- ◆ *Ease of use versus price.* We all make cracks about how people can't program their VCRs just as we do about that awful or nonexistent airline food. Are we really willing to pay for something better? Most people buy the cheapest airline seat and complain about the food afterward. Airlines know that, and that's why you're lucky to get half an ounce of dry-roasted peanuts. It's possible that a similar situation exists in the VCR market. People buy based on price and maybe features, *then* complain that it's hard to use.

  Who exactly is willing to pay for an easy-to-use VCR? If it's wealthy retirees with vision problems, that should inform the whole design process. If it's eight-year-olds who have their own TVs and want a simple VCR of their own, that's something else we want to know. And if it turns out that *no one* is willing to pay for ease of use, then we should scrap the whole idea.

- ◆ *Ease of use versus features.* You *could* design a VCR with one button. Push the button, and it starts recording. Push the button again and it stops recording. There you've got it, a VCR easy enough for everyone.

It's only if you want to do things such as set the VCR to record shows while you're out — or to play tapes, for that matter — that you need other controls. It's unlikely that anyone would opt for a one-button VCR just because it's easy to use. Today's manufacturers cram in a raft of features that require controls to perform different functions depending on the "mode." You can't type in or select a time to start recording; instead, you have to keep pushing a button to increment minutes, hours, A.M. or P.M., the day, the week. This makes programming a VCR difficult.

For the sake of argument, let's assume that consumer studies identify a market niche willing to pay for an easy-to-use VCR. It would also be helpful to know whether these potential customers really use all the features that most VCRs provide. How often do people program to record more than a week ahead? More than twenty-four hours ahead? Dropping some features could lead to an easier interface.

As a rough sketch, here's how a plausible "easy" interface might work: The VCR box has only five buttons (play, pause, fast-forward, rewind, and eject). These are really just backups so that you can play tapes should the remote control fall behind the couch. The VCR box has no display (saving money). All the programming is done with the remote and on-screen menus. The remote has one button and one "joystick." The joystick is like those found on some monitors or on the keyboard in some laptops. It is hardly more than a button itself. You can move it in all directions in order to control an on-screen cursor. The button is for selecting. In essence, the remote is a mouse that you hold in your hand.

To program the VCR, you pick up the remote and touch either the joystick or the button. This "wakes up" the VCR (if it's off) and superimposes a menu/wizard/control panel on the TV screen. This interface lets you play tapes, record a program, and set the time (if for some reason it can't be synchronized automatically). The VCR downloads a graphical TV schedule and lets you simply point and click on the shows you want to record.

Since the selling point for all this is the two-button simplicity, a great deal of attention should go to the look and feel of the remote control. It should *not* look like other remotes. If the market is young people, maybe it should look "cool," sort of like an iMac. If the market is retirees, make sure the joystick and buttons are easy to control for people with limited dexterity.

? Design a remote control for a venetian blind.

A regular venetian blind has two controls. One raises and lowers the blind; the other changes the angle of the slats. So the control will allow those two adjustments, maybe with two rocker switches.

As long as you've got a motorized mechanism to open and close the blinds, you might as well add a feature that lets you program the blind. People rarely open or close blinds for no reason. They (a) open blinds to let in more light; (b) close them when the sun is directly hitting someone's eyes or fading the carpet; and (c) close them at night for privacy.

This raises some of the same ease of use versus features issues that a VCR does. Do you need to program the blind like a VCR, specifying that it opens at, say, 7:30 A.M., adjusts the louvers' angle from 4:45 to 5:05 P.M. so the late-afternoon light doesn't hit you in the eyes, and then closes at 7:45 P.M.? Probably not. Who knows what the right times are? They change throughout the year and even with the weather. On a cloudy afternoon, you want to leave the blinds wide open to get as much light as possible.

The best solution is for the blind to have a photocell. By default, the blind opens its louvers when the light exceeds a certain threshold of indirect illumination (daytime) and closes them when the light falls below this threshold (at night). It partly closes the louvers when it senses sunlight parallel to them (direct sun). A circular dial on the remote allows you to set the threshold. (You can also turn off the photocell control with this dial, as you might do when going on vacation.) The remote control therefore has three controls — the dial to adjust the default programming and the two rocker switches to override it.

? Design a spice rack for a blind person.

You are allowed to intelligently redefine the question. Should you have a strong reason for devising a spice–lazy Susan rather than a rack, then that's what you should do. So all right, we are devising an integrated system for storing and dispensing spices for a blind person. The feature common to almost all answers is braille labels. There is something to be said for putting the braille on the lids. It is hard to read braille on a curved surface. Since most spice jars are cylindrical, the lid is the one accessible flat surface. You could run your finger over a row of lids to find the one you want.

There are several disadvantages to this approach. It's easy to read the lids *only* if you've made meticulously sure that every jar is returned to the rack with the lid in the right orientation. Otherwise, the labels will be in all possible states of rotation. That makes them hard to read.

A second problem is that lids easily get separated from the jars while cooking. A third is that you have to transfer spices from the supermarket's jars to the special jars and lids used with the spice rack.

How about putting the braille on the jar? Then it doesn't matter whether the lids get swapped. But as we've already noted, it's hard to read a curved braille label, and the label might not be facing outward.

Making the jars square in cross section, with identical braille labels on all four sides, can solve these problems. The spice rack itself should be designed so that jars are squared up when returned. It should also have an opening where the labels are, so you can efficiently slide your finger across them to find the right one.

The bumps on paper braille labels would not stand up to repeated use and the humidity of cooking. It would be more practical to emboss the braille labels in the glass (or in whatever the jars are made of). That, however, would prevent using commercially available jars, raising the cost. A better solution is to use self-adhesive labels made of durable yet flexible plastic. These could be attached to any type of jar.

Do you need special jars at all? In many ways, it's simpler to take the supermarket jars as a given and ask how the spice rack may accommodate them. Suppose the spice rack has a number of holes or slots for jars. A label panel in front contains the braille labels, all in one continuous strip, set at the ergonomically optimum angle. By sliding your finger once across the panel, you find the right label, then reach behind it to get the jar.

Of these three options (labels on lid, jar, or rack), the

latter is simplest and probably best. But the decision might be made differently if you add additional features. In practice, a spice rack is almost always used with measuring spoons. Measuring spoons can be tricky for the blind to use. Do you have a heaping 1/8 teaspoon or a level one? To find out, you have to run a finger over the top of the spoon, spilling the spice back into the jar (you hope) — and too bad if you really wanted a heaping 1/8 teaspoon. This action alone can take two hands, meaning that the jar and lid have to be set down somewhere. You don't want to be feeling around for missing lids on a hot range.

There is a lot to be said for designing a jar that dispenses ground spice in measured amounts (say, 1/8 teaspoon) at the push of a button. This would solve a lot of problems. You don't have to remove the lid (except to refill the jar), so there's much less chance of misplacing it or burning your hand feeling for it. You don't have to find measuring spoons, guess how much spice is in them, or clean them afterward. In the long run, these advantages would probably outweigh the initial hassle of transferring the spice from the supermarket containers. This might appeal to sighted people as well.

A reasonable design, then, would include square-sided self-dispensing jars, each with adhesive, tough-plastic braille labels on all four sides (so that you don't have to worry about replacing the jars in the right slot or orientation). The design task reduces to devising a rack that comfortably presents the labels to the user's finger. Regular spice racks are often at eye level to facilitate reading fine print. Here it makes more sense to have the labels positioned more like a keyboard: at counter level, with the labels nearly horizontal, canted at a slight angle. The jars should be nearly reclining, though at enough of an angle that gravity keeps them in line. With this arrangement, you don't need a railing in front, and this makes it easier to remove the jars as needed.

? How would you test a saltshaker? [A toaster? A teakettle? An elevator?]

For testing questions, you are supposed to play *Consumer Reports* and imagine how you might test whatever the interviewer asks you about. Successful answers are not necessarily profound. You just want to show that you're aware multiple criteria apply in evaluating even the simplest artifacts. (A car's merit depends on a lot more than its top speed.)

One place to start is by imagining what might go wrong with the item. That is easy for an elevator. It is more challenging to imagine how a saltshaker might go on the fritz.

Well, a saltshaker can be filled with sugar instead of salt — it can, anyway, if this is a third-grade cafeteria. Or the cap can be left on so loosely that it falls off and all the salt pours out on the unsuspecting victim's plate. In the grown-up world, the main problems are more likely to be design issues. Common complaints are (a) the holes are the wrong size — the shaker dispenses too much or not enough salt; (b) it's hard to tell the saltshaker from the pepper shaker (as in some sleek, minimalist sets, or in those kitschy porcelain numbers where one shaker is a dog and one is a fire hydrant); and (c) it's too hard to refill the shaker.

A reasonable plan is to shake a little salt on a plate, confirming that it comes out without pouring and that what comes out is salt. Then hand it off to a focus group. Let the group use the saltshaker in a realistic situation and compare it to other types of saltshakers. Ask for comments on the above and any other issues.

* * *

For a toaster, you would address things such as how accurate and predictable the darkness settings are, how well it deals with frozen waffles or bagels, how easy it is to clean crumbs, how efficiently it uses energy, how much space it takes up, how attractive the design is, and how safe it is (What if someone spills coffee in it, or tries to get something out with a fork?).

For a teakettle, criteria might include the following: How many cups of hot water does it make? How long does it take to heat up a fixed amount of water? How hot is the water when the kettle whistles (boiling or not quite boiling)? How easy is it to hear the whistle from another room? How hot does the handle get?

With an elevator, the number-one issue is probably safety (so you'd arrange for a detailed safety inspection). Otherwise, the issue is speed, which is probably less a matter of mechanical design than traffic patterns. You should show you realize that elevators are site specific and that people's satisfaction is going to depend on how well the elevator copes with the traffic patterns that exist in the building. You would probably measure how long it takes to get an elevator after pushing the button, and how long it takes to get somewhere for various floors and at various times of day.

? How would you locate a specific book in a big library? There's no cataloging system and no librarian to help you.

Suppose the books are in random order, which they might be, for all you know. In that case, the best you can do is to scan the shelves methodically. That is at least an improvement on wandering the library without a plan. On the average, you would expect to have to scan half the library to find a given book.

There is good reason to believe that the library is *not* in random order, though. Every library big enough to make finding books a chore is going to have a plan for shelving books — just as every building of a certain size is going to have an architectural plan. Your problem is not likely to be the absence of a plan but rather that you have no way of knowing at the outset what the plan is.

Most libraries shelve books by their catalog numbers. The two most popular cataloging systems in U.S. libraries, the Dewey decimal and Library of Congress systems, are different from each other and by no means universal. Rarebook libraries often shelve early printed books by date of publication. Some systems are *strange*. In the library of the Warburg Institute, books on different subjects are purposely juxtaposed, so as to inspire study of unexpected connections. Founder Aby Warburg instituted this system and implemented it until he was taken away to an insane asylum.

The best approach is to first try to learn the system, then use that system to direct your search for the book you want. What you really need is a map of the library. Since you're not given one, it's up to you to make it. A good way to start is to spot-check shelves in a regular grid pattern. You might examine the first few books on the top left shelf of every twentieth bookcase in every other row. The point is, you want to get the lay of the land and not get bogged down in details.

At each spot check, you should pay attention not only to what books you find there but to how they are arranged on the shelf. Are books that are physically close to each other also close in subject matter? (Probably, and if so, that's an important thing to know.) Are they totally random? (We hope not, but again, that is important to know.) Are the books arranged alphabetically (by author, title, or subject), or is this a shelf of oversize books that were put here because they wouldn't fit on the regular shelves? Is the system of shelving books the same everywhere you look, or does it vary?

Pretend the book you're looking for is *The Seattle Junior League Microwave Cookbook.* Should you come across a shelf of cookbooks, you're (probably) in luck. The book is likely to be somewhere nearby. Depending on how many cookbooks the library has, you might be ready to forget about the map and just scan the cookbooks. But if the cookbook section is huge, it might be necessary to continue the mapmaking. Do more spot checks, now on a finer grid centered on the shelf of cookbooks you found. This might allow you to identify sections devoted to American cooking, microwave cooking, cuisine of the Pacific Northwest, or charity cookbooks.

What if your first pass through the library doesn't turn up *any* cookbooks, or anything remotely connected to cooking? In that case, you need to survey the whole library again, at a finer scale. Instead of checking every twentieth bookcase, you might check every tenth or every fifth. If need be, you keep surveying the entire library at an ever-finer scale until you find books that are related to the one you're looking for.

Failing to find recognizably "nearby" books is not the only problem that might arise. A big library might keep widely consulted cookbooks in its reference section, newly published cookbooks in a "new arrivals" section, very old cookbooks in a rare-books and manuscripts division, foreign-language cookbooks with other books of the same language, braille cookbooks with other braille books, and maybe a few cookbooks for children in a children's section — and most cookbooks in the cookbooks section of the general stacks. These sections of the library are not normally adjacent. That means that locating a cache of cookbooks is no guarantee the one you're looking for will be in it.

The general plan, then, is this: Using systematic spot checks, survey the library at progressively smaller scales until you start to find books "close" to the desired one (close by the prevailing arrangement of books on shelves). Once you detect "nearby" books, focus the search. Systematically spot-check the vicinity of the most promising find at progressively smaller scales, until you either find the book or determine that it is unlikely to be there. In the latter case, move on to another promising region and continue searching; if there are no other promising regions, resume reconnaissance of the entire library until more promising regions are identified.

That is approximately the kind of answer Microsoft's interviewers want. A more concise reply was offered on the acetheinterview.com website: "I would leave the library, drive to the exact location of the person who wrote this question, and slap them."

? Suppose you're hired as an IRS agent. Your first job is to find out whether a nanny agency is cheating on its taxes. How would you do it?

There are two main ways that businesses cheat on taxes: overstating expenses and understating income. The nanny agency's tax form gives its claimed income and expense. You want to find an independent way of deciding whether these figures are reasonable or way out of the ballpark — in which case further scrutiny is called for.

There should be no problem in estimating a nanny agency's expenses. The IRS generally has a good idea of how much a particular size and type of business will spend on staplers and phone bills; office rent and salaries; advertising and a website. If there's any doubt, a trip to the place of business can tell you whether the claimed number of employees and office rent are reasonable.

Income is more difficult. A nanny agency screens nannies and places them with families for a fee paid by the families. Thereafter the nanny becomes a household employee of the family. That means that all subsequent tax issues are the responsibility of the family and nanny. The family is required to file W-2 forms and pay employment taxes.

This provides one way of checking up on a nanny agency's income using data already available to the IRS. The IRS can compile, from W-2 forms and 1040s, a list of the nannies working in a given region. By comparing that list to the names on the previous year's W-2s and 1040s, the IRS can determine how many *new* nannies entered the profession in a year's time.

It's a reasonable guess that the vast majority of *new* nannies are placed by agencies. There may be seasoned nannies who move from one family to another through a network of recommendations. Much nannylike work is done by grandmothers and other relatives, with or without compensation, and probably not reported to the IRS. But most parents who look outside their family for child care, and who are unable to find a nanny through the recommendation of friends, are going to go through an agency. No one wants to trust his or her child to an unscreened stranger.

Therefore, nearly every nanny entering the workforce earns a fee for *some* nanny agency. Should the agency in question be the only one in the area, it should get nearly all the revenue. Should there be more than one agency in the area, you have to apportion the revenue between them (but note that you then would be able to pull up the records on the competing agencies and use them as guidelines).

That provides an independent check on nanny-agency

income — assuming the families and nannies are honest. What if they're not?

Well remember, it's the IRS's business to know how honest people are. There should be compliance statistics you can consult. If it's known that, in general, 90 percent of nannies report their salaries and 10 percent get paid under the table, then your estimates of the agency income can be revised upward to account for that. You are dealing with a lot of nannies and only one nanny agency. By the law of large numbers, chances are that the nannies' compliance will be close to the mean.

? You have eight billiard balls . . .

A balance is the simple two-pan setup, like the one the blindfolded figure of Justice holds. It tells you which of the two pans is heavier, though not by how much. It can also tell you when the two pans are of equal weight.

The obvious approach will not work. That would be to weigh four balls against four balls. The heavier pan would have to contain the defective ball. Split that group's balls into two pairs and weigh the pairs against each other. Again, the heavier pan has to contain the defective ball. You're then out of your two allotted weighings. There is no way to decide which of the two suspect balls is heavier.

The solution is to make full use of the fact that the balance can tell you two pans are equal. Whenever the two pans are of equal weight, you can conclude that the defective ball is not in either pan.

For the first weighing, pick any three balls and weigh them against any other three balls. This has two possible outcomes.

One is that the balance finds the two pans equal. In that case, the defective ball must be one of the two you *didn't* weigh. For the next and last weighing, just compare the two still-untested balls. The heavier one *has* to be the defective ball.

The other possible outcome of the first weighing is that the balance finds one of the two pans heavier. The defective ball must be in the heavier pan. For the final weighing, pick any two of the balls in the heavier pan and compare them. If one is heavier, it's the defective ball. If both are equal, the defective ball has to be the third ball that you didn't weigh this time.

This puzzle is known throughout the world. It appeared, for instance, in Boris Kordemsky's *Mathematical Know-How* (1956), the bestselling puzzle book of the Cold-War Soviet Union.

? You have five jars of pills . . .

The scale in this puzzle gives you an actual weight (unlike the balance in the billiard-balls puzzle).

In a more normal situation, you'd probably weigh a pill from each jar until you found one that weighed 9 grams. That won't work here, since you've got only one measurement. Chances are four in five that the first and only pill you get to weigh will be of normal weight.

That means you must weigh pills from more than one jar in your single measurement. Take the simplest case: You weigh five pills, one from each jar. The result will necessarily be $10 + 10 + 10 + 10 + 9 = 49$ grams. The trouble is, you know that before making the measurement. The 49-gram result cannot tell which bottle contributed the 9-gram pill.

You need to manufacture a situation in which the weight measurement *is* informative. One solution is to call the bottles #1, #2, #3, #4, and #5. Take one pill from #1, two from #2, three from #3, four from #4, and five from #5. Weigh the whole lot. Were all the pills normal, the result would be 10 + 20 + 30 + 40 + 50 = 150 grams. In fact, the weight must fall short of this by a number of grams equal to the number of the contaminated bottle. Should the total weight be 146 (4 grams short), then bottle #4 must contain the lighter pills.

An alternate solution, with the arguable virtue of weighing fewer pills, is to weigh 1 + 2 + 3 + 4 pills from the first four bottles only. Then, if the weight is less than 100 grams, the shortfall amount points to the rogue bottle. Should the measurement be 100 grams on the nose, the fifth bottle must be contaminated.

Having answered the question, you might ask the interviewer who the pills are intended for. A good answer is "a horse." A 10-gram pill is over thirty times the size of the usual (325-milligram) aspirin tablet.

This puzzle was mentioned (as a coin weighing) in Martin Gardner's *Scientific American* column in the mid-1950s. Gardner described it as a "new and charmingly simple variation" on the weighing puzzles popular "in recent years."

? There are three ants at the three corners of a regular triangle . . .

There are only two ways the ants can avoid running into each other. Either they all travel clockwise, or they all travel counterclockwise. Otherwise, there has to be a collision.

Pick one ant and call him Bill. Once Bill decides which way to go (clockwise or counterclockwise), the other ants have to go in the same direction to avoid a collision. Since the ants choose randomly, there is a one-in-two chance that the second ant will move in the same rotational direction as Bill, and a one-in-two chance that the third ant will. That means there is a one-in-four chance of avoiding a collision.

? There are four dogs, each at a corner of a large square . . .

To make things easy, let's say the square is 1 mile on each side, and the dogs are genetically enhanced greyhounds that run exactly 1 mile per minute. Pretend you're a flea riding on the back of Dog 1. You've got a tiny radar gun that tells you how fast things are moving, relative to your own frame of reference (which is to say, Dog 1's frame of reference, since you're holding tight to Dog 1's back with five of your legs and pointing the radar gun with the sixth). Dog 1 is chasing Dog 2, who is chasing Dog 3, who is chasing Dog 4, who in turn is chasing Dog 1. At the start of the chase, you aim the radar gun at Dog 4 (who's chasing you). It informs you that Dog 4 is approaching at a speed of 1 mile per minute.

A little while later, you try the radar gun again. What does the gun read now? By this point, all the dogs have moved a little, all are a bit closer to each other, and all have shifted direction just slightly in order to be tracking their respective target dogs. The four dogs still form a perfect square. Each dog is still chasing its target dog at 1 mile per minute, and each target dog is still moving at right angles to the chaser. Because the target dog's motion is still at right angles, each chasing dog gains on its target dog at the full running speed. That means your radar gun must say that Dog 4 is still gaining on you at 1 mile per minute.

Your radar gun will report that Dog 4 is approaching at that speed throughout the chase. This talk of fleas and radar guns is just a colorful way of illustrating what the puzzle specifies, that the dogs perpetually gain on their targets at constant speed.

It makes no difference that your frame of reference (read: dog) is itself moving relative to the other dogs or the ground. One frame of reference is as good as any other. (If they give you a hard time about that, tell 'em Einstein said so.) The only thing that matters is that Dog 4 approaches you at constant speed. Since Dog 4 is a mile away from you at the outset and approaches at an unvarying 1 mile per minute, Dog 4 will necessarily smack into you at the end of a minute. Fleas riding on the other dogs' backs will come to similar conclusions. All the dogs will plow into each other one minute after the start.

Where does this happen? The dogs' motions are entirely symmetrical. It would be strange if the dogs ended up two counties to the west. Nothing is "pulling" them to the west. Whatever happens must preserve the symmetry of the original situation. Given that the dogs meet, the collision has to be right in the middle of the square.

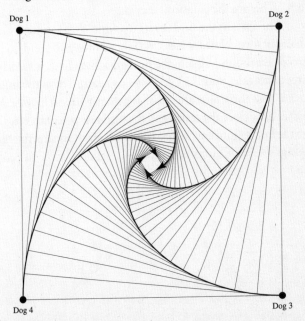

Dog 1

Dog 2

Dog 4

Dog 3

Seen from above, each of the dogs' paths is a graceful spiral. You don't need to know that to solve the problem. Nor do you need to use calculus, as many people assume. This question tests whether you're so wrapped up in using what you learned in school that you miss an easier solution.

Once again, Martin Gardner mentioned this puzzle in the 1950s.

? A train leaves Los Angeles for New York at a constant speed . . .

The bird is always the fastest object in this puzzle. Nothing the bird does affects the trains in the least.

Call the trains Eastbound and Westbound. The bird sets out with Eastbound. Since the bird is faster than Eastbound, it will intercept Westbound before Eastbound does — before the collision, that is.

The instant the bird meets up with Westbound, it does a hairpin turn. Now it races west, ahead of Westbound, to intercept Eastbound. Again, the bird gets there first. It switches direction again, and the cycle repeats again. The only difference is that the trains are closer together with each cycle. No matter how close the trains get, the bird always completes the next leg of its journey before the crash. That means the bird zigzags an *infinite* number of times.

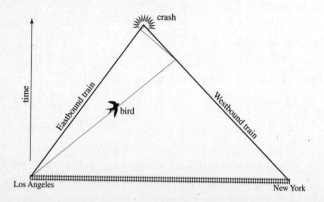

Theoretically, anyway. A moment before the collision, the bird is going to get wedged between the fronts of the trains and crushed. You can ignore that grisly detail.

It is harder to ignore the infinite series. Most of the people interviewing at Microsoft have learned the way to sum an infinite series somewhere in their education. Many of them have forgotten this technique by the time they find themselves in Redmond for an interview.

You don't need to worry about the infinite series at all. The two trains are approaching one another at a *relative* speed of 35 miles per hour (15 + 20 miles per hour). Suppose the rail distance between New York and Los Angeles is 3,500 miles. Then the collision will take place 3,500/35, or 100, hours later.

All during that time, the bird is in the air, flying at its constant speed of 25 miles per hour. Though it changes direction, it is always traveling at that speed. The bird must therefore fly a total distance of 25 miles per hour times 100 hours, or 2,500 miles. Or if d is the rail distance between Los Angeles and New York, the collision takes place in $d/35$ hours, in which time the bird flies $25d/35$, or $5d/7$, miles.

It's said that someone once posed a version of this puzzle to mathematician John von Neumann (1903–57). He announced the answer so quickly that his friend said, "Oh, you spotted the trick."

"What trick?" von Neumann asked. "I summed the infinite series."

? You have 26 constants . . .

In English, you read from left to right, so let's say you fall into the *trap* of evaluating the expression from the left. What is this constant X?

X is the twenty-fourth letter of the alphabet. The constant X must equal 24 raised to the power of the previous constant, W. Since W is the twenty-third letter, W equals 23 to the power of U, which is 22 to the power of T, which is 21 to the power of . . .

What all this means is that X is going to be 24 raised to the power of 23 to the power of 22 to the power of 21 . . . and so on, all the way up to 3 to the power of 2 to the power of 1. That's 23 nested exponentiations.

X is a *very big number*.

The Google Web search engine takes its name (though not quite its spelling) from that of a number, the googol, defined as the quantity that can be written as a 1 followed by 100 zeros. There is also a vastly bigger number called the googolplex, which would be written as a 1 followed by a *googol* zeros. Both the googol and the googolplex have no practical use save as illustrations of absurdly large numbers. There is not a googol of any physical object in the known universe. The googolplex is so large a number that it cannot even be written down in full. Since its decimal expansion has a googol zeros, and there are not nearly a googol of atoms or quarks or anything else in the universe, you are not going to write it down on paper, no matter how much paper you have or how small you write.

$$\text{Googol} = 10^{100} \qquad \text{Googolplex} = 10^{10^{100}} \qquad X = 24^{23^{22^{21^{\cdot^{\cdot^{\cdot^{3^{2^{1}}}}}}}}}$$

The googolplex is insignificantly miniscule compared to Microsoft's X. Intel has not made enough microprocessors to compute the value of X in full. Should Moore's Law hold to the end of time, and should you fill the whole universe with Super-Hyper-Pentium chips, they would still be pathetically inadequate to deal with the unimaginable vastness that is X.

The fact that the interviewer is asking you for the *exact numerical value* of an expression that contains lots of Xs should tell you that something funny is going on.

The correct answer is zero. Among the 26 terms being multiplied must be $(X - X)$. That's 0, of course. It doesn't matter what all the other terms are. Multiply anything by 0 and you get 0.

Trick questions can take many forms. This one is kind of like a *Where's Waldo?* picture. There is no surefire rule for zeroing in on a hidden trick — like Waldo, tricks can be anywhere. How quickly you realize the trick depends a lot on where your mental gaze happens to land first, and second, and third. The key $(X - X)$ term is of course "hidden" under the ellipsis when Microsoft's interviewers write out the expression.

It is reasonable to want to know whether a job candidate is someone who looks at the big picture before investing time and energy in something that may be pointless. But for many people, the "big picture" is that they're in a high-pressure interview where every hesitation counts. Even if their natural inclination is to scope out a problem first — and even if they correctly surmise a trick — many conscientious people plunge right in with the algebra. Most likely, these people will start from the left. They may continue down the "wrong" path for some time before perceiving the simple solution.

? Count in base *negative* 2.

This silly request has long been used in Microsoft interviews. There is no "base negative 2," really. It's like asking someone to diagram sentences in Klingon.

It is nevertheless possible to invent a reasonable and self-consistent base -2 notation. That's what you're supposed to do.

The ordinary way of writing numbers is base 10. That means we break down numbers into powers of 10. A number such as 176 means $1 \times 10^2 + 7 \times 10^1 + 6 \times 10^0$. (By convention, any number raised to the power of 0 equals 1.) Another feature of base 10 is that we use *ten* digits (0, 1, 2, 3, 4, 5, 6, 7, 8, and 9).

Computers use base 2, or binary notation. That uses just two digits (0 and 1). In a multidigit number (such as 10010), each position stands for a successive power of 2: 1, 2, 4, 8, 16, 32 . . . A binary number such as 10010 means $1 \times 2^4 + 0 \times 2^3 + 0 \times 2^2 + 1 \times 2^1 + 0 \times 2^0$. That adds up to the number we call 18 in regular, base 10 notation.

In general, any base works like a set of building blocks of different sizes. In base 10, the blocks come in sizes 1, 10, 100, 1,000, etc. In base 2, the blocks come in sizes 1, 2, 4, 8, 16, etc. Combining units in these standard sizes creates any desired number.

So what would base −2 notation be?

Reasonably enough, a base −2 number would have to be expressed as a sum of powers of −2. The successive powers of −2 are 1, −2, 4, −8, 16, −32 . . .

The novelty is that the odd-numbered powers are negative ($-2 \times -2 = +4$, but $-2 \times -2 \times -2 = -8$). You therefore have to break numbers down into this fixed set of positive *and* negative numbers.

You might wonder whether that's even possible for all numbers. It is. You can express all positive and negative numbers this way (without having to append a negative sign onto the whole quantity like you do to express negatives in regular bases). Base −2 numbers generally require more digits than regular binary notation does.

Before we can start counting, there's a separate issue to settle. What digits should be used in base −2? 0 and 1? 0 and −1? Something else entirely?

With normal bases, there are as many digits as the number of the base itself. In base 10 there are ten different digits; in base 2 there are two.

Should you try to apply this rule literally, you would conclude that base –2 should have negative two digits — less than no digits at all.

Rules are made to be broken. Still, there are cool ways of breaking rules and sloppy ways. You want to capture the spirit of positional notation while translating it into the heretofore-alien domain of negative numbers. The rule about the number of digits equaling the base just doesn't translate when the base is negative.

The most obvious approach is to use 0 and 1 as the digits. These are the same digits you use in regular binary notation. An alternative, arguably even more in the spirit of things, is to use 0 and –1, the latter understood to be a single symbol. That's more cumbersome, though. You might as well make it as simple as possible. Let's use 0 and 1 as the digits.

Then one would be written simply as 1 [meaning $1 \times (-2)^0$].

Two is trickier. The next position to the left counts as –2. That means that 10 (in base –2) would be $1 \times (-2)^1 + 0 \times (-2)^0 = -2 + 0$, or –2.

Try 111. That's $1 \times (-2)^2 + 1 \times (-2)^1 + 1 \times (-2)^0 = 4 + (-2) + 1 = 3$. Okay, substitute 0 for the rightmost 1: 110 is $4 + (-2) + 0 = 2$. So 110 is how we have to write two in base –2.

We just figured above that three is 111 in base –2.

Four is easy. The third position counts as 4, just as it does in regular binary notation. Four is written as 100.

Add a 1 in the rightmost place and you get the base –2 version of five, or 101.

To express six, it does no good to put a 1 in the second or fourth positions from the right, for these count negative quantities (−2 and −8 respectively). You have to leapfrog to the fifth position, which counts as +16. So 10000 is 16. That's too big. But 11000 is 16 + (−8) = 8. Subtract two from that by putting a 1 in the second column (11010) and you've got the base −2 version of six.

Adding 1 gives seven (11011).

We already figured that 11000 is eight.

Add 1 to get nine (11001).

Ten requires more juggling. Start with eight (11000). Add four by putting a 1 in the third position (11100). Then subtract two by putting a 1 in the second position (11110). This is ten.

The first ten numbers in base −2 are written as follows: 1, 110, 111, 100, 101, 11010, 11011, 11000, 11001, and 11110.

? You have two jars and 100 marbles . . .

At first glance, it looks impossible to stack the odds one way or another. The number of red and blue marbles is exactly equal. You have to use them all; you cannot "lose" a few blue marbles. The way a marble is chosen is entirely "random." Shouldn't the chance of drawing a red marble be fifty-fifty?

It is when you put 25 marbles of each color in each jar. In fact, the odds are fifty-fifty when there are 50 marbles in each jar, regardless of how the colors are mixed. Put all the red marbles in jar A and all the blue marbles in jar B. Then the chance of drawing a red marble is still exactly 50 percent, for that is the chance that jar A is chosen (guaranteeing that the marble selected at random from it will be red).

This suggests the puzzle's answer. You really don't need all 50 red marbles in jar A. One marble would do just as well. In that case, there is still a 50 percent chance that jar A, containing a lone red marble, will be chosen. Then the 1 red marble will be "chosen" at random — not that there is any choice.

That yields a 50 percent chance of choosing a red marble just for jar A. You still have 49 more red marbles, which you can and must put in jar B. In the event jar B is chosen, you have nearly an even chance of drawing a red marble. (Actually the chance is forty-nine in ninety-nine.) The total chance of selecting a red marble with this scheme is just under 75 percent (50 percent + 1/2 of 49/99, which comes to about 74.74 percent).

This is how they draw up voting districts.

? You have a 3-quart bucket, a 5-quart bucket, and an infinite supply of water. How can you measure out exactly 4 quarts?

Let's look at the quantities you can measure out. Dunk the 3-quart bucket in the infinite well and pull it out: there's your 3 quarts. Dunk the other bucket and there's 5 quarts.

To measure any other quantity, you need to resolve an ambiguity in the statement of the problem. What operations are you allowed to do in order to "measure out exactly" a quantity?

Had you super–graduated cylinder vision, you might, just by eyeballing it, pour exactly 1 quart out of the full 5-quart bucket. That would solve the problem. Evidently, you can't do that or there'd be no puzzle.

Surely you're allowed to *add* two quantities. Should you contrive to get 2 quarts in the 3-quart bucket and 2 quarts in the 5-quart bucket, you could pour the 3-quart bucket's contents into the 5-quart bucket, giving you 4 quarts.

Adding quantities, by itself, doesn't get you anywhere. You can't even use it to get 3 + 3 = 6 quarts, for the 5-quart bucket isn't big enough to hold 6 quarts. You might think of pouring the measured water into a bathtub, empty swimming pool, dry lakebed, anything. Your interviewer won't allow this. You have to imagine you're on a planet consisting entirely of ocean, and these two buckets are the only vessels in the world.

Since there is no way of proceeding by adding quantities alone, you must also be permitted the slightly more difficult operation of subtracting. Fill the 5-quart bucket to the brim and carefully pour the water into the empty 3-quart bucket until it is full. Then stop! As long as you didn't spill anything, you've then got 2 quarts in the 5-quart bucket.

Leave the 2 quarts in the 5-quart bucket and you'll never get any farther. The only way to move forward is to empty the 3-quart bucket and pour the 2 quarts from the 5-quart bucket into the 3-quart bucket.

Now all you need to do is refill the 5-quart bucket to the brim. Carefully pour it into the 3-quart bucket until the water reaches the top. That drains off exactly 1 quart, leaving 4 quarts in the 5-quart bucket.

An alternate solution (requiring one additional pouring operation) is to fill the 3-quart bucket and pour it into the 5-quart bucket. Refill the 3-quart bucket and use it to top off the 5-quart bucket (leaving 1 quart in the 3-quart bucket). Now empty the 5-quart bucket. Pour the 1 quart of water into the empty 5-quart bucket. Refill the 3-quart bucket and transfer its contents into the 5-quart bucket, making 4 quarts.

W. W. Rouse Ball mentions this puzzle in his *Mathematical Recreations and Essays* (1892), a popular Victorian-era collection. Ball believed it went back to medieval times.

Though Lewis Terman used a simpler version of this

puzzle in the first IQ test (page 26), he reported that two-thirds of "average adults" failed to solve it in the allotted five minutes. "If the amount of invention called for seems to the reader inconsiderable," Terman wrote, "let it be remembered that the important inventions of history have not as a rule had a Minerva birth, but instead have developed by successive stages, each involving but a small step in advance."

Minerva, Schminerva, Terman's version is *easy*. This may reflect the long-term trend of increasing "average" IQ scores (when you test people by the same set of questions used in the past). Contrary to Terman's belief, environment appears to make a substantial difference in IQ scores.

The harder Microsoft version figures in the movie *Die Hard with a Vengeance* (1995). There, a criminal mastermind has rigged a bomb to go off unless Bruce Willis and Samuel L. Jackson can solve the puzzle. They are at a park fountain with two plastic jugs of the specified sizes. The measured amount of water must be placed on a scale. They can't estimate because the bomb is rigged to go off if the weight of the filled jug is more than an ounce off. They can't just walk away because, uh, the bomb has a "proximity detector." Willis and Jackson work out the solution while trading buddy-movie banter ("You don't like me because I'm white!" / "I don't like you because you're gonna get me killed!").

? One of your employees insists on being paid daily in gold . . .

You need a one-unit piece to pay the employee for the first day's work. The obvious way to do that is to slice off a one-unit end piece. The not-so-obvious way is to cut a piece somewhere out of the middle, using up *both* your permitted cuts. Try the obvious plan (reserving the right to reconsider). You lop one unit off the end and hand it to the employee.

This leaves you with a six-unit bar and one more permitted cut.

On day two, you *could* slice another single unit off the end. But that would give you a five-unit bar and no more permissible cuts. You would have no way of paying on the third day.

The alternative is to cut off a two-unit piece. At the end of the second day, you hand over the two-unit piece to the employee and get the one-unit piece back as change. (You have to hope the employee hasn't already spent it.)

This leaves you with a four-unit bar, the one-unit piece you got in change, and no more cuts. On the third day, you return the one-unit piece. On the fourth day, you hand over the four-unit piece and get the two smaller ones as change. Use them to pay the worker on the fifth, sixth, and seventh days.

? You have b boxes and n dollar bills . . .

The basic idea is the same as with the gold-bar puzzle. You exploit the binary number system. Put \$1 in the first box, \$2 in the second, \$4 in the third, and so on. A requested amount can be broken down into a sum of powers of 2.

Unlike the gold-bar puzzle, this version tests your "exception handling." One complication is that n is not necessarily the sum of successive powers of 2. You will probably have some money "left over" after breaking n into powers of 2. This changes how you dispense larger amounts. Another problem is that you may not have enough boxes.

Suppose you've got \$100. You will have boxes containing \$1, \$2, \$4, \$8, \$16, \$32 . . . and then there's not enough to put \$64 in a seventh box. The first six boxes contain $1 + 2 + 4 + 8 + 16 + 32 = 63$ dollars. That means you have \$37, not an even power of 2, to go in the seventh box.

How do you supply any requested amount of money,

from $0 to $100? Using the first six boxes, you can deliver any amount from $0 to $63. (For $0 you "hand over" no boxes at all!)

What if you need $64? First hand over the seventh box with $37. Then subtract $37 from the desired $64, getting $27. Hand over another $27 using the powers-of-2 system of the first six boxes. In this case, that would mean you use the boxes containing $37, $16, $8, $2, and $1. A similar scheme will work for any amount up to the full $100, in which case you hand over all the boxes.

In asking about the "restrictions" on b and n, the interviewer means "How can you tell whether this plan will work, for specific values of b and n?" For example, if you have a million dollar bills and just one box, the plan won't work. You don't have enough boxes for that many bills. Notice that the converse is not a problem. It's okay if you have more boxes than you need for a given amount of money.

You need a general expression relating b and n. Make a quick table of how many dollar bills you can handle for the first few values of b.

b	n
1	up to 1
2	up to $2 + 1 = 3$
3	up to $4 + 2 + 1 = 7$
4	up to $8 + 4 + 2 + 1 = 15$

As a first stab at an answer, you can see that each additional box approximately doubles the number of dollars that can be handled. Two boxes can handle up to $3 while three boxes are good for up to $7. More exactly, b boxes are good for up to $2^b - 1$ dollar bills. For the plan to work, n must be less than or equal to $2^b - 1$.

This is an acceptable answer. You make it slightly more graceful by adding 1 to each side: $n + 1 \leq 2^b$. This is then the same as saying $n < 2^b$.

As much as it reflects our digital zeitgeist, this puzzle has been around in one form or another since the Renaissance. It is usually called Bachet's weights problem, after its mention in Claude Gaspar Bachet's *Problèmes plaisans et delectables* ("Pleasant and Delectable Problems") of 1612. Bachet asks for the minimum set of weights needed to balance any whole number of pounds from 1 to 40. An earlier version, also involving weights, appears in Nicolò Tartaglia's treatise on measurement (Venice, 1556). The answer was of course 1, 2, 4, 8, 16, and 32 pounds. The use of powers of 2 must have been much less obvious to Venetian humanists than to twenty-first-century Microsoft interviewees.

? You have a bucket of jelly beans in three colors — red, green, and blue . . .

Four. Pick just three jelly beans, and it's possible you'd have one of each color and therefore no match. With four jelly beans, at least two *have* to be the same color.

This is Microsoft's twist on the older puzzle asking how many socks you have to pull out of a drawer in the dark to be sure of getting a matching pair. Bankers Trust, for one, asks its interviewees the sock puzzle. When there are two colors of socks, the answer, of course, is three.

? You have three picnic baskets filled with fruit . . .

Pretend you pick a piece of fruit from the basket labeled "Apples." What can you learn from that? You get exactly one bit of information telling whether the sampled fruit is an apple or an orange. Say it's an apple. The sampled basket, being labeled "Apples," cannot *really* be the all-apples basket. If you draw an apple from it, it *must* be the apples-and-oranges-mix basket. Fine. That leaves two baskets, labeled "Oranges" and "Apples and Oranges." "Oranges" cannot be oranges (since all the labels are false), nor can it be apples and oranges (since we have already determined that the sampled basket, "Apples," contains the apples-and-oranges mix). Therefore, "Oranges" must contain apples. That leaves "Apples and Oranges," and it must contain oranges only.

Does this solve the puzzle? No. We made what is actually an optimistic supposition, that you would draw an apple from the basket labeled "Apples." That permitted the conclusion that this basket was the mixture. You might just as well have drawn an orange from "Apples." There would then be no way of telling whether "Apples" was all oranges or the mix.

It's necessary to make certain that the sampled fruit tells what's in the sampled basket. The only way to do that is to pick a fruit from the basket labeled "Apples and Oranges." Since every label is wrong, this *must* contain one type of fruit only. The fruit you pick tells you which.

If it's an orange, the basket has to be all oranges. That leaves two baskets, labeled "Apples" and "Oranges." One of these baskets is *really* apples, and the other is really the combination. Again, since every label is guaranteed to be wrong, the apples cannot be in the basket labeled "Apples." They have to be in the one labeled "Oranges." That means the combination is in the basket labeled "Apples." Parallel though opposite reasoning applies if you draw an apple from the "Apples and Oranges" basket.

? Every man in a village of fifty couples has been unfaithful to his wife . . .

Start with the situation that exists in the village before the queen's announcement. *Every* man has been unfaithful.

The women, who are aware of rampant adultery in the village, have a law that requires them to kill unfaithful husbands. Why hasn't every woman killed her husband?

The answer is that only the wife of an unfaithful husband is supposed to kill him. Each wife knows of the philandering of the *other* forty-nine husbands in the village, but not of her own husband's. Etiquette prevents anyone from informing a wife of her own husband's unfaithfulness.

That's a weird situation, but it's what we're dealing with in this puzzle. Then one day, the queen comes into town and says that at least one husband has been unfaithful. How does that change things?

It doesn't. *At least one???* the wives must be thinking, each ticking off her own private list of forty-nine unfaithful husbands. The queen's pronouncement doesn't tell *anyone anything* not already known.

That is where many interviewees get stuck. Since the queen's announcement has no information value, what more is there to say? No woman is going to kill her husband because of it. Nothing happens.

And "nothing happens" is correct — for the rest of the day on which the queen made her announcement.

Nothing happens the next day, either. Or the next day.

Skip to the forty-ninth day. Take one particular woman, Edna. Edna knows of forty-nine cheating husbands. Among them is Max, the husband of Edna's friend Monica. Given the way that gossip gets around, Edna also knows that Monica must know of (at least) forty-eight cheaters. They are the forty-nine that Edna knows about, minus Max. No one would dare tell Monica what Max has been up to.

Now here's where it gets tricky. By day forty-nine, Edna is able to conclude that Monica can conclude that Max has been unfaithful. Monica can conclude this (reasons Edna) because there have been no killings on *any* of the previous days.

Had there been just *one* philandering husband in the village, his wife should have killed him on the day of the queen's announcement (call it day one). For in that case, every wife would have known about the one philandering husband *except* his wife. His wife alone would have been aware of no adulterous husbands whatsoever. The queen's announcement would have hit her like a ton of bricks. Since she would have known of no adulterers, the "at least one" unfaithful husband would have had to be her own. She would have killed her husband that very day, as required by law. If, that is, there had been exactly one philandering husband.

Instead day two dawns with no husband killed. That informs one and all that there is *not* exactly one adulterer in the village. That, plus the infallibility of the queen, implies there must be at least two.

And had there been exactly two, their wives would have killed them on day two. Had there been three, their wives would have killed them on day three. Etc., etc. . . . And had there been forty-eight, their forty-eight wives would have killed them on day forty-eight.

Now it's day forty-nine, and Monica, who knows of forty-eight adulterous husbands, has to be mystified at why there was no mass execution the previous day. The only possible explanation (this is still Edna's analysis of what Monica must be thinking) is that Monica's own husband must be a forty-ninth adulterer.

Edna therefore concludes that ever-logical Monica will kill Max by midnight of day forty-nine. Edna can come to the same conclusion about all the other women in the village. *Yes,* thinks Edna, *there is going to be a bloodbath on day forty-nine.*

Then it's day fifty, and still nothing has happened. The only possible explanation *now* is that Monica (and all the other women) *was* aware of a forty-ninth cheater after all. It can't be Max. There's only one other man it can be: Edna's own husband, Edgar!

So on the fiftieth day, Edna is able to conclude that *her* husband is unfaithful. All the other women come to the same conclusion.

The answer to the puzzle is that nothing at all happens for forty-nine days. Then on the fiftieth day, all fifty wives kill their husbands.

As a logic puzzle, this is a masterpiece. It is questionable whether it is equally good as a hiring tool. The puzzle's earliest mention in print appears to be a 1958 book, *Puzzle-Math*, by physicist George Gamow and mathematician Marvin Stern. Their version is about cheating wives. Since then it has appeared widely. By the 1980s, it had become cheating husbands, and the puzzle was the subject of a technical paper at IBM Research Laboratory. John Allen Paulos's *Once upon a Number* (1998) gives a cheating husbands version so similar to Microsoft's that it may be the proximate source.

I suspect that the average reader of the above publications read the puzzle, thought about it a bit without getting anywhere, and then turned to the answer. "Wow! What a great puzzle!" Maybe they tried it out on a few friends, who didn't get it either, but thought the solution was great when they heard it. The popularity of a logic puzzle is in no way dependent on anyone actually solving it.

That is an issue only when someone tries to use the puzzle to decide whom to hire. While the zany "recursive" logic has some parallel to coding issues, this puzzle tends to penalize people for having a practical understanding of human behavior (a worthwhile attribute even for a coder). When people fail to solve it, it is usually because they conclude, correctly, that nothing happens in the immediate aftermath of the queen's announcement and intuit that the chance of dramatic consequences diminishes with time. That is normally a reasonable assumption outside of a logic puzzle.

? An evil demon captures a large, unspecified number of dwarfs . . .

What can a perfectly logical dwarf deduce in this situation? Probably nothing. Most likely a typical dwarf sees some fellows with green gems and others with red gems. He still hasn't a clue about his own gem.

But suppose there's a dwarf who sees *only* red gems or *only* green gems on the other dwarfs' foreheads. Since the demon has informed all that there is at least one red gem, a dwarf who sees *only* green gems can conclude that *he* is the lone dwarf with a red gem. And vice versa: A dwarf who sees only red gems can conclude that he is the lone dwarf with a green gem.

Consider a hypothetical dwarf who sees only green gems. He knows he's got a red gem. All that dwarf has to do is to step forward on the first lineup after the demon's announcement. He can be confident that his logical fellow dwarfs, with green gems, will remain in line. This will be the correct response the demon has requested.

You might ask why the other dwarfs remain in line. Is it because they know they have green gems? No. Each of those dwarfs sees one red gem (on the fellow who's about to step out of line) and lots of green gems (on everyone else). That does not permit them to deduce their own gem's color. There has to be at least one gem of each color, and they see at least one gem of each color. Their own gem could be either color.

These dwarfs remain in line because they're clueless. Remember, if anyone makes a wrong move, everyone dies. Being logical, the only safe course is to remain in line until and unless one can deduce that one has a red gem.

This does not solve the problem. It is one scenario, picked because it's easy to analyze. That doesn't mean it's actually the case. We're told only that there are a large, unspecified number of dwarfs with a mix of red and green gems.

If the above scenario *doesn't* play out on the first lineup (as it probably *won't*), then all the dwarfs can conclude that there are at least *two* gems of each color. This may well have been obvious all along (if all the dwarfs saw many gems of each color). But should there be any dwarf who sees just one gem of a given color, he can, at the second lineup, conclude that he is the other guy with that color of gem. He and the other dwarf of that color (who reasons identically) will both step forward on the second lineup. . . . This chain of reasoning and metareasoning continues until the number of lineups corresponds to the actual number of dwarfs with the less common color of gems. Then, that many logical dwarfs step forward, and (if an evil demon's promise is any good) all will be freed.

Any computer-science major will recognize the name Alonzo Church. In the 1930s Church formulated the so-called Church-Turing thesis, a cornerstone of AI. (The gist of it is that a computer can be programmed to do anything a human can do.) Church is also one of the few people who can be identified as the author of a world-class logic puzzle. At just about the time he was formulating his thesis, he came up with a puzzle about three gardeners who have gotten smudges of dirt on their foreheads. Someone sees them and remarks that at least one has a smudge on his forehead. They must deduce their own smudge or absence thereof from the others' actions.

This puzzle has spawned a genre about people who have to deduce the color of hats they're wearing or of stamps pasted on their foreheads. In recent years, Raymond Smullyan has produced many clever variations. One way or another, virtually all such puzzles' solutions involve hyper-logical beings drawing conclusions from the *failure* of fellow hyper-logical beings to draw conclusions within a given time frame.

The adulterous-village puzzle is probably the most baroque example. The demons-and-dwarfs version differs from it mainly in that you're asked to put yourself in the place of one of the participants and strategize. I have not come across this particular story line elsewhere. It shows more than passing familiarity with the travails of working in a big organization with a flat organizational chart.

? Four people must cross a rickety footbridge at night . . .

No one knows why the travelers are named after the members of U2.

Since there is only one flashlight — this flashlight being indispensable — the only way to make progress is for two people to cross the bridge together to the farside and then to have one return to the nearside with the flashlight. The net effect of a round-trip is to convey one person across the chasm.

When two people travel together, they go at the speed of the slower person. Should Adam cross with Bono, Adam must slow down to Bono's pace, and it takes ten minutes to get across.

You might think that four round-trips would be needed to get all four people across. Luckily, that's wrong.

The last trip is one-way and can convey two people across. You need two and a half round-trips, the final one-way taking two people across.

The most appealing idea is probably to have Adam, who takes just one minute to cross, escort the slower people in succession.

On trip one, let Adam escort the slowest traveler, Bono (ten minutes needed), across the bridge. This takes ten minutes.

Then Adam returns with the flashlight (taking a mere minute).

Adam next takes second-slowest Edge across (five minutes) and returns (one minute).

Finally, Adam and Larry cross the bridge (two minutes.) Total time: 10 + 1 + 5 + 1 + 2 = 19 minutes. That's two minutes too long.

Were this situation to arise in real life, most people would probably conclude that it's hopeless. They'd draw straws, or oust Bono. It is probably only the fact that you know this is a puzzle *guaranteed* to have a solution that convinces you to seek it.

Try the old trick of listing the assumptions. The most basic assumption is that people backtrack. Somebody has to return the flashlight to the people still waiting to cross on the nearside, right?

It's tough to see how you can get around that. The puzzle makes it clear that no one goes anywhere without the flashlight. (Should you suggest trick solutions, like tossing the flashlight across the chasm, or retrieving it with string, you'll be told that it's cheating.)

We also assume that *two* people cross toward the farside and only *one* returns with the flashlight. Would it do any good to try different numbers?

Well there's no point in a "trip" where *no one* crosses. We're told that the bridge won't hold three or more people. That leaves just two possibilities: one person, or two. While you might conceivably do a "backward round-trip," sending one person across to the farside and then having him escort back someone who is already on the farside — that just makes things harder. We're back to where we started.

Why not send the two slowest people across together? Bono is going to eat up most of the allotted seventeen minutes all by himself. At least kill two birds with one stone by sending Edge across with him. Then Edge won't be slowing anyone else down.

This idea is the keystone of the solution. There's a good chance you're reading this and saying "I thought of that already! It doesn't work!"

That's because this is one of those good ideas that gets easily derailed. Most people's next thought is to imagine starting with Bono and Edge crossing together. Then what?

Then you've got two insufferably slow people on the farside *with the only flashlight.* That means that one of them, presumably Edge, has to backtrack (slowly) to return the flashlight to the nearside. Time elapsed: fifteen minutes. Now there are three people on the nearside, including Edge, who alone dashes all hope of a seventeen-minute solution.

Some people give up there. It's easy to assume that this fiasco means the basic idea was wrong. Others are willing to take the next step and try the five/ten-minute trip at the very end. The last crossing is special in that no one has to go back and return the flashlight.

This idea fares no better. How do Edge and Bono end up on the nearside, *with the flashlight,* and with no one else with them? One of them (Edge most likely?) must have *already* returned from the farside with the flashlight — in which case we're talking about a minimum ten-minute round-trip to the farside and back — or else the flashlight has been returned by one of the swifter travelers, who must also be waiting to cross again. This leads to the same time problems as the previous case.

This is where many people throw in the towel. They have examined the two extreme cases (the slow pair setting off first, and setting off last) and shown them to be unworkable.

The extremes are not the only possibilities. The slow pair's trip can be in the middle. That is what leads to the solution.

Round-trip one: The fastest pair, Adam and Larry, cross, taking two minutes. One of them (let's say Adam — it doesn't matter) immediately returns with the flashlight (one minute). Elapsed time: three minutes.

Round-trip two: The slow pair, Edge and Bono, cross, taking ten minutes. As soon as they reach the farside, their bridge-crossing days are over. They hand the flashlight to the faster person who is already there. (That's Larry, assuming that Adam returned in the first round-trip.) Larry returns the flashlight to the nearside (two minutes). Elapsed time: fifteen minutes.

Final, one-way trip: The fast pair is now reunited on the nearside. They cross for the second and last time (two minutes). Elapsed time: seventeen minutes.

This puzzle has roots in early medieval times. Abbot Alcuin (735–804 A.D.) wrote a puzzle collection including an early version of the long-familiar brainteaser about a man taking a basket of cabbages, a goat, and a wolf across a river (the man mustn't leave the goat alone with the wolf, or the cabbages with an unsupervised goat). Many variations have been devised in the past dozen centuries. The river is sometimes replaced with a bridge that threatens to collapse or a pulley and bucket that the people use to escape from a tower. The constraints may be a weight limit, a time limit, not allowing unchaperoned females, and the aforementioned predator-prey issues. A puzzle about cannibals and missionaries crossing a river in a two-seat boat (any time the cannibals outnumber the missionaries, the cannibals eat them) played a role in early AI research. Early AI programs were able to identify solutions.

The Microsoft puzzle is one of the hardest of the genre. It has circulated as a much-forwarded e-mail, complete with its own "urban legend." The e-mail claims, "Reportedly, one guy solved it by writing a C program, although that took him 17 minutes to develop. Another guy solved it in three minutes. A group of 50, at Motorola, couldn't figure it out at all. . . . Note: Microsoft expects you to answer this question in under 5 minutes." (They don't.)

? In front of you are two doors. One leads to your interview, the other to an exit . . .

Since you have no way of knowing whether the consultant will tell you the truth, it is pointless to ask something such as "Is this the right door?" or "Do you work here?" You will get an answer that may or may not be correct. Having used up your one and only question, you cannot determine which.

Instead, you have to invent a question where it doesn't matter whether the person tells the truth or lies. The way to do that is to use a double negative. An example is to point to one door (it makes no difference which) and ask "*If* I asked you whether this is the way to my interview, *would* you say it is?"

The basic idea is, a perfect liar would lie about what he *would* say *if* you asked him straight-out whether this was the door to the interview (which, technically, you haven't asked!). So the perfect liar would say the opposite of what he would say to the direct question — which in turn would be the opposite of the truth. The two opposites cancel out, and the liar ends up saying yes if and only if it is the right door. And a truthful consultant also says yes to the right door, for, of course, he *would* give you that correct answer to the direct question. You don't find out whether the consultant is a liar or a truth-teller, but you do find the right door.

There are a number of alternate solutions. One is "If I asked a consultant of the *other* consulting firm whether this was the door to my interview, would he or she say it was?" All such solutions require that the consultants be willing to parse a convoluted question and answer it in the spirit intended. But such questions risk tipping off the liar that something funny is going on. The liar had better be a "perfect liar," of a sort found only in logic puzzles. Should the liar be less mechanical and only concerned with misleading people, he might do a triple switcheroo just to throw you off.

There is a way around that. Point to a door and say "Excuse me, I'm trying to get to an interview at your company — will this door get me there?"

The double-negative gimmick is the same, but this is a much more natural question. It permits a liar to lie without having to do a lot of analysis. That is because you toss in a lie of your own (but only when speaking to a liar!), for you are *not* interviewing at the liar's firm. So if you point to an exit (which really *is* the way to get to the liar's firm, presumably somewhere across town), the liar will lie and say "No, that's not the right door." And if you point to the door that leads to your interview at the truthful firm — that is, a door that does *not* lead to an interview at the lying, rival firm — then the consultant will have to lie and say that it *does*.

This "one question" version of older liar-and-truth-teller puzzles seems to date from the 1950s. The 1950s version usually involved "tribes" of truth-tellers and liars on a remote island. However, a bogus "Microsoft Interview Question" circulated on the Internet puts yet another spin on it. You come to a crossroad. One way leads to Microsoft, the other to Utopia. You want to get to Utopia. There is a man with a Microsoft Windows box on his head. You don't know if he is a liar, a truth-teller, or Bill Gates. You are allowed to ask him only one question. What would it be?

When this puzzle was posted on the rec.puzzles newsgroup, it elicited a flurry of facetious answers, many of them rabidly anti-Microsoft. If you see Bill Gates as a complex person about whose truthfulness we can make no assumptions, then the puzzle is strictly insoluble. It amounts to saying "You find yourself on the island of Manhattan, where some people tell the truth and some don't." If you instead assume that Gates — whatever his truthfulness while being grilled by the Feds — wouldn't lie to *you* about road directions, then he "counts" as an honorary truth-teller and the same solutions apply.

Most of the answers posted on rec.puzzles were more creative. One proposed solution was to ask the man "Where do I want to go today?" and do the opposite (on the grounds that "they've yet to get that one right"). Another suggested asking "Which path would a member of the opposite tribe tell me to take?" and then *punching* the guy. "If the guy was a truth-teller or liar, you get to go to Utopia. If not, you got a free punch at Bill Gates."

? Why are beer cans tapered at the top and bottom?

If you guess it's to make the can stronger, you're *sort of* right. The tapered ends are an architectural issue. Cans, like suspension bridges, work together as a whole. That often means it's difficult to supply a simple explanation for a particular feature.

From a historic perspective, the tapers were *not* added to make cans stronger. Beer cans were already strong enough to hold beer. What more can you ask of a beer can? The tapers are instead a feature of a design that minimizes the amount of metal used. That may not seem like such a big deal, but it is when you consider how many cans are produced and recycled each year.

There was a time when beer and carbonated soft drinks came in heavy steel cans whose cross sections were nearly rectangular. The steel had to be fairly thick to keep a carbonated beverage under pressure. These cans were three-part, meaning that a circular top and bottom were attached by a crimp to a cylindrical middle.

As can companies became more cost and environment conscious, they figured out ways to switch to thinner aluminum cans. The thin aluminum is less strong. Like eggshells, today's cans are just about as thin as they can be and still reliably enclose their contents. This demands architectural tricks that weren't necessary with the steel cans.

The thickest and strongest part of the can is the top, attached separately with a crimp. The top has to stand the stress of someone ripping open the flip top. Because the top is thicker metal, the manufacturers found it desirable to minimize its diameter. So they shrunk the top a little. This meant adding a bevel at the top to connect it to the rest of the can. (They couldn't shrink the diameter of the whole can, or it would hold less beer.) Once you shrink the top, you also have to shrink the bottom, for the cans are supposed to stack. Both top and bottom are tapered.

There are other reasons why the bottom is tapered. The bottom and middle are pressed from a single piece of thin aluminum, eliminating the extra step of attaching a separate bottom to the can. This is easiest to do when there is a bevel rather than a sharp right angle. The bevel also makes the can a little more dent-proof at the ends.

A similar interview question goes "Why are Coke cans concave at the bottom?" (Beer cans have concave bottoms too.) The answer is that the metal on the bottom is so thin that, were it flat, it would be prone to deformation. The concave metal is stronger, just as an eggshell is stronger than a cubical egg would be. You could get a similar strengthening effect with a convex bottom, but then the cans wouldn't stack.

? How long would it take to move Mount Fuji?

The consulting firm Booz, Allen and Hamilton seems to have originated this question. There are two possible approaches. If you can conceive a plan for moving Mount Fuji all in one piece — the way European monarchs had their engineers move Egyptian obelisks to their capitals — good luck. Otherwise, it's a Fermi estimation. You treat moving Mount Fuji as if it were an ordinary excavation job. You need to estimate the volume of Mount Fuji in truckloads.

The starting point of that estimation is likely to be the famous profile of Fuji. Most Americans have a mental picture of Fuji as a shallow cone, maybe five times as wide at the base as it is high. Most people have a much hazier idea of

Fuji's height. Fuji is not in a class with the world's tallest mountains (Mount Everest being about 35,000 feet high). It is surely thousands of feet tall. Let's settle for the nicely round figure of 10,000 feet. (A lucky guess, for the summit of Mount Fuji is actually 12,387 feet above sea level.) That means we've got a cone 10,000 feet high and 50,000 feet across at the base.

Were Fuji a tuna can–shaped cylinder rather than a cone, its volume would be its base area times its height. The base is a circle 50,000 feet in diameter. A *square* 50,000 feet on a side would have an area of 50,000 × 50,000 feet. That's 2.5 billion square feet. But a circle has less area than a square of equal breadth ($\pi/4$ as much, or 79 percent), so let's say about 2 billion square feet.

Multiply this by the 10,000-foot height, and you've got 20 trillion cubic feet as the volume of a cylinder exactly enclosing Mount Fuji.

Fuji is more like a cone, though. If you remember that a cone has a volume exactly one-third of the equivalent cylinder, give yourself extra credit. Whether you remember that or not, a cone obviously has less volume than the associated cylinder. Since we like round figures so much, let's cut the 20 trillion to 10 trillion and say that's the volume of Fuji's cone: 10 trillion cubic feet of volcanic rock.

How many truckloads is that? A truck might be able to carry something like a 10-foot by 10-foot by 10-foot cube of excavated rock and soil. That's 1,000 cubic feet to the truckload. So Fuji represents 10 billion truckloads.

The question leaves a lot unspecified. We don't know *where* we're moving Mount Fuji. See if the interviewer will supply this information. We also don't know how much of the mountain is loose topsoil and how much is solid volcanic rock that might have to be excavated with dynamite.

At best, the excavation and transport of a truckload is probably going to be a good day's work for somebody. Equating truckloads with worker-days, we estimate it will take on the order of 10 billion worker-days to move Fuji.

The project's time frame depends on how many people are on the job. In the implausible event that a lone individual is charged with the task (to be replaced successively, like lighthouse keepers, over the millennia), then it would take 10 billion days, which comes to something like 30 million years. (Fuji is probably not that old, and won't exist in its present form for that span of time. It would vanish through natural processes before one guy could move it.)

In the also-implausible event that all the world's 6 billion people pitched in (and had suitable equipment, and avoided getting in each other's way), you could move Fuji in a couple of days.

Pretend that the Japanese government wants to move Fuji and marshals more or less realistic resources for the task. Ten thousand people, the size of a large corporation, might be a reasonable workforce. It would take them 10 trillion / 10,000 days. That's a million days, or about 3,000 years.

? There are three switches in a hallway . . .

This is another problem that looks impossible as stated. If you set all the switches off, the light will be off (and the trip to the room will tell you nothing). If you set *one* switch on, there is a one-in-three chance it will be the right one. The light will be on, and you will know that the on switch controls it. There is also a two-in-three chance you will find the light off and have no way of telling which of the other two switches controls the light. Setting two switches on, or all three on, produces comparable problems.

To put it another way, it takes two bits of information

to identify one switch out of three. Your single trip to the room produces only one bit of information.

It would be simple to tell which switch works the light if dimming switches were involved. You could have one switch off, one on, and one 50 percent on. The state of the bulb would then tell which switch controls it.

That would work; of course, the puzzle would be lame if it neglected to mention the vital fact that the switches dim. This false start makes an important point. If there were a way of setting one switch to an "intermediate" position, not on and not off, that would solve the problem.

The solution is this: Call the switches 1, 2, and 3. Turn switch 1 on and 2 and 3 off. Wait about ten minutes. Then turn switch 1 off and switch 2 on. Immediately go to the room.

If the light is on, it's controlled by switch 2. If the light is off but *warm,* it's controlled by switch 1. If the light is off and *cold,* it's controlled by switch 3.

? You play this game with one other player . . .

Game strategies are normally complex. The very fact that they're asking for one in a job interview suggests that the intended strategy is simple. An interviewer wouldn't ask you for a winning strategy in chess.

The first move is often an advantage. In ticktacktoe, you want to occupy the center square on your first move. You ought to ask yourself "Is there any *unique* first move I might make here that would give me a strategic advantage?"

There's no center square. Instead, there's an infinity of possible positions in which to place the first quarter. Suppose you decide to put your first coin on the northwest corner of the table — on the grounds that it's a *distinctive,* if not quite unique, position. Does that give you a strategic advantage?

It's hard to say. This is evidently a game of many moves (it takes a lot of quarters to cover a table so densely that you can't add another coin without touching one already placed). It might be that the first player can secure an advantage that persists throughout the game. And maybe not.

It seems unlikely that there is any overwhelming strategic advantage to occupying the northwest corner. This isn't Monopoly, where Boardwalk has higher rents than any other property. Here, one corner is as good as any other. In fact, if there *was* some great benefit to occupying a corner, your opponent could respond by putting her first quarter on one of the remaining corners. If corners are so great, then the first four moves might consist of occupying the four corners. Each of you would have two, eliminating the putative advantage. Then what? It's your move again. Does this fundamentally change anything?

No matter what you do on your first move, your opponent seems to be able to effectively duplicate it on her first move. All she has to do is place her quarter at a position 180 degrees rotated from your quarter. If you take the northeast corner, she takes the southwest corner, and so on.

Wait! There is one exception only — a move your opponent can't duplicate. That is to put your first quarter in the *exact center of the table.* While there is no "center square," there is only one center of the table. Once covered by a quarter, the spot cannot be taken by anyone else.

This doesn't itself mean that the center is a good first move. It is simply the only unique first move, the only one that exploits your status as first player to do something your opponent will not be able to copy.

Hold that thought . . .

No matter what you do, the other player has freedom to put her quarters almost anywhere on the table throughout the early phase of the game. So if you've got a *good* strategy that is also a *simple* strategy, it has to involve a no-brainer, tit-for-tat response to any possible move your opponent might make.

Now put all of the above reasoning together. As first player, you should begin by placing your quarter in the precise center of the table. Thereafter, you "mirror" your opponent's previous move. Draw a line from her last quarter, through the center of the table, and beyond. Place your next quarter on the extension of that line, exactly as far from the center as the opponent's quarter (but on the opposite side of the center).

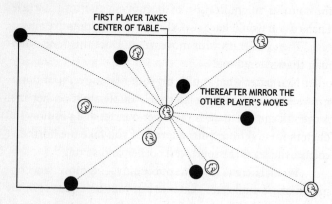

FIRST PLAYER TAKES
CENTER OF TABLE

THEREAFTER MIRROR THE
OTHER PLAYER'S MOVES

You will always be able to do this, for you are only duplicating your opponent's last action (given the symmetry of the table). Eventually, your opponent will be the one who's unable to place an additional quarter without touching one already placed.

British puzzle expert Henry E. Dudeney created a stir with this game at his London club (he played it with cigars). The game is described in Dudeney's 1917 book, *Amusements in Mathematics.* Dudeney's cigar version was especially clever. His unbeatable gambit was to set a cigar straight up, on its trimmed end, in the center of the table. Subsequent cigars may be placed horizontally or vertically — it makes no difference as long as symmetry is observed. Dudeney's American rival, Sam Loyd, ripped off the idea but added a creative twist: eggs. In order to make the first egg stand upright, you have to make a slight dent in the flatter end.

? Five pirates on an island have one hundred gold coins to split among themselves . . .

As far as we know, all five pirates have equal claim to the coins. The simplest plan is to split the coins five ways. That's twenty coins each. What's wrong with that?

The answer is that nothing is wrong with that, other than it might get you killed. Propose an even split, and the other four pirates are apt to feel that while twenty coins are fair, twenty-five coins are fairer. That is what they might expect if they voted in a bloc against your plan and killed you. Then they would start over with the same one hundred coins and only four pirates.

You can argue till you're blue in the face that an even split is the fairest plan conceivable. The only thing is, the puzzle says nothing about the pirates being fair. Fairness is usually not a core competency with pirates.

Not only is your proposal for an even split likely to be rejected, but also future proposals will run up against the same resistance. Isn't it better to split the loot three ways rather than four? Two ways rather than three? Where does the slippery slope end?

The puzzle is something like the TV game show *Survivor.* On that show, contestants "vote each other off the island" in hopes of being the sole winner of a cash prize. *Survivor* contestants generally succeed by forming short-lived voting alliances. A similar approach is called for here. Since you are at risk of forfeiting your life and not just fifteen minutes of media fame, you want to be as certain as you can be that your division plan will be accepted.

The puzzle is another exercise in recursive reasoning. The solution depends on realizing that the situation with n pirates can be analyzed in terms of the situation with $n - 1$ pirates, and so on, until you reach a "base case" where the situation is unmistakably clear.

The base case here is that of one surviving pirate. Obviously a lone pirate would propose to take all one hundred coins for himself. Motion carried!

What if there were two pirates? The senior one has to propose the division. The puzzle stipulates that a proposal carries if "at least half" vote for it. That means that the senior pirate's own vote is enough to carry his proposal. Consequently, the senior pirate of two has nothing to fear and no need to care about what the other guy thinks. Greedy devil that he is, the senior pirate will propose to take all one hundred coins for himself. The vote will be one for and one against, and the proposal will carry.

It's beginning to look like the most senior pirate always gets everything. Not quite. Suppose the senior pirate tried to pull that stunt in the three-pirate case. Let's number the pirates from least to most senior: #1, #2, and #3. It's up to #3 to propose a division. If the division were "everything for me and nothing for you two guys," the next pirate in succession (#2) would certainly vote against it. Pirate #2 knows that he would get *everything* in the two-pirate case that would result after putting #3 to the sword. The least-senior pirate (#1) is the swing voter. He gets nothing under #3's plan and would also get nothing in the two-pirate case. He has no reason to vote one way or another.

So if #3 is as smart as the puzzle implies, he will want to buy #1's support. Pirate #3 is also greedy. He isn't about to give #1 any more than he has to. Pirate #3's proposal logically would be to give #1 one gold coin, #2 nothing at all, and himself — ahem! — the other ninety-nine gold coins. Being logical, #1 will realize that a pittance is better than the nothing he would get if #3 were executed. Pirate #1 will vote for the plan (along with #3 of course) and it will pass two to one over #2's rum-soaked curses.

Now look at the four-pirate case. Four is another even number. That means that the senior pirate's proposal needs *just one vote other than his own* to pass. His question ought to be "which one of the three other pirates' votes can be bought the cheapest?"

Look at the three-pirate case. Pirate #2 is totally screwed. So if Pirate #4's plan gives Pirate #2 anything at all, #2 will logically have to vote in favor of it.

And with #2's vote in his pocket, Pirate #4 couldn't care less what #1 and #3 think. Pirate #4's plan should be nothing for #1, one coin for #2, nothing for #3, and ninety-nine coins for himself.

We are now seeing a pattern. In each case, the senior-most pirate should "buy" only the votes he needs, and buy them as cheaply as possible. He then keeps everything else for himself.

Apply this to the five-pirate case, the one the puzzle asks about. You are Pirate #5. You need three votes, your own and two of the others. You therefore want to toss a bone to the two pirates worst off in the four-pirate case. That's #1 and #3. Both will be empty-handed if you are killed and four pirates remain. Both can be induced to vote for your plan as long it allots them *something*. You should propose to give nothing to Pirate #4, one coin to #3, nothing to #2, and one coin to #1. You keep the remaining ninety-eight coins for yourself.

This is one of those commonsense-defying solutions that convince people of the absurdity of logic puzzles. Should the pirates form alliances based on friendship (which seems to be the determining factor on *Survivor*-type game shows), all bets are off. Even without alliances, the solution is dicey. What pirate (or drug dealer or mafioso or whomever you may think of as a more realistic egoist) would sit still for a scheme where you get ninety-eight coins and they get one or none at all? The other four would shoot now and make deductions later.

This question is used at Fog Creek Software in New York. "I bet the CEO of Fog Creek keeps 98% of the profits for himself," went one newsgroup post. "That's the real reason for the question, to find the dweebs who will put up with it under some bogus mathematical explanation."

? A high school has this ritual on the last day of school . . .

The first thing to realize is that this puzzle almost *has* to be simpler than it looks. Your interviewer is too busy to sit there while you run through all 100 steps. There must be a simplifying trick, and the answer must be relatively uncomplicated. Either all 100 lockers are open — or none are — or there's some high-concept pattern that makes it easy to figure out how many are open.

Your fidgety interviewer will sit still for a quick white board trial with the numbers 1 through 10. Write out the first ten numbers and make a tally of how many times each is toggled. For instance, on the very first run, all 100 lockers are toggled open. You put a mark beneath all the locker numbers.

For the second toggle, you add a mark beneath the even numbers 2, 4, 6, 8, and 10. Continue on, all the way up to the tenth toggle, where you add a mark under 10 (you would add marks for 20, 30, 40, and so on, were you making a full chart). By this point, the tally looks like this:

1	2	3	4	5	6	7	8	9	10
/	//	//	///	//	////	//	////	///	////

Further toggles will not affect the first ten lockers at all. The eleventh toggle affects only lockers 11, 22, 33 . . . The above tallies are final and complete for the first ten lockers. Since the lockers started out *closed*, any locker toggled once is open. Any locker toggled an odd number of times is open. A locker toggled an even number of times is closed.

This means that lockers 1, 4, and 9 above are open, while all the others above are closed. One, 4, and 9 are perfect squares. Each is a number multiplied by itself ($1 = 1 \times 1$; $4 = 2 \times 2$; $9 = 3 \times 3$). That's a pretty good pattern.

Do you see *why* the perfect square–numbered lockers are open? You toggle each locker once for every factor its number has. Factors come in pairs. Twelve, for instance, is 1×12 or 2×6 or 3×4. Since there are three ways of breaking it down into two factors, it has six factors in all. That means locker 12 is toggled six times. The only way a number can *avoid* having an even number of factors is when two of its factors are identical. Nine is 1×9 and also 3×3. That gives it just three distinct factors (1, 3, and 9). Only the perfect square–numbered lockers are toggled an odd number of times, and only they are left open.

The perfect squares up to 100 are 1, 4, 9, 16, 25, 36, 49, 64, 81, and 100. The answer is that ten lockers are open.

? You have two lengths of fuse . . .

A simpler version of this question, also asked in interviews, has you measure thirty minutes with the same two fuses. Since that *is* simpler, let's start with it.

There are not many options. Light either fuse at the end, and you won't know how much time has elapsed until the lighted fuse reaches the other end: sixty minutes. No good.

Notice that you can find the middle (by length) of either fuse without a yardstick. Just bend it in half. But light either fuse in the middle, and you won't learn anything. Because the fuse burns unevenly, the burn will reach one end before the other. While the *combined* burn times of the two halves must sum to sixty minutes, that is unhelpful here. To give an extreme case, it might be that the right half of the fuse is super–fast burning and will reach the right end in one minute. Then the left half would have to be super–slow burning and take fifty-nine minutes to reach the left end. That doesn't help you decide when thirty or forty-five minutes have passed.

Have we exhausted all the possibilities? No. A clever scheme is to make an X with the two fuses. Set them out so that they cross and touch in the middle of each fuse's length. Then if you light one corner of the X, the flame will burn to the middle and branch out in three directions at once.

All this does is to light the crossing fuse in the middle (something we've already decided is useless) at an unknown time in the future (however long it takes for the lit end to burn to the crossing point). It's garbage in, garbage out.

Does this exhaust all the possibilities? No, you can also light a fuse at both ends.

The burn rate of the two flames means nothing in itself, and there is no guarantee that the two flames meet in the middle. But they do meet, obviously. When that happens, two flames will have traversed the full sixty-minute length of fuse. That means that the time interval must be half of sixty minutes, or thirty minutes.

Great! That solves the simpler version of the problem. It also gives us a start on the forty-five-minute version. By burning one fuse at both ends, we measure thirty minutes. If we could measure fifteen minutes with the second fuse, the problem would be solved.

What we've established is that you can halve the burn time of any fuse by lighting it at both ends. Had we a thirty-minute fuse, we could light it at both ends the instant the sixty-minute fuse's two flames met. This would give us fifteen minutes more, for a total of forty-five minutes.

We don't have a thirty-minute fuse. We can make one by burning the second fuse, from one end, while we time thirty minutes with the first fuse.

Here's the whole procedure: At time zero, light both ends of fuse A and one end of fuse B. The fuses must not touch each other. It takes thirty minutes for fuse A's two flames to meet. When they do, there is exactly thirty minutes left on fuse B. Instantly light the other end of (still-burning) fuse B. The two flames will now meet in fifteen minutes, for an elapsed time of forty-five minutes.

? You are in a boat in the exact center of a perfectly circular lake . . .

Just so you understand the problem: The obvious plan is to make a beeline for the shore at the point farthest from where the goblin is right now. This gives you a substantial distance advantage. You have only to travel a radius (r) of the circular lake. The nonswimming goblin has to run in a semi-circular arc along the shore, amounting to half the lake's circumference. This comes to πr. The goblin thus has to cover π times the distance you do.

Pi is a little more than three. Were the goblin only three times as fast as your boat, you could narrowly beat him to the far shore. That's why the puzzle says the goblin is *four* times as fast. No matter where you choose to land, the goblin will be there to grab you.

Like many puzzles, this one asks you to sort out some significant ambiguities. Is the goblin just a mindless "magnet" sliding along the shore at the nearest point to you — or is he a thinking being? That business about the goblin being "extremely logical" implies the latter. It would seem you've got to fake out the goblin. But the scope of any "faking out" is restricted. There is no place to hide in the middle of a lake. An extremely logical goblin must carefully consider all possible strategies on your part and cannot truly be taken by surprise.

For the moment, pretend the goblin is a mindless magnet tracking your every motion and trying to stay as close to you as possible. Here's one way to rattle his cage: Make a tiny circle about the center of the lake. This will drive the goblin nuts. He will want to circle the entire lake (while your boat is making a circle of a few feet). The goblin won't be able to keep up with your boat since his circle is so much larger than yours. This means you can, by circling, put yourself beyond the halfway point of a line drawn from the goblin through the lake's center to the far shore.

That suggests a solution. Ask yourself "What is the *largest* circle, concentric with the lake, I can travel on, such that the goblin can *just* keep up with me?"

It must be a circle where you cover only 1/4 the distance of the four-times-faster goblin. It's a circle with radius $r/4$.

Travel clockwise on this circle, and the goblin will be forced to run at top speed clockwise, just to stay at the point closest to you onshore. Travel counterclockwise, and the goblin has to run counterclockwise. Here's the clever part. Should you travel on a path of radius just *under* $r/4$, the goblin will be unable to keep up with you. He will lag gradually behind.

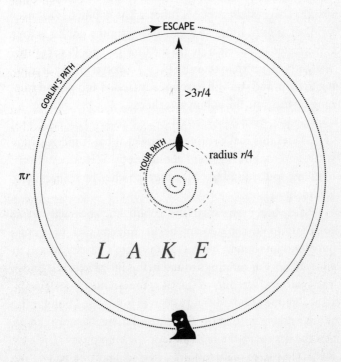

That means that you can manage to put yourself 1 1/4 radii from the goblin. One way to do it is to spiral out from the center of the lake, approaching yet not quite attaining the circle of radius $r/4$. As long as you stay within that charmed circle, the goblin will be unable to keep up with you. You can keep playing him out until the goblin falls a full 180 degrees behind you. That puts your boat opposite the goblin and nearly 5/8 of the way across the lake from him (the lake's center is halfway across the water from the goblin, and you are almost but not quite a 1/4 radius or 1/8 diameter beyond that). This geometry allows you to escape. You abruptly stop your circling and make a beeline to the far shore. The distance you need to cover is just over 3/4 times r. The goblin has to cover πr. That is $4\pi/3$ times as great, and since the goblin is four times faster, he covers it in $\pi/3$ the time you do. Pi over three is slightly bigger than one (1.047 . . .). Do everything according to plan, and you will have already landed and started running by the time the goblin gets there.

Does this really solve the puzzle? What if the goblin is smart and has already heard about this plan? He doesn't *have* to follow you around like a lapdog, not when he realizes what you're up to.

Yes, but even when the goblin knows exactly what you're up to, he can't do any better. You can pick up a bullhorn and announce "Hey, Goblin! Here's exactly what I'm going to do. I'm running around in this little circle just under one-quarter the radius of the lake. You do the math! The instant I'm one hundred eighty degrees from you, I bolt for the shore, and we both know I'll beat you there. Now we can do this the easy way, the hard way, or the stupid way. The easy way is for you to realize you're defeated. Stay put, and let me swing around to the other side and make my escape. The hard way is for you to chase me. That's more work for both of us. The outcome will be exactly the same. Finally, there's the stupid way. Should you try and pull a 'contrary' strategy — such as chasing at less than your top speed, chasing in the wrong direction, running back and forth, or even running away from the water — *any* of those things will just make it easier for me to get one hundred eighty degrees away from you, at which point I'm out of here."

At various companies, the anecdote takes other forms. Sometimes you're in the middle of a circular field, surrounded by barbed wire, with a killer dog on the outside trying to get you. Another version has a fox attempting to get a duck in the middle of a circular lake (though it's hard to imagine a duck knowing the geometry).

? Does the sun always rise in the east?

The answer has to be no. Some people toss out cosmic counterexamples. Venus and Uranus rotate in the opposite direction from Earth. From a hypothetical nonrotating platform in space, the sun doesn't rise or set at all. A difficult interviewer will disallow these answers and rephrase the question as "Does the sun always rise in the east on Earth?" The answer is still no. At the North Pole, there is no such thing as east. Every direction is south. During the six-month polar "day," the sun rises in the south and sets in the south. The opposite holds for the South Pole, where every direction is north.

? You've got six matchsticks. Arrange them so they form four equilateral triangles.

The intended solution (a) is to arrange the matchsticks to form a three-sided pyramid (tetrahedron). Nearly everyone resists the idea of a three-dimensional solution.

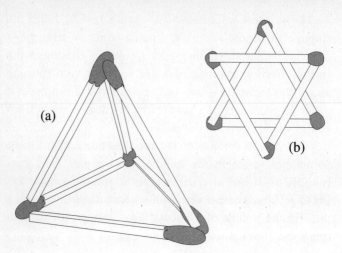

(a)

(b)

There are two-dimensional solutions; they just seem mundane next to the pyramid. One is to make a Star of David (b) by overlapping two triangles of three matches each. The points of the star make six small equilateral triangles (plus the two big equilateral triangles, for a total of eight). Perfectionists can shift one of the matches to get exactly four (small) equilateral triangles.

GROUCHO: Now, listen here. I've got a swell job for you, but first you have to answer a couple of important questions. Now . . . what is it that has four pair of pants, lives in Philadelphia, and it never rains but it pours?

CHICO: 'At'sa good one. I give you three guesses.

GROUCHO: Now lemme see. . . . Has four pair of pants, lives in Philadelphia. . . . Is it male or female?

CHICO: No, I no think so.

GROUCHO: Is he dead?

CHICO: Who?

GROUCHO: I don't know. I give up!

CHICO: I give up too.

> — Groucho and Chico Marx in *Duck Soup* (1933), written by Bert Kalmar, Harry Ruby, Arthur Sheekman, and Nat Perrin

Acknowledgments

I have drawn on the expertise of an unusually diverse spectrum of people: hirers, entrepreneurs, psychologists, human resources experts, historians, cognitive scientists, and logic-puzzle aficionados. A few of the most helpful must be mentioned here. Joel Shurkin was kind enough to share material from his then-unpublished biography of William Shockley. This helped establish a historic precedent for puzzle interviews at high-technology companies and tied it to the intelligence-testing movement (and its demise) in a most unexpected way. Conversations with Joel Spolsky and Adam David Barr were especially helpful in sketching in the history and practice of these interviews and formulating the advice for hirers in chapter nine. Chris Sells, Kiran Bondalapati, and Gene McKenna were an inspiration and provided invaluable anecdote and analysis. Officially, Microsoft refused to have anything to do with my research for this book. The company's position is that its interviewing techniques are proprietary. Ironically, the interview questions themselves were easy to obtain. More difficult was tracing just what goes on "behind-the-scenes" in that complex performance known as a Microsoft interview. For this I have to thank the cooperation of a number of individual Microsoft employees. I have found them to be generous with their time and thoughtful in their assessment of their way of hiring. Some of these people must go unnamed here. Thanks also go to Steve Abell, Joe Barrera, Linda Bates, John Brockman and Katinka Matson, Astrid De Kerangal, Terry Fonville, Ryan Harbage, Larry Hussar, Philip Johnson-Laird, Asya Muchnick, Alex Paikin, Michael Pryor, Jerome Smith, Norman Spears, Noah Suoja-nen, Rod Van Mechelen, Bob Weide, and Tim Young.

Notes

3 make a million dollars: Hiltzik, "The Twisted Legacy."

4 did not care for other people: Joel Shurkin, e-mail to author, April 25, 2002. Gibbons, later dean of Stanford's engineering school, helped convince Bill Gates to fund the William Gates Computer Science Building at Stanford.

5 Gene McKenna signed up for an interview: McKenna, "An Interview with Microsoft."

7 interview questions are reported from Italy, Russia, and India: Kiran Bondalapati, e-mail to author, March 27, 2002.

9 Microsoft's turnover rate: Microsoft Corporation, *Inside Out,* p. 134.

9 scanned for keywords: Lieber, "Wired for Hiring."

9 "We look for original, creative thinkers": Microsoft Corporation <http://www.microsoft.com>.

10 Six recent hires are pictured: Microsoft Corporation <http://www.microsoft.com/college/fulltime/default.asp>.

10 "Get over your fear of trick questions": Microsoft Corporation, *Inside Out*, p. 130.

10 "You never know when they are going": Crack, *Heard on the Street*, p. 18.

11 man-eating she-monster . . . *Godfather* trilogy: Andrew Wilson, "Oedipus and the Sphinx" <http://www.users.globalnet.co.uk/~loxias/sphinx.htm>.

13 The court added . . . $1.9 million: *Frank B. Hall & Co. v. Buck,* 678 S.W.2d 612 (Tex. App. 1984), mentioned in Adler, "Encouraging Employers."

13 "We tell our clients not to get involved": Perry, "Cut Your Law," p. 54.

14 "Social Security Number Decoder for Recruiters": *MBA Style Magazine* <http://members.aol.com/mbastyle/web/ss.html>.

15–17 Nalini Ambady and Robert Rosenthal . . . Tricia Prickett: Gladwell, "The New-Boy Network," pp. 70–1.

19 "The most important thing we do": Microsoft Corporation, *Inside Out,* p. 130.

19 "We fully know how bogus": Barr, *Proudly Serving My Corporate Masters,* p. 33.

20 "Microsoft really does believe": Ibid., p. 27.

20 the National Football League's annual draft: Adam David Barr, telephone conversation with author, April 6, 2002.

23 IQ is all that matters: See, for instance, Munk, "Think Fast!" p. 146, and Isaacson, "In Search," pp. 51, 57.

24 The phrenologist predicted good things: Gould, *The Mismeasure of Man,* p. 204.

26 When a man says, "I have never solved a puzzle": Dudeney, *Amusements in Mathematics,* p. v.

26 A mother sent her boy to the river: Terman, *The Measurement of Intelligence,* pp. 345–6.

26 An Indian who had come into town: Ibid., p. 316.

26 claimed that he invented the first puzzle: Ibid., p. 348.

27 girls scored higher: Block, *The IQ Controversy,* pp. 461–2.

29 "helped to win the war": See Gould, *The Mismeasure of Man,* p. 224.

29 "Anything above 85 IQ in the case of a barber": See ibid., p. 212.

31 "If Shockley had been a better manager": Joel Shurkin, quoted at <http://www.pbs.org/transistor/album1/addlbios/shurkin.html>.

33 Lewis Terman had believed . . . Yerkes had wanted to keep Jews: See discussion in Gould, *The Mismeasure of Man.*

34 Shockley's estranged children learned of his death: Hiltzik, "The Twisted Legacy."

40 "There are Mensans on welfare": Mensa International <http://www.mensa.org/info>.

41 the young William Shockley was tested: Leslie, "The Vexing Legacy."

41 "Mensa member mucks up": *Independent,* December 22, 2000.

44 "I enjoy puzzles, but I would really be cheesed off": cpt kangarooski, Online posting, July 6, 2000 <http://www.kuro5hin.org>.

44 "In general, I think logic puzzles": Chris Sells, e-mail to author, November 26, 2001.

44 "Performance on brainteasers says a lot about your experience": Mongan, *Programming Interviews Exposed,* p. 159.

44 "cheap shots that don't prove much of anything": Ibid., p. 167.

44 "Everyone who works there": Chris Sells, telephone conversation with author, November 30, 2001.

44 "The weird thing was": Microsoft Corporation, *Inside Out,* p. 154.

45 these interviews are more "fun": Spolsky, "The Guerrilla Guide."

45 "The [Microsoft] interviewing process really emphasizes": Sells, telephone conversation.

45 to prove the validity of Microsoft's interview: Philip Johnson-Laird, e-mail to author, December 11, 2001.

49 The first question put to Abell: Steve Abell, telephone conversation with author, March 20, 2002.

50 "The play was quite serious": Isaacson, "In Search," p. 47; see also Auletta, *World War 3.0,* p. 142.

51 at home with jigsaw puzzles . . . draw a map: Ibid., pp. 153–4.

51 "sing down" game: Isaacson, "In Search," p. 52.

51 the game was a scavenger hunt: Microsoft Corporation, *Inside Out,* p. 192.

52 accusing another player of cheating: Auletta, *World War 3.0,* p. 36.

52 "The miserable little cheat unplugged his computer": Bank, *Breaking Windows,* p. 158.

52 "Basically what Microsoft is trying to do": Gleick, "Making Microsoft Safe."

52 "full concepts": Jim Allchin, quoted in *Los Angeles Times,* March 5, 2002, C3.

53 "THAT'S THE STUPIDEST THING": Isaacson, "In Search."

53 "Why don't you just give up your stock options": Bank, *Breaking Windows,* p. 75.

53 potbellied pig: Gimein, "Smart Is Not Enough."

54 anniversary couple dropped the pretense: Auletta, *World War 3.0,* p. 161.

54 The Redmond campus is itself an amazing place: Microsoft Corporation, *Inside Out,* p. 133.

54 Victorian outfits: Gimein, "Smart Is Not Enough."

55 porn images installed as wallpaper: "Women Behaving Badly?" <http://www.nwlink.com/~rodvan/msft.html>. (Defunct.)

55 salaries are relatively modest: Auletta, *World War 3.0,* p. 164.

55 "a lot more shrimp than weenies": Microsoft Corporation, *Inside Out*, p. 145.

56 "Just in case anyone is in danger": Ibid.

56 "Excess destroys success": Ibid.

56 "If we make the wrong decisions": Ibid., p. 127.

56 "One day, somebody will catch us napping": Bank, *Breaking Windows*, p. 33.

56 "Our next competitor could come out of nowhere": Microsoft Corporation, *Inside Out*, p. 71.

57 "If we don't continue to innovate": Ibid., p. 186.

57 toting copies of Christensen's book: Bank, *Breaking Windows*, p. 228.

57 Out of seventeen companies making hard drives: Christensen, *The Innovator's Dilemma*, p. 7.

58 transistor radios became the first breakout: Ibid., p. 201n.

58 "Markets that do not exist": Ibid., p. 143.

59 "Microsoft cannot make great products": Gleick, "Making Microsoft Safe."

59 "Microsoft just needs a set of taillights": See, for instance, Microsoft Corporation, *Inside Out*, p. 14, where Tom Button mentions this claim.

59 "don't always realize all the innovative things": Lieber, "Wired for Hiring."

60 Gates was loath to hire nonprogrammers: Microsoft Corporation, *Inside Out*, p. 72.

64 "lower life-form": Barr, telephone conversation.

65 "Is there a program manager in the house?": Barr, *Proudly Serving My Corporate Masters*, p. 48.

66 "If you ever say anything even vaguely implying": Ibid., p. 65.

66 "totally bogus": Ibid., p. 67.

66 "The most successful testers just think differently": Microsoft Corporation, *Inside Out*, p. 89.

66 "Actually, you forgot to ask this": Spolsky, "The Guerrilla Guide."

69 "People who are smart": Ibid.

69 "Sometimes candidates will drift": Ibid.

69 "Good candidates have a tendency": Ibid.

70–71 when Carl Tashian arrived . . . Tashian could go: Tashian, "The Microsoft Interview."

71 three-act play": See Weinstein, "Landing a Job at Microsoft."

72 "No hire, unless everyone else thinks hire": Barr, telephone conversation; Barr, *Proudly Serving My Corporate Masters*, p. 15.

73 "A false negative is bad": Joel Spolsky, telephone conversation with author, March 12, 2002.

73 "The best thing we can do for our competitors": Lieber, "Wired for Hiring."

74 "There's always a problem": Spolsky, telephone conversation.

74 "As the day goes on it's tempting": Microsoft Corporation <http://www.microsoft.com/college/joinus/tips.asp>.

75 characterized as a "frat boy" . . . Frat Boy was not hired: Spolsky, telephone conversation.

76 "It's sort of a status thing": Barr, telephone conversation.

76 Stanford student . . . walked out of the building: Noah Suojanen, telephone conversation with author, March 26, 2002; McCarty, "It's Not a Job Interview."

79 Steve Ballmer was jogging: Barr, telephone conversation.

80 a 1983 book by Martin Gardner: Gardner, *Wheels, Life and Other,* pp. 79, 87–8.

86 "A friend of mine was not hired at Microsoft": Spolsky, telephone conversation.

87 "You know, of course, that water holds up a fish": Terman, *The Measurement of Intelligence,* pp. 334–5.

88 "If the subject keeps changing his answer": Ibid., p. 335.

88 "Throughout the interview": Spolsky, "The Guerrilla Guide."

88 Chris Sells was interviewing: Sells, telephone conversation.

90 "I always reply": Sells, e-mail to author.

91 physicist Murray Gell-Mann: Kim, "TRIZ."

94 "clueless plateau": Perkins, *Archimedes' Bathtub,* p. 54.

98 Do you buy the Hawaiian trip: Tversky, "The Disjunction Effect."

99 a similar effect in the stock markets: Shafir, "Thinking Through Uncertainty."

99 "When I walked in and looked at the screen": *New York Times,* November 10, 1988, cited in Shafir, "Uncertainty and the Difficulty."

107 "Not-so-smart candidates will get flustered": Spolsky, "The Guerrilla Guide."

110 "I can't make the suit out": Bruner, "On the Perception of Incongruity," p. 218.

112 "I enjoyed meeting you": "How to Stay Graceful in a Stress Interview" <http://www.wetfeet.com/asp/article.asp?aid=168&atype=Interviewing>.

112 Do you choose to sit: Crack, *Heard on the Street,* p. 12.

112 Lewis mentions the tale: Lewis, *Liar's Poker,* p. 27.

113 How common are these devices?: <http://www.vault.com/nr/ht_list.jsp?ht_type=10>.

114 "It was difficult because it was a shiny chair": quoted in Frase-Blunt, "Games Interviewers Play"; also see transcript of the Diane Sawyer interview at <http://www.analytictech.com/mb021/rickover.htm>.

115 "I'd put them in there for a couple of hours": Ibid.

115 Another puzzle is to scale a wall: Freedman, "Corps Values."

115 Elites, Managers, and Immigrants: Bank, *Breaking Windows*, pp. 97–8.

116 "competency-based recruitment": <http://www.ddiworld.com/hiring/hiringmain.asp>.

116 "We take all the crises": Munk, "Think Fast!" p. 150.

116 "a fad diet": Sells, telephone conversation.

117 tossing out a hand grenade: Munk, "Think Fast!" p. 146.

117 "sparked some great conversations and insights": Frase-Blunt, "Games Interviewers Play."

121 "roaring with indignation and disdain": *Washington Post*, March 3, 1998. For a description of Gates's "eruption," see Auletta, *World War 3.0*, p. 14.

123 "Not-so-smart candidates think that design": Spolsky, "The Guerrilla Guide."

124 "the point of the question is to generate": Spolsky, telephone conversation.

129 the candidate decided that a blind person: Ibid.; see also Spolsky, "The Guerrilla Guide."

131 "You're going in there": Spolsky, telephone conversation.

134 "To college kids, this way of interviewing": Barr, telephone conversation.

134 "based on one thing": Sells, telephone conversation.

139 "You want a question that's not just right": Barr, telephone conversation.

149 Microsoft has stopped using it: Barr, *Proudly Serving My Corporate Masters*, p. 36.

149 "Candidates showed up in the lobby": Ibid.

149 Consolidated Edison's manhole covers are square: Gardner, *Wheels, Life and Other*, p. 88.

149 "That's easy": Barr, *Proudly Serving My Corporate Masters*, p. 36.

154 He wrote a whole book: Gardner, *Mathematical Puzzles and Diversions*, pp. 162–73; Gardner, *The Ambidextrous Universe*.

157 On the passenger side, a counterclockwise turn: Jerome Smith of General Motors was kind enough to explain this convention.

158 "There's a sheet of hot boiling chocolate": Spolsky, telephone conversation.

166 Trade statistics: Adapted from "Marketing History of the Piano" <http://www.cantos.org/Piano/History/marketing.html>.

175 "not so long ago someone made the discovery": Gardner, *Mathematical Puzzles and Diversions,* p. 23.

180 "Some of these future scenarios": Microsoft Corporation, *Inside Out,* p. 271.

181 They couldn't get it to work: Corcoran, "The House."

193 "I would leave the library": soney, Online posting, 2001 <http://www.acetheinterview.com>.

196 Boris Kordemsky's *Mathematical Know-How:* Kordemsky, *The Moscow Puzzles,* p. 117.

197 "new and charmingly simple variation": Gardner, *Mathematical Puzzles and Diversions,* p. 26.

200 Martin Gardner mentioned this puzzle: Ibid., p. 113 (where it's about "four amorous bugs").

209 "If the amount of invention called for": Terman, *The Measurement of Intelligence,* p. 347.

212 Bachet's weights problem: See Ball, *Mathematical Recreations and Essays,* p. 50.

216 a 1958 book, *Puzzle-Math:* Gamow, *Puzzle-Math,* pp. 20–3.

216 IBM Research Laboratory: Dolev, "Cheating Husbands."

216 Paulos's *Once upon a Number:* Paulos, *Once upon a Number,* pp. 109–11.

222 Abbott Alcuin (735–804 A.D.) wrote a puzzle: See Ball, *Mathematical Recreations and Essays,* p. 118.

223 "Reportedly, one guy solved it": Barr, *Proudly Serving My Corporate Masters,* p. 34. A slightly different version of the "legend" is at <http://www.grand-illusions.com/puzzle2.htm>.

225 date from the 1950s: Martin Gardner called it "a recent twist on an old type of logic puzzle" (Gardner, *Mathematical Puzzles and Diversions,* p. 25).

225 a bogus "Microsoft Interview Question": littlegreenrat@lycos.com, Online posting, May 25, 2001 <rec.puzzles>.

225 "they've yet to get that one right": Michael Will, Online posting, May 26, 2001 <rec.puzzles>.

225–26 "If the guy was a truth-teller": Fay Aron Charles, Online posting, May 25, 2001 <rec.puzzles>.

233 Dudeney's cigar version: Dudeney, *Amusements in Mathematics*, p. 119.

233 added a creative twist: Loyd, *Mathematical Puzzles*, p. 62.

236 "I bet the CEO of Fog Creek": Jeremy Singer, Online posting <http://www.realrates.com>.

Bibliography and Web Links

Websites Listing Puzzle and Technical Interview Questions

The most comprehensive websites covering Microsoft-style interview questions are:

Bondalapati, Kiran. "Interview Question Bank" <http://halcyon.usc.edu/~kiran/msqs.html>.

Pryor, Michael. "Techinterview" <http://techinterview.org>.

Sells, Chris. "Interviewing at Microsoft" <http://www.sellsbrothers.com/fun/msiview>.

Wu, William. "Riddles" <http://www.ocf.berkeley.edu/~wwu/riddles/intro.shtml>.

All four sites include puzzles and riddles. Bondalapati's and Sells's sites focus on Microsoft specifically (though most questions are asked at other companies) and include programming questions as well. Pryor's site gives answers; the others have few or none.

Other sites with shorter lists of questions include

"How to Hack the Microsoft Interview," 1997 <http://www. howdyneighbor.com/zephyr>. (Programming questions only.)

"Microsoft Interview Questions" <http://www.4guysfromrolla.com/ misc/100798-1.shtml>.

"Microsoft Interview Questions," 2001 <http://www.acetheinterview. com/qanda/microsoft_interview.html>. (A short list of Microsoft questions submitted by Andrew Smith. See also the section on "Analytical" questions that includes more Microsoft questions with answers [right and wrong!] posted by readers.)

Bibliography

Adler, Robert S., and Ellen R. Pierce. "Encouraging Employers to Abandon Their 'No Comment' Policies Regarding References: A Reform Proposal." *Washington and Lee Law Review* 53, no. 4 (1996): 1,381+.

Auletta, Ken. *World War 3.0: Microsoft and Its Enemies.* New York: Random House, 2002.

Ball, W. W. Rouse, and H. S. M. Coxeter. *Mathematical Recreations and Essays.* 1892. Reprint, New York: Dover, 1997.

Bank, David. *Breaking Windows: How Bill Gates Fumbled the Future of Microsoft.* New York: Free Press, 2001.

Barr, Adam David. *Proudly Serving My Corporate Masters: What I Learned in Ten Years as a Microsoft Programmer.* Lincoln, Nebr.: iUniverse.com, 2000.

Block, N. J., and Gerald Dworkin. *The IQ Controversy.* New York: Pantheon, 1976.

Bruner, J. S., and Leo Postman. "On the Perception of Incongruity: A Paradigm." *Journal of Personality* XVIII (1949): 206–23.

Christensen, Clayton M. *The Innovator's Dilemma.* Rev. ed. New York: HarperCollins, 2000.

Corcoran, Elizabeth, and John Schwartz. "The House That Bill Gates's Money Built." *Washington Post,* August 28, 1997. A01.

Crack, Timothy Falcon. *Heard on the Street: Quantitative Questions from Wall Street Job Interviews.* N.p.: Timothy Falcon Crack, 2001. (Available from Web booksellers or by contacting author at timcrack@alum.mit.edu.)

Dolev, Danny, Joseph Halpern, and Yoram Moses. "Cheating Husbands and Other Stories." *Distributed Computing* 1, no. 3 (1986): 167–76.

Dudeney, Henry Ernest. *Amusements in Mathematics.* 1917. Reprint, New York: Dover, 1970.

Frase-Blunt, Martha. "Games Interviewers Play." *HR Magazine,* January 2001.

Freedman, David H. "Corps Values." *Inc Magazine,* April 1, 1998.

Gamow, George, and Marvin Stern. *Puzzle-Math.* New York: Viking, 1958.

Gardner, Martin. *The Ambidextrous Universe: Left, Right, and the Fall of Parity.* New York: New American Library, 1969.

———. *Mathematical Puzzles and Diversions.* New York: Simon and Schuster, 1959.

———. *Penrose Tiles to Trapdoor Ciphers.* New York: W. H. Freeman, 1989.

———. *Wheels, Life and Other Mathematical Amusements.* New York: W. H. Freeman, 1983.

Gates, Bill. *Business @ the Speed of Thought.* New York: Warner Books, 1999.

Gates, Bill, Nathan Myrhvold, and Peter M. Rinearson. *The Road Ahead.* Rev. ed. New York: Penguin, 1996.

Gimein, Mark. "Smart Is Not Enough." *Fortune,* January 8, 2001.

Gladwell, Malcolm. "The New-Boy Network." *The New Yorker,* May 29, 2000, 68–86.

Gleick, James. "Making Microsoft Safe for Capitalism." *New York Times Magazine,* November 5, 1995.

Gould, Stephen Jay. *The Mismeasure of Man.* Rev. ed. New York: W. W. Norton, 1996.

Hiltzik, Michael A. "The Twisted Legacy of William Shockley." *Los Angeles Times Magazine,* December 2, 2001.

Isaacson, Walter. "In Search of the Real Bill Gates." *Time,* January 13, 1997, 45–57.

Johnson-Laird, Philip N. *Human and Machine Thinking.* Hillsdale, N.J.: Lawrence Erlbaum, 1993.

Kane, Kate. "The Riddle of Job Interviews." *Fast Company,* November 1995, 50+.

Kim, Eugene Eric. "TRIZ: The Theory of Inventive Problem Solving." *Dr. Dobb's Journal,* May 17, 1999.

Kordemsky, Boris A. *The Moscow Puzzles.* Translated by Albert Parry and edited by Martin Gardner, adapted from a 1956 Russian book whose title translates *Mathematical Know-How.* New York: Dover, 1992.

Kuhn, Thomas. *The Structure of Scientific Revolutions.* Chicago: University of Chicago Press, 1962.

Langley, Pat, Herbert Simon, Gary Bradshaw, and Jan Zytkow. *Scientific Discovery: Computational Explorations of the Creative Process.* Cambridge, Mass.: MIT Press, 1987.

Leslie, Mitchell. "The Vexing Legacy of Lewis Terman." *Stanford Magazine,* July/August 2000 <http://www.stanfordalumni.org/news/magazine/2000/julaug/articles/terman.html>.

Lewis, Michael. *Liar's Poker: Rising Through the Wreckage of Wall Street.* New York: Penguin, 1990.

Lieber, Ron. "Wired for Hiring: Microsoft's Slick Recruiting Machine." *Fortune,* February 1996.

Loyd, Sam. *Mathematical Puzzles of Sam Loyd.* New York: Dover, 1959.

McCarty, Ellen. "It's Not a Job Interview, It's a Subculture!" *Fast Company,* August 2000, 46.

McKenna, Gene. "An Interview with Microsoft," 2001 <http://www.meangene.com/essays/microsoft_interview.html>.

Microsoft Corporation. *Inside Out: Microsoft — In Our Own Words.* New York: Warner Books, 2000.

"The Micro$oft Hate Page" <http://www.enemy.org>.

Mongan, John, and Noah Suojanen. *Programming Interviews Exposed: Secrets to Landing Your Next Job.* New York: John Wiley, 2000.

Munk, Nina, and Suzanne Oliver. "Think Fast!" *Forbes*, March 24, 1997, 146–51.

Newell, Alan, and Herbert Simon. *Human Problem Solving.* Englewood Cliffs, N.J.: Prentice Hall, 1972.

Paulos, John Allen. *Once upon a Number: The Hidden Mathematical Logic of Stories.* New York: Basic Books, 1998.

Perkins, David. *Archimedes' Bathtub: The Art and Logic of Breakthrough Thinking.* New York: W. W. Norton, 2000.

Perry, Phillip M. "Cut Your Law Practice's Risks When Giving References for Former Support Staff." *Law Practice Management*, September 1994, 54.

Shafir, Eldar. "Uncertainty and the Difficulty of Thinking Through Disjunctions." In *COGNITION on Cognition*, edited by Jacques Mehler and Susana Franck. Cambridge, Mass.: MIT Press, 1995.

Shafir, Eldar, and A. Tversky. "Thinking Through Uncertainty: Nonconsequential Reasoning and Choice." *Cognitive Psychology* 24 (1992): 449–74.

Shurkin, Joel. *Broken Genius: A Biography of William B. Shockley.* Work in progress.

Smith, Rebecca. *The Unofficial Guide to Getting a Job at Microsoft.* New York: McGraw-Hill, 2000.

Spearman, Charles. "General Iintelligence Objectively Determined and Measured." *American Journal of Psychology* 15 (1904): 201–93.

Spolsky, Joel. "The Guerrilla Guide to Hiring," 2000 <http://www.joelonsoftware.com/articles/fog0000000073.html>.

Sternberg, Robert, and Janet E. Davidson, eds. *The Nature of Insight.* Cambridge, Mass.: MIT Press, 1995.

Tashian, Carl. "The Microsoft Interview," 2001 <http://www.tashian.com/microsoft.html>.

Terman, Lewis M. *The Measurement of Intelligence.* London: Harrap, 1919.

Tversky, Amos, and Eldar Shafir. "The Disjunction Effect in Choice Under Uncertainty." *Psychological Science* 3 (1992): 305–9.

Van Mechelen, Rod. "Sex, Power and Office Politics at Microsoft" <http://www.nwlink.com/~rodvan/msft.html>. (Defunct.)

Weinstein, Bob. "Landing a Job at Microsoft: One Techie's Story of Interviewing for the Software Giant," 2001 <http://home.techies.com/Common/Content/2000/11/2career_landingjobmicrosoft.html>.

Index

Abell, Steve, 48–49

absurdist interviews, 116–17

adulterous village question, 85, 126, 213–17, 219

Alcuin, Abbot, 222–23

algorithms, 68, 100, 143–44

Allard, J, 54–55

Allen, Paul, 12, 60

Altair 8800, 60

Ambady, Nalini, 15–16, 47

analogies, 25, 43

answers: adulterous village question, 213–17, 219; ants question, 197; bathroom design for Gates question, 179–82; beer can question, 226–27; boat and goblin question, 239–43; boat and suitcase question, 160–63; boxes and dollar bills question, 210–12;

car-door key question, 154–57; clock's hands question, 175–76; count in base *negative* 2 question, 203–06; crossing bridge question, 219–23; demon and dwarfs question, 217–19; dogs at corner of square question, 198–200; employee paid daily in gold question, 209–10; fuses' burning time question, 238–39; gas stations question, 166–67; high school lockers question, 236–38; hot water in hotel question, 157–58; jars and marbles question, 206–07; jelly beans in three colors question, 212; library-book loca-

answers (*cont.*)

tion question, 190–93;
Manhattan phone book
question, 176–78; man-
hole covers question,
148–50; matchstick and
equilateral triangles
question, 243–44; micro-
wave oven controlled by
computer question,
182–83; mirror question,
150–54; Mississippi
River question, 168–69;
M&Ms question,
158–60; moving Mount
Fuji question, 227–29;
nanny agency cheating
on taxes question,
193–95; piano tuners
question, 163–66; picnic
baskets filled with fruit
question, 212–13; pirates
splitting gold coins
question, 233–36; points
on globe question,
173–75; quarter on
rectangular table game,
230–33; rectangular
cake question, 178–79;
Russian roulette ques-
tion, 147–48; saltshaker
testing question, 189–90;
spice rack for blind
person question, 186–89;
state removal question,
170–73; sun always rises
in east question, 243;
3-quart bucket, 5-quart
bucket measuring ques-
tion, 207–09; three
switches in hallway
question, 229–30; train
question, 200–01;
$21 between Mike and
Todd question, 176; 26
constants question,
201–03; two doors ques-
tion, 223–26; VCR con-
trols question, 183–85;
venetian blind remote
control question, 185–
86; weighing billiard
balls question, 195–96;
weighing jars of pills
question, 196–97; weigh-
ing jet plane question,
148; weight of ice in
hockey rink question,
169–70

ants question, 82–83, 99,
197

Appraises, Vincent J., 13

Armstrong, Louis, 92

artificial intelligence (AI), 91,
92, 94, 101, 102, 218,
223

as-appropriate interviews, 72,
142–43

assumptions: of intelligence
tests, 39–40; and inter-
view techniques, 139,
145; and paradigm shifts,
109, 132–33; and
problem-solving ability,
102–06; and strategies
for puzzle interviews,
127–28, 220

AT&T, 58

Bachet, Claude Gaspar, 212

Bachet's weights problem, 212

Ballmer, Steve: and competition, 56, 57; and hiring,
  19, 60; and puzzle interview questions, 79–80;
  and Simonyi, 63; and
  traditional interview
  questions, 78; and U.S.
  map game, 51

Ball, W. W. Rouse, 208

Barr, Adam David: and hard
  interviewers, 76; and
  hiring, 72; and interview
  as workout, 20; and job
  candidates' experience,
  134; and manhole covers
  question, 149; and pro-
  gram managers, 65, 66;
  and secrecy of questions,
  139

bathroom design for Gates
  question, 82, 126,
  179–82

beer can question, 7, 118, 126,
  226–27

behavioral interview questions,
  17–18, 46, 78

Bell Labs, 31, 32, 58

Bernieri, Frank, 16, 47

Binet, Alfred, 24–25, 28

blacks, and intelligence tests,
  27, 33

Blair Television, 117

Blumenthal, Jabe, 53, 64, 67–68

boat and goblin question, 120,
  239–43

boat and suitcase question, 81,
  160–63

Bondalapati, Kiran, 89

Booz, Allen and Hamilton,
  227

boxes and dollar bills question,
  70, 84, 210–12

brainteasers. *See* puzzles

Brigham, Carl, 35–36

Bruner, J. S., 108–10

Buffett, Warren, 52

Bush, George H., 99

Bush, George W., 36

Bush, John, 149

Byham, William, 116

car-door key question, 67, 81,
  94, 154–57

case questions, 113–14, 123

Challenge [interview tech-
  nique], 43, 86–88

Christensen, Clayton M.,
  57–58, 59, 144

Church, Alonzo, 218–19

Church-Turing thesis, 218

clock's hands question, 61, 81,
  175–76

cluelessness, 57, 94, 95

coding ability, 47, 60, 61,
  62–63, 64, 66, 78

Codrescu, Andrei, 149–50

cognitive illusion, 98

competency-based recruit-
  ment, 116

computer models, 92

computer software: and disjunction effect, 100; and
  solution space, 93

corporate culture, 7, 138–39

count in base *negative* 2 question, 83, 203–06

creativity: and logic, 59; and
     Microsoft Corporation
     interviews, 9, 42; and
     Microsoft's value system,
     56; and open-ended
     questions, 141; and
     problem-solving ability,
     12, 42, 92; and program
     managers, 65; and
     Shockley, 33
crossing bridge question, 86,
     99, 219–23
crossword puzzles, 25
cultural bias, and intelligence
     tests, 24, 27, 28, 33, 35,
     38, 39, 138

demon and dwarfs question,
     85–86, 99, 126, 217–19
design questions: answers for,
     157; and innovation, 69;
     and Microsoft Corpora-
     tion interviews, 10,
     67–68; and project com-
     pletion, 137; strategies
     for, 67–68, 121, 123–24,
     126, 129, 180, 182–83
developers: and coding ability,
     62–63, 78; and disjunc-
     tion effect, 100; and
     Microsoft Corporation,
     60–68; and program
     managers, 64–65; and
     programming questions,
     78; and testers, 66
Development Dimensions
     International (DDI),
     116
DevelopMentor, 88–89

dialogue [answer expecta-
     tions], 122–24
disjunction effect, 97–98, 99,
     100, 128, 144
Disney, Walt, 30
displacement, 160–63
disruptive technologies, 57–58,
     144
dogs at corner of square ques-
     tion, 83, 198–200
Dudeney, Henry Ernest, 25–26,
     27, 232–33
Dukakis, Michael, 99

egalitarianism, and puzzles,
     11–12
elevator testing question, 82,
     126, 189, 190
employee paid daily in
     gold question, 84,
     209–10
Equal Employment Opportu-
     nity Commission, 36
equal opportunity employment
     law, 46
ergonomics, 157
eugenics, 34

Fairchild Semiconductor, 33
Fermi, Enrico, 163–64
Feynman, Richard, 91–92
first impressions, 140–41
Fog Creek Software, 68, 137,
     236
framing problems, 101–08,
     128, 170
Frank B. Hall and Company,
     13
Fries, Karen, 75

fuses' burning time question, 120, 238–39

Gada-Jain, Neha, 16, 47
Gamow, George, 216
Gardner, Howard, 40
Gardner, Martin, 80, 149, 154, 175, 197, 200
gas stations question, 81, 106–07, 166–67
Gates, Bill: and artificial intelligence, 91; attitude toward education, 19; competitiveness of, 31, 50, 51–52, 53, 61; and fairness, 121; as founder of Microsoft, 12; and global marketplace, 48; and hiring, 23, 60–61; and importance of intelligence, 41, 143; on IQ, 23; obsessions of, 21; and paradigm shifts, 108; and puzzles and games, 50–54; Shockley compared to, 31; and Simonyi, 63; values of, 55, 56, 57
Gates, Mary, 50
Gates, Melinda, 51
Gates, William, II, 50
Gehry, Frank, 65
Gell-Mann, Murray, 91–92
gender, and intelligence tests, 27–28, 39
George, Grant, 66–67
Gibbons, Jim, 3–4
Gleick, James, 59
global marketplace, 7, 48

Goldman Sachs, 112
Goodenough, Florence, 51
Google Web search engine, 202

Hewlett-Packard, 49
Hewlett, William, 30
hierarchy, suspicion of, 11
high school lockers question, 119–20, 126, 236–38
high-technology industries, 6–7, 19, 24, 43–44
Hippocrates, 73
hiring: changes in Microsoft's approach to, 67; Gates's philosophy on, 23, 60–61; and intelligence tests, 29, 35; and Microsoft Corporation interviews, 12, 72, 73, 75, 134; priorities of, 12, 14, 19–20, 46, 68–70, 130–31, 136–38, 144–45; and puzzle interviews, 7–8, 22, 46, 47–48, 61–62, 130–33, 143–45, 216–17; and Shockley, 31–32. *See also* interview techniques
hot water in hotel question, 81, 157–58
human resources departments: and developers, program managers, and testers, 66; and hard interviewers, 76, 77; and intelligence testing, 29; and interview techniques, 17; and puzzle interviews, 7, 12, 48; and screening interview, 71

hypothetical questions, 6, 67, 79, 98, 113

IBM, 56, 57
immersive interviews, 114–16
immigrants, 27, 29, 33
impossible questions: and assumptions, 106; and disjunction effect, 99–100; and interview techniques, 7–8, 20; and project completion, 137; sources of, 80; strategies for, 121; and Wall Street culture, 112
infinite series, 201
innovation: and Christensen, 57–58, 59; and hiring, 48, 130–33; and logic puzzles, 20, 69; and Microsoft Corporation, 57, 59
Intel, 32, 33
intelligence tests: assumptions of, 39–40; and cultural bias, 24, 27, 28, 33, 35, 38, 39, 138; and definition of intelligence, 25, 39–40, 143; and Mensa, 40–42; and puzzle interviews, 42–43, 135–36; and puzzles, 26–27; and race, 27, 33–34, 35, 39, 42; and Shockley, 31–34, 35, 39, 41; validity of, 37–39, 40, 46, 136; and workplace, 20–21, 28–30, 35, 36. See also IQ; Stanford-Binet intelligence scale

interviewers: fallibility of, 14–17; and first impressions, 16, 17, 18, 140–41; and hard interviewers, 75–76, 77, 123, 243; and hiring decisions, 131–33; and job candidates' strategies for puzzle interviews, 68, 122, 123–24, 126, 128, 129, 170, 176, 182, 193, 203, 228; and peer interviewing, 76; and puzzle interviews, 8–9, 21, 132, 150–51, 155; and stress interviews, 112
interview techniques: and assumptions, 139, 145; comparison of, 46–47; in computer industry, 6–7; evaluating during interview, 72–75, 142; and first impressions, 140–41; guidelines for, 134–43; and honesty, 142–43; and impossible questions, 7–8, 20; and intelligence tests, 135–36; and interview plan, 135; and job candidates' experience, 134–35; and logic puzzles, 9, 20, 48, 49; and preventing bad hires, 12, 46, 73, 130–31, 136–38; and puzzles, 7, 8, 9; and riddles, 10–12, 20; and secrecy of questions, 139–40; and Shockley, 3–4, 31–34; and stress

interview, 8, 9, 141–42;
traditional interview
questions, 12–13, 17–18,
46, 47, 71, 78, 130–31,
134. *See also* hiring;
Microsoft Corporation
interviews; puzzle inter-
views

IQ: disenchantment with,
35–36; and environment,
209; and intelligence test
scores, 27, 36; and Microsoft Corporation, 23, 42;
and sterilization, 34;
Lewis Terman on, 23–28.
See also intelligence tests

jars and marbles question,
83–84, 206–07
jelly beans in three colors question, 84, 212
Jews, and intelligence tests, 33
job candidates: experience of,
19, 61, 134–35; first
impressions of, 16, 17,
140–41; information
about, 14, 19, 45, 74, 131,
136; and puzzle inter-
views, 8, 45, 46, 61–62,
132, 134–35; and self-
awareness, 102; Spolsky
on, 68–70; strategies for
puzzle interviews, 21–22,
67–70, 121–29, 170, 176,
182, 193, 203, 228; and
traditional interview
questions, 17–18; and
websites of puzzle ques-
tions, 89

job experience, 19, 61, 134–35
job interviews: absurdist interviews, 116–17; as-
appropriate interviews,
72, 142–43; and assess-
ment, 13–14; exhaustiv-
ity of, 8; immersive
interviews, 114–16;
importance of, 12–13;
stress interviews, 8, 9,
111–12, 114–16, 141–42;
two-second interviews,
14–17, 18. *See also* interviewers; interview tech-
niques; job candidates;
Microsoft Corporation
interviews; puzzle inter-
views
job references, 13
Johnson-Laird, Philip, 45

Kepler, Johannes, 93
Koch, Zeke, 44
Kordemsky, Boris, 196
Kuhn, Thomas, 108, 144
Kummert, Ted, 180

Last, Jay, 32
Lego blocks, 117
Lehman Brothers, 112
Lewis, Michael, 112
library-book location question,
82, 95, 190–93
logic: and Christensen, 58, 59;
and intelligence, 144;
and Microsoft Corpora-
tion interviews, 12; and
problem-solving ability,
92, 95

logic puzzles: absurdity of, 236; and competitiveness, 62; and computer-industry interviews, 6; and disjunction effect, 99, 100, 128; effectiveness of, 44; and first impressions, 141; and framing problems, 102, 106; and innovation, 20, 69; and intelligence tests, 25, 38; and interview techniques, 9, 20, 48, 49; invention of, 80; and management consultant industry, 113; mental tricks of, 22; and Microsoft Corporation interviews, 43, 45, 67, 79, 121; and puzzle interviews, 21; Shockley's use of, 32; strategies for, 121, 123, 124, 125–29; variations of, 140; verification of answers, 147; Zen riddles compared to, 11. *See also* puzzles

Loyd, Sam, 25, 27, 233

management consulting industry, 113–14

Manhattan phone book question, 81, 176–78

manhole covers question, 79–80, 89, 112, 148–50, 160

Mars Company, 158–59

matchstick and equilateral triangles question, 132–33, 243–44

McKenna, Gene, 5–6

meaningless decisions, 155

measuring questions, 26, 112, 207–09

Mensa, 36, 40–42

meritocracy, 12, 29

Mexicans, and intelligence tests, 27

Microsoft Corporation: antitrust suit of, 12, 52; attitude toward winning, 52, 62; and developers, 60–68; and egalitarianism, 11–12; future focus of, 19–20; and games, 51–52, 53, 54, 115–16; and IQ, 23, 42; and math camp, 52–54; value system of, 55–58

Microsoft Corporation interviews: and behavioral interview questions, 18, 78; and Challenge [interview technique], 43, 86–88; and coding ability, 47, 60, 61, 62; controversy surrounding, 43–45; exposés of, 88–90; and fairness, 10, 11, 46, 121; and Hewlett-Packard, 49; and hiring, 12, 72, 73, 75, 134; impressions of, 117; and intelligence, 23, 25; and intelligence tests, 42–43; and job candidates' experience, 19; and logic puzzles, 43, 45, 67, 79, 121; and motivation, 43;

and peer interviewing, 131; and problem-solving ability, 10, 12, 20, 42, 43; and programming questions, 78–79; and puzzles, 10, 61, 67, 79; and recruiting, 5–6, 50; sample questions, 80–86; secrecy of questions, 78; and Spolsky, 68; structure of, 9–10, 20, 70–77; and traditional interview questions, 23, 78; and trick questions, 10, 79; validity of, 45–46; Wall Street interviews compared to, 111, 112
microwave oven controlled by computer question, 5–6, 82, 182–83
mirror question, 7, 81, 126, 150–54
missing information, 95, 99, 100, 128
Mississippi River question, 81, 168–69
M&Ms question, 68, 81, 158–60
Mongan, John, 44, 47
monologue [answer expectations], 122–24
Moore, Gordon, 32
Moore's Law, 202
Morita, Akio, 58
motivational factors: and intelligence tests, 42, 43; and perfectly logical beings (PLBs), 126–27; and puzzle interviews, 6, 62, 137, 145

moving Mount Fuji question, 7, 118, 227–29
Murray, Mike, 55–56
Myhrvold, Nathan, 55

nanny agency cheating on taxes question, 82, 193–95
National Football League, 20, 36
Nazism, 34
Newell, Alan, 92–93
number puzzles, 25, 93

Oden, Melita, 41–42
Oedipus, 10, 11
open-ended questions, 147; effectiveness of, 141; and framing problems, 106–08; sources of, 80; strategies for, 68, 123, 124, 129
organizational structure, 131, 219
Osborne, Tom, 54
outside-the-box thinking, 7, 11, 42, 101

Packard, David, 30
paradigm shifts, 108–10, 132–33, 144, 154
Paterson, Tim, 62
Paulos, John Allen, 216
peer interviewing, 76, 131
perfectly logical beings (PLBs), 126–27, 138
Perkins, David, 94
Perry, Susan, 117
piano tuners question, 7, 8, 81, 100, 163–66

picnic baskets filled with fruit
    question, 84, 99, 212–13
pirates splitting gold coins
    question, 119, 126,
    137–38, 140, 233–36
Planck, Max, 93
points on globe question, 81,
    173–75
Policy, Carmen, 36
polygraph exams, 32–33, 37
Postman, Leo, 108–10
Prickett, Tricia, 16, 47
Pritchard, David, 59, 73
problem-solving ability: and
    artificial intelligence, 91;
    assessment of, 20; and
    assumptions, 102–06;
    and framing problems,
    101–07, 128, 170; and
    intelligence tests, 43; and
    job candidates' experi-
    ence, 134; and logic, 92,
    95; and Microsoft Cor-
    poration interviews, 10,
    12, 20, 42, 43; and para-
    digm shifts, 108–10; and
    puzzle interviews, 46, 47,
    62, 130, 139; and self-
    awareness, 102; and
    Shockley, 33; study of,
    91–98
programming: and logic, 144;
    and master program-
    mers, 63–64; and pro-
    gram managers, 64–66,
    67, 87; and program-
    ming questions, 78–79;
    and testers, 65–67. See
    also developers

project completion, and puzzle
    interviews, 136–38, 145
Pryor, Michael, 89, 137
psychometrics, 30
puzzle interviews: and absurd-
    ist interview, 116–17;
    and calculus, 125, 200;
    and competitiveness, 7,
    12, 48, 62, 79, 111, 118;
    effectiveness of, 21,
    43–48, 132–33; and
    fairness, 10, 11, 134,
    138–39; and hiring, 7,
    22, 46, 47–48, 61–62,
    130–33, 143–45, 216–17;
    history of, 20, 48–49; and
    intelligence tests, 42–43,
    135–36; and job candi-
    dates, 8, 45, 46, 61–62,
    132, 134–35; and man-
    agement consulting
    industry, 113–14; most
    difficult interview ques-
    tions, 118–20; and non-
    programmers, 67;
    rationale for, 45–46; and
    repeating questions, 72;
    sample questions, 80–86;
    and secrecy of questions,
    139–40; and simple
    answers, 125–26; and
    software industry, 43, 62,
    143; sources of puzzles,
    79–80, 159; strategies for,
    21–22, 121–29, 170, 176,
    182, 193, 203, 220, 228;
    and Lewis and Frederick
    Terman, 24; and Wall
    Street culture, 111, 112

puzzles: and artificial intelligence, 92; case questions as, 113; and clueless plateau, 94–95; and disjunction effect, 100; effectiveness of, 44, 135; and egalitarianism, 11–12; experience with, 122; and first answer pitfall, 124–25; Bill Gates's affinity for, 50–51; and hiring, 7; and intelligence tests, 26–27; and interview techniques, 7, 8, 9; and Microsoft Corporation interviews, 10, 61, 67, 79; and paradigm shifts, 108–10; popularity of, 25–26; and project completion, 137; and solution space, 93–94, 95; sources of, 79–80; and uncertainty, 95, 97, 98, 100; and U.S. Marines' Officer Candidate School, 115. *See also* logic puzzles; riddles; trick questions

quarter on rectangular table game, 119, 230–33

race, and intelligence tests, 27, 33–34, 35, 39, 42
Raikes, Jeff, 54, 57
reading-comprehension questions, 25

rectangular cake question, 81–82, 178–79
Rickover, Hyman G., 114–15
riddles: and absurdist interviews, 117; and computer-industry interviews, 6; and first answer pitfall, 124–25; and interview techniques, 10–12, 20; and management consulting industry, 113; and nonprogrammers, 67; and solution space, 94; Zen riddles, 11, 95, 154. *See also* puzzles
Roberts, Sheldon, 32–33
robots, 101–02
role-playing games, 115–16
Rosenthal, Robert, 15, 16
Russian roulette question, 8–9, 147–48

saltshaker testing question, 71, 82, 189–90
Sawyer, Diane, 114
Scholastic Aptitude Test, 35–36
school systems, and intelligence tests, 24, 29, 30, 35
science education, 30
self-awareness, 102
Sells, Chris, 44, 47, 88–90, 116, 134
semiconductor technology, 33
sentence-completion tasks, 43
Shafir, Eldar, 98
Shin'ichi Hisamatsu, 95
Shockley, Emily, 32

Shockley Semiconductor Laboratory, 3, 4, 32, 33
Shockley, William: and intelligence tests, 31–34, 35, 39, 41; and polygraph, 32–33, 37; and puzzle interviews, 3–4, 43, 47, 48; and transistor, 3, 5, 31, 34, 58
Shurkin, Joel, 31
Shuzan (Zen master), 11
silicon, 3, 33
Silicon Valley, 5, 21, 24, 43, 49
Simon, Herbert, 92–93, 94
Simonyi, Charles, 63
smart packaging, 182
Smullyan, Raymond, 219
software industry, 43, 52, 55, 62, 69, 143
solution space, 93–94, 95
Sony, 58
Sophocles, 11
sphinx, 10–11
spice rack for blind person question, 82, 129, 186–89
Spolsky, Joel: and Challenge [interview technique], 87, 88; and design questions, 123–24, 129; and framing problems, 107; and hiring, 68–69, 73; and information from interviews, 45, 74, 131; and M&Ms question, 68, 159, 160
standards, 157
Stanford-Binet intelligence scale: and composite

IQ scores, 40; Microsoft Corporation interviews compared to, 43, 87–88; and national IQ obsession, 28; and Lewis Terman, 24, 25, 26, 33, 38
Stanford University, 24, 30, 31, 34
Star Trek transporter question, 7, 113–14
state removal question, 7, 67, 81, 107, 124, 170–73
Stern, Marvin, 216
Stern, William, 27
stock markets, 99
stock options, 55, 61
stress interviews, 8, 9, 111–12, 114–16, 141–42
structured interviewing, 135
sun always rises in east question, 132, 243
Suojanen, Noah, 44, 47, 76
Survivor, 233–34
synonyms/antonyms, 25, 43

Tartaglia, Nicolò, 212
Tashian, Carl, 70–71, 74, 75
teakettle testing question, 82, 190
tennis match question, 4
Terman, Frederick, 24, 30–31
Terman, Lewis M.: and Challenge [interview technique], 88; and concept of intelligence,

39–40, 43; and intelli-
gence tests, 35, 37, 39,
143; on IQ, 23–28; and
measuring question, 26,
208–09; and meritocracy,
29; prestige of, 30; and
race issues, 27, 28, 33–34;
study of high-IQ chil-
dren, 41–42
testers, 65–67
thermometer, 37
3-quart bucket, 5-quart bucket
measuring question, 84,
112, 207–09
three switches in hallway question, 118–19, 229–30
toaster testing question, 82,
190
trade-offs, 123, 137, 183
traditional interview questions,
12–13, 17–18, 46, 47, 71,
78, 130–31
train question, 83, 200–01
Traitorous Eight, 33
transistor radios, 58
transistors, 3, 5, 31, 34, 58
trick questions: and computer-
industry interviews, 6;
and interview tech-
niques, 8, 139–40; and
Microsoft Corporation
interviews, 10, 79; and
puzzle interviews, 22,
132; and solution space,
95, 96; strategies for,
121, 176, 203. *See also*
puzzles
Trudeau, Garry, 36

Tversky, Amos, 98
$21 between Mike and Todd
question, 81, 176
26 constants question, 83,
201–03
two doors question, 113,
223–26

uncertainty: and puzzle inter-
views, 144, 145; and
puzzles, 95, 97, 98, 100;
and stock markets, 99
Unisys, 116
U.S. Army, 28–29, 35–36
U.S. Justice Department, 12
U.S. Marines' Officer Candi-
date School, 115
U.S. Supreme Court, 35

VCR controls question, 82,
183–85
venetian blind remote control
question, 82, 185–86
von Neumann, John, 201

Wall Street culture, 8, 21,
111–12
Warburg, Aby, 191
Wason, Peter, 97
Wason selection task, 97
websites: and case questions,
113–14; and Microsoft
Corporation interview
questions, 79, 80, 88,
89–90, 225–26; and
strategies for puzzle
interviews, 122; and
stress interviews, 112

weighing billiard balls question, 5, 49, 82, 112, 195–96

weighing jars of pills question, 82, 103–06, 196–97

weighing jet plane question, 80, 148

weight of ice in hockey rink question, 81, 169–70

white supremacists, 33

Winblad, Ann, 51

Wonderlic, 36

word puzzles, 25, 93

Xerox PARC, 63

Yerkes, Robert M., 28, 33, 35

Zefer Corp., 117

Zeno's Paradox, 175

Zen riddles, 11, 95, 154

About the Author

William Poundstone is the author of nine books, including *Carl Sagan: A Life in the Cosmos; Prisoner's Dilemma; Labyrinths of Reason;* and the popular Big Secrets series that inspired two television network specials. He has written for *Esquire, Harper's, The Economist,* and the *New York Times Book Review,* and his science writing has been nominated twice for the Pulitzer Prize. He lives in Los Angeles.